DYING AND DEATH IN CANADA

DYING AND DEATH IN CANADA
SECOND EDITION
HERBERT C. NORTHCOTT
AND DONNA M. WILSON

broadview
press

LIBRARY AND ARCHIVES CANADA CATALOGUING IN PUBLICATION

Northcott, Herbert C., 1947–
      Dying and death in Canada / Herbert C. Northcott and Donna M. Wilson. — 2nd ed.

Includes bibliographical references.

ISBN 978-1-55111-873-4

      1. Death — Canada. 2. Death — Social aspects — Canada. 3. Death — Psychological aspects.
I. Wilson, Donna M. (Donna Marie), 1955– II. Title.

BF789.D4N67 2008   306.90971   C2008-901947-4

BROADVIEW PRESS is an independent, international publishing house, incorporated in 1985. Broadview believes in shared ownership, both with its employees and with the general public; since the year 2000 Broadview shares have traded publicly on the Toronto Venture Exchange under the symbol bdp.

We welcome comments and suggestions regarding any aspect of our publications — please feel free to contact us at the addresses below or at: broadview@broadviewpress.com / www.broadviewpress.com.

Broadview Press acknowledges the financial support of the Government of Canada through the Book Publishing Industry Development Program (BPIDP) for our publishing activities.   ·

Cover & Interior Design by Michel Vrana, Black Eye Design.
Printed in Canada

This book is printed on paper containing 100% post-consumer fibre.

10 9 8 7 6 5 4 3 2 1

North America
Post Office Box 1243,
Peterborough, Ontario, Canada K9J 7H5

2215 Kenmore Ave.
Buffalo, New York, USA 14207

tel: (705) 743-8990; fax: (705) 743-8353

customerservice@broadviewpress.com

UK, Ireland and continental Europe
NBN International
Estover Road, Plymouth, UK PL6 7PY
tel: 44 (0) 1752 202300
fax: 44 (0) 1752 202330
enquiries@nbninternational.com

Australia and New Zealand
UNIREPS, University of New South Wales
Sydney, NSW, Australia 2052
tel: 61 2 96640999; fax: 61 2 96645420
infopress@unsw.edu.au

This book is dedicated to my students, both undergraduate and graduate, who have taught me as much as I have taught them. — HN

I would like to dedicate this book to those dear friends and family who, through their life and through their dying and death, helped bring special meaning and purpose to life. I would also like to thank my family and acknowledge my nursing career for providing me with the opportunities to see dying and death for what it is — a fundamentally important challenge and thus opportunity for growth. — DW

CONTENTS

ACKNOWLEDGMENTS..11

PREFACE..13

PART I: THE DEMOGRAPHY AND EPIDEMIOLOGY OF DYING AND DEATH

CHAPTER 1
THE HISTORY OF DYING AND DEATH IN CANADA...19
    Dying and Death among Aboriginal People in Canada
        in the Pre-Contact Era...20
    Dying and Death in Canada Following the Arrival of the Europeans.........25
    Dying and Death in Canada in the Twentieth and
        Twenty-First Centuries 31
    Summary 37

CHAPTER 2
DYING AND DEATH IN CANADA TODAY 39
    Causes of Dying and Death...39
    Causes of Death by Age 45
    The Dying Process...46
    Factors Affecting the Dying Process 48
    Age at Death..52
    Premature Dying and Death 56
    Other Influences on Dying and Death in Canada 57
    Location of Death...60
    Summary 63

PART II: THE SOCIAL AND CULTURAL RESPONSE TO DYING AND DEATH

CHAPTER 3
**DYING AND DEATH IN THE CONTEXT OF
CANADIAN SOCIAL INSTITUTIONS**...67
    The Family 68
    Religion...71
    The Health Care System..73
    Legal System..80
    The Funeral Industry 87
    Summary 90

CHAPTER 4

DYING AND DEATH IN THE CONTEXT OF CANADIAN CULTURE 91

Selected Works of Literature 92

Language 95

Folklore, Popular Culture, and Contemporary Media 96

The Secularization, Professionalization, Medicalization,
and Bureaucratization of Dying and Death 102

Making Sense of Death 104

Different Types of Death 106

Dying and Death as Social Stigma 108

Social Rituals Accompanying Dying and Death 109

Cultural Constructions of Dying and Death 110

Coast Salish 110

Cree 111

Dene 111

Inuit 112

Muslim 112

Jewish 114

Chinese 115

Ethnic Viet and Lao Hmong 116

Western European and Euro-North American 117

Summary 118

PART III: THE INDIVIDUAL RESPONSE TO DYING AND DEATH

CHAPTER 5

INDIVIDUAL PERSPECTIVES ON DYING AND DEATH 123

Expectations of Dying and Death 123

Dying Trajectories 125

Preferences for Dying and Death 126

Fear of Dying 129

Awareness of Dying 130

The Dying Process 131

Personal Accounts of "Brushes with Death" 132

Fear of Death and Denial of Death 140

The Religious Solution 141

The Spiritual Solution 141

Risking Death 142

Choosing Death 143

Preferred Location of Dying and Death 145

Living with Dying 147

Summary 149

CHAPTER 6

SURVIVOR PERSPECTIVES ON DYING AND DEATH.. 151

Grief and Bereavement 153

Death of a Child... 154

Death of a Spouse 163

Death of a Parent 167

Death of a Grandparent 170

Death of a Friend... 170

A Second-Order Account of Dying 173

Pathways for the Grieving 175

Summary 176

CONCLUSION.. 177

APPENDIX: SELECTED SOURCES OF INFORMATION

ON DYING AND DEATH 181

REFERENCES 185

INDEX 213

ACKNOWLEDGMENTS

For the first edition of this book, Wendy Maurier and Michael Stingl reviewed the entire manuscript, Kathryn Wilkins reviewed Chapters 3 and 4, and Christy Nickerson conducted library research for and also reviewed Chapters 4 through 6. All of these reviewers provided helpful suggestions. Chapters 1 through 3 benefited from statistical data analysis and research assistance provided by Corrine Truman. Data access and analysis for Chapters 1 to 3 were made possible by a National Health and Research Development Program operational research grant (#6609-2096-96) and the University of Alberta, which provided a Social Science Research grant and an EFF Support for the Advancement of Scholarship grant. Chapters 5 and 6 include personal accounts concerning dying and death provided by persons who must remain anonymous; we are very grateful to them for sharing their stories. Finally, the authors are grateful to Barbara Tessman for her excellent editorial work and to Peter Saunders of Garamond Press for his support of this project. For the second edition of this book, Jennifer Northcott assisted with the literature search to update Chapters 4 through 6. The authors are grateful to Betsy Struthers for her excellent editorial work and to Anne Brackenbury of Broadview Press for her support of this second edition.

·PREFACE

Until the 1960s, death, like sexuality, was present but rarely discussed. While dying and death have long been a focus of attention in religion, philosophy, popular culture, and the arts, it has nevertheless been argued that dying and death were among the last taboos to be explored by twentieth-century social science. Since the 1960s, this taboo has been breached, and the social science discourse on dying and death in North America has begun to develop (Aiken, 2001: ix; see also Lucas, 1968: 15).

This book focuses on Canada and on Canadian work in the area of dying and death. The first edition was published in 2001; this second edition updates the previous work by incorporating research on dying, death, and bereavement published in Canada since 2000. It is meant to serve as a supplement to larger texts such as Kastenbaum (2007), Leming and Dickinson (2007), or DeSpelder and Strickland (2005), all of which were written outside of Canada but often used in this country. Although *Dying and Death in Canada* is written primarily for students who wish to learn about dying and death and for practitioners who work with the dying and the bereaved, it can also be used by the dying and the bereaved themselves, as well as by others interested in the topic.

Dying is a process; death is an event. For the dying person, the process of dying culminates in the event of death. For that reason, throughout this book the term dying typically precedes the term death and discussions of dying typically precede discussions of death. This is in contrast to the more common usage that curiously focuses first on death and adds dying almost as an afterthought.

Dying and death in a society reflect the material and social conditions of that society. For example, dying and death come frequently and early in life in a society where there is widespread poverty, austere living conditions, inadequate nutrition, unclean water, inadequate sewage and garbage disposal, war and civil unrest, and underdeveloped medical technology and health care delivery systems. In contrast, dying and death typically come late in life in a more "developed" society such as Canada in the twenty-first century. How we live influences how and at what age we die. And the society and culture in which we live influences what we think and do about dying and death.

Dying is both a personal experience and a social role given shape and meaning by social practices and cultural definitions (Lucas, 1968). Death itself is both a personal event and an event with social significance. The same is true for the bereaved person who loses a loved one to death. The bereaved grieve and mourn in both personal and social terms, and the meaning assigned to dying and death is both personally and socially constructed.

Dying and Death in Canada is divided into three parts. Part I explores the causes of dying and death in Canada both historically and at present. It contains two chapters. Chapter 1 focuses in particular on factors affecting changes in death and dying among different groups at different times throughout the country's history, while Chapter 2 examines trends in and causes of dying and death in Canada in the early years of the twenty-first century.

Part II examines the collective constructions of — that is, the social and cultural response to — dying and death in Canada. The social and cultural context is important because it, in part, shapes the meaning that an individual assigns to the experience of dying and death. Chapter 3 discusses dying and death from the point of view of Canadian social institutions such as family, religion, health care, and the legal system. Chapter 4 investigates the cultural constructions of the meaning of dying and death and the social rituals that attend death and help to give it a collectively shared meaning.

Part III discusses dying and death from the personal points of view of the dying and the bereaved. Chapter 5 examines individual perspectives on dying and death from the point of view of the person who is dying, while Chapter 6 discusses dying and death from the point of view of persons who are associated with the dying and the dead as surviving family members and/or caregivers.

PART I
THE DEMOGRAPHY AND EPIDEMIOLOGY OF DYING AND DEATH

CHAPTER 1
THE HISTORY OF DYING AND DEATH IN CANADA

Death is inevitable. Death occurs at the end of a process of dying that can range in length from only a few minutes to many years. The typical course of dying, the causes and timing of death, and social responses to death tend to vary from one society to another and also from one historical time to another. Perhaps the greatest challenge in writing about dying and death historically is finding sufficient meaningful information from the past. Despite such early efforts as a 1678 Quebec law mandating the keeping of vital statistics (Harding le Riche, 1979) and more recent efforts such as the development of a quality improvement organization for social data called the Vital Statistics Council of Canada (2007), historical information on dying and death in Canada is limited. In the past, information on any given death, and the dying process that led to it, was often restricted to a single line on a church's burial roster or a hospital's daily record of admissions and discharges

(Fair, 1994). Even today, information on dying and death continues to be sparse and incomplete, despite more consistent data collection and sophisticated computerization procedures.

Although death is becoming less of a taboo subject, most people today do not dwell on their own death or on the potential death of others close to them. In large part, this avoidance is a natural outcome of death having become a circumstance primarily of advanced old age (Health Canada, 2002; Statistics Canada, 2002a). Dying and death can thus be dismissed as topics for which little information and research is needed. They are also uncomfortable topics for many people, as they bring out fears and in some cases unpleasant memories of loss or of dying processes that were not optimal. In short, dying and death are topics that people would much rather not think about nor personally experience in the near future. Yet, death used to be a common life event, and high death rates among larger families until around the second half of the twentieth century meant bereavement was experienced much more frequently in Canada than it is today. The public health movement prior to World War II, and advances in health care and in the health care delivery system post World War II, brought about radical changes in both the circumstances and likelihood of dying and death. As a result of these changes, most Canadians have come to expect to live a long life.

At the same time that death was becoming increasingly associated with old age, it also became increasingly associated with the hospital. That is, death was moved from the home, family, and community into the hospital, where the process of dying was largely removed from public scrutiny and consciousness (Wilson et al., 2001, 2002). It is not surprising, then, that dying and death became neglected topics.

This chapter examines the history of dying and death in Canada. It begins with dying and death among the Aboriginal people of Canada in the pre-contact era and then reviews the situation in colonial Canada before progressing to the twentieth and twenty-first centuries. Trends in life expectancy, historical changes in the causes of death, and historical contexts relevant to dying and death in Canada are presented.

DYING AND DEATH AMONG ABORIGINAL PEOPLE IN CANADA IN THE PRE-CONTACT ERA

Prior to the arrival of European explorers and settlers, dozens of Aboriginal or First Nations lived across Canada, from the Arctic to the Great Lakes, from the East Coast to the West, each with its own unique lifestyle and culture. Centuries after contact between the Norse and the Aboriginal peoples of Newfoundland, Jacques Cartier landed on the Gaspé Peninsula and claimed the land for France in 1534 (Morton, 2006); more than half a century later, the first French settlement was founded in Acadia (that is, Nova Scotia and New Brunswick). Given the sheer size of the land, and the limited number of Europeans who first settled it, many Aboriginal groups were not greatly influenced by the Europeans until decades or even centuries after these events. Indeed, almost 250 years after Cartier's landing, fur traders in western Canada remarked on meeting Aboriginal groups that had never before encountered a white man (Bryce, 1902).

In the pre-contact era, shamans and other Aboriginal healers in Canada provided health care to their people. Since "medicine to the Indians was not only physical but spiritual" (Stone, 1962: 6), they were adept at gathering and using medicines and at employing a "supernatural article or agency which may be of aid in curing disease" (Stone, 1962: 5). Aboriginal peoples in those days were aware of and used the medicinal properties of plants, roots, leaves, herbs, barks, and other substances.

Although death frequently came early in life for Aboriginal peoples in the pre-contact era, not all deaths were premature; an unknown proportion reached advanced age. The historian Eric Stone (1962) believed that, as a consequence of clean environments, natural foods, ongoing physical labour, and other positive lifestyle factors, a "considerable" number of Aboriginal people reached old age in pre-colonial North America. Longevity was also noted after the arrival of the Europeans. For instance, an Aboriginal woman who died in 1800 at a Hudson's Bay fort in Manitoba was said to have been "upwards of one hundred years old" (Brown, 1980: 68). In 1884, three Aboriginal men on a western Canadian reserve were said to be in their mid-nineties (Carter, 1973). Despite instances of advanced age, existence could be precarious for Aboriginal groups. Since food supplies often were limited (Stone, 1962), starvation would especially have threatened seniors and children. Abandonment of seniors may have also been practiced to some degree (Burch, 1988; de Beauvoir, 1973; Brown, 1980; Dickason, 1984) and may have occurred when a person began to require care or assistance in activities of daily living, could no longer perform a necessary function within the community, or developed a serious health problem.

It is unlikely that older Aboriginal persons were free of disabling arthritis, limitations in eyesight, and any number of other disorders that commonly affect senior citizens today. Stone (1962) reported that Aboriginal people tended to develop rheumatism and arthritis as a result of injury, repetitive physical labour, and bouts of scurvy. They also developed eye infections as a result of smoke irritation from cooking and heating fires; colds, pleurisy, and pneumonia; and gastro-intestinal problems due to bouts of starvation alternating with times of plenty (Stone, 1962). These conditions would have contributed indirectly or directly to death. For example, if older Aboriginal persons had limitations such as reduced eyesight, arthritis, loss of teeth, or dementia, then their ability to procure, prepare, and eat food would have been considerably impaired. Their ability to migrate with a nomadic tribe would have also been compromised. The seriousness of this issue is illustrated by a report that Aboriginal people were relieved to leave their weak, elderly, and disabled dependants at a fur trading fort instead of leaving them behind in the wilderness to fend for themselves until death (Brown, 1980). Olive Dickason (1984), a noted Canadian historian, also reported that infants, as well as weak and elderly Aboriginal people, were left at early hospitals to be cared for.

Life expectancy among Aboriginal peoples would have been considerably lower than is currently the case for all Canadians. On the eve of the arrival of the Europeans, Aboriginal life expectancy would likely have been only 30 to 40 years, as it was in Europe at the time. It is not surprising then that Corlett reported in 1935 that cancer seldom afflicted Aboriginal peoples; cancer then and now occurs more often in old age (Canadian Cancer Society/National Cancer Institute of Canada, 2007). Moreover, Aboriginal persons then would not have been exposed to many of the environmental and lifestyle factors that are associated with cancer today.

Although there may have been some gender differences in life expectancy among Aboriginal groups, the majority of deaths for both sexes would have occurred prior to old age. Death from injury sustained in the course of hunting or war-related activities would have been common, with younger men and boys most prone to such injuries. Men were sometimes tortured to death following capture by an enemy group (Dickason, 1984), although it is not known how often death occurred under such circumstances. By contrast, captured women and children were typically not tortured or killed in intertribal conflict; instead, they were usually kept to perform various functions within the adopting tribe (Dickason, 1984).

Women may also have been more vulnerable than men during times of food shortages. Hunters, who were primarily male (Kelm and Townsend, 2006), may have survived when those dependent on them for sustenance did not. Hunters had more immediate access to food sources than did women or children; moreover, hunters may have been given preferential access to food when it was in short supply. According to Bryce (1902: 103), one fur trader was told by an Aboriginal chief that, on fur-trade expeditions, women "are maintained at a trifling expense, for as they always stand cook, the very licking of their fingers in scarce times is sufficient for their subsistence."

Children, too, would have been vulnerable in times of shortages. Children, then, as now, are particularly susceptible to insults on their health. Starvation has a more serious impact on younger children in comparison to older children and adults, either through loss of life or permanent damage to growing organs, muscles, and bones. Infanticide was practiced by some Aboriginal groups in response to unwanted children, multiple births, and "in defence against privation and hunger" (Brown, 1980: 150). There is no evidence to suggest that male children were favoured during times of food shortages or that female children were more deliberately euthanized. Generally, children of both sexes were highly valued, considered nec-essary to ensure the continuance of the groups and to provide assistance to their elders (Morton, 2006). Nonetheless, it is likely that Aboriginal children had a high death rate.

As a consequence of a much higher death rate than today and the greater vis-ibility of dying and dead people in smaller, more intimate communities, dying and death would have been a relatively common life circumstance for Aboriginal peoples. There is no evidence that dying people or dead bodies were shunned. Other evidence suggests an acceptance of, if not reverence for, the dead. For instance, Dickason (1984: 115) indicated that "burial customs formed the most distinctive aspect of Huron culture." Whenever a village moved, the bones of deceased per-sons were exhumed, cleaned, wrapped, and reburied in a common grave during a 10-day ceremony. An ossuary (a burial site for the bones of the dead) could hold between 800 and 4,000 skeletons (Carter, 1973).

W.H. Carter (1973), who studied the burial customs of Aboriginal peoples in Canada, indicated that many tribes regularly revisited their dead every eight to twelve years in a "Feast of the Dead." He relates an eyewitness account of an Aboriginal woman caressing the bones of her children and father. This revisiting was made possible by careful storage of the body, which was prepared so that the bones, and at times skin or hair, would be preserved. It was apparently common for the deceased to be bound tightly together by straps so that the knees were touching the chest, although at times the body was wrapped in a prone position. Women prepared the bodies for burial and in some cases performed the burial unaided by men (Carter, 1973).

Aboriginal burial customs varied across Canada and included cremation (partial or full body), mummification (a few mummies consisting of skin wrapped around bones after the flesh had been removed have been found on the West Coast), grave burials, surface burials (using stones, furs, and/or wood to cover the body), tree or scaffold burials, water burials (the body was sent downstream in a canoe), urn burials of cremated remains or bones, and ossuarial (group) burials (Carter, 1973).

According to Carter (1973), the most common burial involved a round grave dug approximately five feet deep with the tightly bound body placed to rest sitting on the heels and facing east. Bark and furs were used to keep the earth from touching the body, and various articles, such as clothing, were placed next to it. Loud wailing and other displays of grief continued for approximately 10 days after the rapid burial (within one day of death) had taken place. Mourning continued for one year, during which time remarriages did not occur, in part, perhaps, because isolation of the bereaved was common.

Dying Aboriginal persons frequently participated in preparing for their own death by praying, calling their family together, and making other preparations. If unable to effect a cure, then the healer's role was to call upon the spirits to help the dying person and to assist the soul on its journey into the afterlife (Carter, 1973).

It is likely that, in the past, dying was considered a normal life process among Aboriginal peoples. The folklore surrounding elderly, disabled, or starving Inuit, and their apparent willingness to sacrifice their own life for the good of the family or community, is but one example (Burch, 1988). Indeed, at times death may have been welcomed if it occurred during a battle to defend territory or kinfolk, during a hunt to test manhood, or as an end to suffering (Carter, 1973; Heagerty, 1928). Folklore about ancestral souls revisiting earth provides another example of how death was perceived (Burch, 1988). If Aboriginal peoples considered death to be a part of the natural cycle of life, just as the seasons ebb and flow, then it may not have been as unexpected or as unacceptable as it is to most Canadians today. Morton (2006) makes the point that Aboriginal North Americans saw themselves as one with nature, not masters of nature. While death would have precipitated grief and mourning, it nevertheless could have been perceived as more of a practical issue: an unfortunate loss of hunters, gatherers, or defenders would threaten the lives and well-being of others in a community, and the loss of women and children would threaten its continuity.

In summary, for Aboriginal people in Canada during the pre-contact era, death often came early in life. Nevertheless, some individuals survived to old age. In contrast to persons dying in relatively short time frames at an early age, elderly persons were more likely to die over a period of months or years from chronic ailments or frailty. Dying and death were familiar in early Aboriginal societies because death was a common, expected, and visible occurrence.

DYING AND DEATH IN CANADA FOLLOWING
THE ARRIVAL OF THE EUROPEANS

In general, associations between Aboriginal peoples and newcomers initially followed a pattern of sporadic contact, later followed by more sustained relations
between the First Nations and European explorers, fur traders, missionaries, and
then farmers and other settlers. Permanent Aboriginal camps were often established
close to missions and fur trading posts. Both the missions and the trading posts
had an enormous impact not only on Aboriginal ways of life but also on ways of
dying and death.

It is estimated that, in the 1500s, the Aboriginal population of Canada numbered
between 200,000 and 500,000, the majority living in central and eastern Canada
(Morton, 2006). By 1867, only 100,000 to 125,000 were left, 10,000 of whom were
Métis and 20,000 Inuit (The Canadian Encyclopedia, 2007a). What happened to
so drastically reduce the Aboriginal population?

The most significant factor was disease. Contact with European fur traders and
missionaries meant exposure to infectious pathogens to which Aboriginal peoples
had little or no natural resistance (Decker, 1991). Because the first European settlements were in eastern and central Canada, a rise in the death rate for Aboriginal
peoples started in these areas and then spread to the north and west. Trading
posts that opened across the northwest following the formation of the Hudson's
Bay Company in 1670 served to widen contact between Europeans and Aboriginal
groups (Morton, 2006; Wilson, 1983) and thus to widen exposure to deadly infectious diseases.

Reductions in Aboriginal populations were dramatic. Morton (2006) reports
that one-half of the Huron, who lived near the Great Lakes, died of contagious illnesses within the first five years of contact with Europeans. By 1650, the Huron had
ceased to exist as a nation, victims of disease and starvation; by 1680, their rivals,
the Iroquois, were also reeling from the effects of European diseases (Heagerty,
1928). Smallpox was the deadliest of the epidemics. The first such epidemic likely
occurred in 1627, and recurrences afflicted both Aboriginal peoples and Europeans
until well after the cowpox inoculation was developed in 1806 (Heagerty, 1928).
According to Bryce (1902: 98), smallpox completely blotted out entire Aboriginal
bands as illustrated by this example: "Of one tribe of four hundred lodges, only
10 persons remained; the poor survivors, in seeking succour from other bands,
carried the disease with them."

Recurring epidemics radiated outward as European explorers and traders fanned
across the country (Decker, 1991). Beginning in the eighteenth century and during

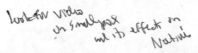

the nineteenth century, many of the Aboriginal peoples living on the Prairies suc-
cumbed to infectious diseases (Statistics Canada, 2006). In the far North, the first
epidemic of measles did not reach the Inuit until 1952, at which time it brought
death to seven out of every 100 cases (Coleman, 1985).

The ineffectiveness of traditional Aboriginal healing methods for treating the
new infections is thought to have been a powerful factor in their adoption of
European health care measures, although these were no more effective against
the raging epidemics (Dickason, 1984; Heagerty, 1940; Stone, 1962). An alternative
explanation for the adoption of European medicine by First Nations peoples is
that many healers died of infection, perhaps in greater numbers than the general
Aboriginal population, due to their more frequent exposure to the infectious agents.
Their store of knowledge, which had been gained over centuries (Erichsen-Brown,
1979), would have been decimated.

In the days before public health, immunization, and antibiotics, contagious diseases also took the lives of many Europeans. Ewart's (1983) study of the daily records
of York Factory, a Hudson's Bay Company fur trading post in northern Manitoba,
reveals a continuously high death rate from infections among the European inhabitants — but higher still among their Aboriginal contacts. Not surprisingly,
cemeteries typically grew quite large around fur trade forts (Brown, 1980).

Unquestionably, infectious disease imported by Europeans was the most important factor in the considerable reduction in life expectancy among Aboriginal
populations. Yet this was not the only cause of death that could be traced to the
Europeans' arrival. Territorial disputes also resulted in Aboriginal deaths. Outright
wars and ongoing skirmishes between Aboriginal and European factions, and among
Aboriginal groups, continued throughout the colonial period (Morton, 2006). Much
of the conflict concerned trade with the French and English or land claims.

The displacement of Aboriginal peoples from their traditional lands by European
settlement and the reduction of food sources as a result of the growing European
presence in Canada were two important reasons for the decline and, in some cases,
the total destruction of Aboriginal populations. The last surviving Beothuk, a nation native to Newfoundland, died in 1829. Although the direct cause of her death
was tuberculosis, the disappearance of the nation as a whole "was at least partly
owing to their loss of access to the coast and its food resources" (Dickason, 1984:
100), as the Beothuk were effectively barred from sea access by the presence of
European fishers and, later, settlers. On the Prairies, the destruction of the bison
herds by overhunting throughout the nineteenth century had a major impact on
local First Nations and Métis, depriving them of their primary source of food and
trade goods (Wilson, 1983).

summary of the 1 death in Native

Thus, the impact of the Europeans on the Aboriginal peoples of Canada was devastating. Infectious diseases previously unknown to First Nations increased death rates and ravaged whole populations. Armed conflict, and the gradual destruction of Aboriginal economies and ways of life further contributed to high rates of death.

Largely as a result of inadequate provisions, misadventure, and infectious diseases, early European settlers in Canada also had a very high rate of death (Morton, 2006). The incidence of death would have been much higher initially if Aboriginal people had not provided direct assistance in the form of food and shared knowledge about survival in the new land (Morton, 2006). For example, over the winter of 1535-36 local people showed Cartier how to brew white spruce and hemlock bark to treat scurvy (Roland, 1985; Stone, 1962). Prior to this intervention, Cartier had resorted to prayer when European medicines failed to prevent death from this disease (Jack, 1981). The Aboriginal peoples who demonstrated this rapid and effective cure to Cartier were annihilated by disease soon after. It would be another 300 years before Europeans began to use a Vitamin C food supplement to prevent scurvy (Stone, 1962); thus, the disease remained a major cause of death in Canada until the nineteenth century (Heagerty, 1928).

The adoption of the Aboriginal treatment for scurvy seems to have been something of an exception. Although folklore hints at the adoption of some Aboriginal medicines by the early Europeans in North America (Dickason, 1984), it is not evident that there was much transfer of health care knowledge between the two peoples. In general, Europeans neither understood nor valued Aboriginal peoples' health care knowledge (Erichsen-Brown, 1979; Stone, 1962). This is unfortunate, as some Aboriginal health care practices, such as suturing, keeping wounds clean, reducing dislocations, splinting fractures, and physiotherapy, were observed by the Europeans to be very effective (Heagerty, 1928; Stone, 1962).

The harsh climate, tough pioneer existence, low standard of living, and unsanitary habits of settlers contributed to many early deaths in the colonies. Between one-quarter and one-third of all Europeans who immigrated to Canada before 1891 died of infectious diseases (Marsh, 1985). Virtually every ship that arrived from Europe brought a new wave of infection. The death rate on these transatlantic voyages was high; one in three travellers became ill and one in seven died (Heagerty, 1928). To try to protect the inhabitants of the colonies from imported diseases, quarantine was established in 1720. Later in that century, legislation was passed to authorize quarantine hospitals and screening centres in strategic parts of the country (Amyot, 1967). After immigrant-bearing ships introduced cholera to British North America in 1832, a permanent quarantine station was set up on

Grosse Ile near Quebec City in an ultimately unsuccessful attempt to stop its spread (Heagerty, 1940).

The death rate from infections was high among all of the Europeans who came to Canada. Although the existence and significance of germs began to be understood as a result of the development of the microscope by Zacharias Janssen in 1590 and its refinement in the mid-1600s by Antony van Leeuwenhoek, it was not until much later that information about germ transmission and avoidance (asepsis) was applied in society. Although surgeons in Canada were first introduced to the principles of asepsis in the 1890s, the medical profession showed considerable resistance to the introduction of aseptic technique (Roland, 1985). At the time of World War I, some Canadian physicians were still performing surgery with their bare hands (Agnew, 1974).

Inadequate health care was another major contributor to the low life expectancy and high death rate in colonial Canada. From the 1500s through the 1800s, health care was often more of a liability than an asset in preserving life (Coleman, 1985; Dickason, 1984). Although Europeans possessed only rudimentary knowledge of the human body and health care, they were interventionist in their approach to treatment (Bettmann, 1956). This could be a deadly combination. European health care was based on reducing imbalances in the four humours (blood, phlegm, bile, and lymph) of the body, and treatment usually consisted of blood letting, enemas to induce the passage of stool, and emetics to induce vomiting (Lessard, 1991); bleeding was a common treatment for a range of ills. Through this, or a variety of other questionable health care practices, a well-intentioned healer could weaken a person further and could spread an infectious agent from one site of the body to another or from one person to another (Heagerty, 1928; 1940).

Most people could not afford either the expense of a hospital stay or the services of the very small number of doctors in colonial Canada. Given the primitive state of both medical knowledge and health care technology, this was not entirely to their disadvantage. It is not surprising that the few hospitals that existed then were considered places of death (Heagerty, 1940; Stone, 1962).

Reducing suffering during the dying process does not appear to have been a common focus of care by European healers in early Canada. For many centuries, healers across Europe are thought to have shunned dying people because the death of patients would negatively affect their reputations (Veatch, 1989). Palliative knowledge and skills consequently remained undeveloped. Trade with the Far East did bring opium to Europe in the mid to late 1600s, and the substance is thought to have been one of the few early analgesics used in Europe (Bettmann, 1956). It is not clear how available opium actually was, particularly for use by the vast majority of people. Instead, alcohol was a common analgesic. Healers in colonial Canada were thus unlikely to have either the tools or the expertise to effectively reduce any unpleasant symptoms during the dying process. Religious doctrine may also have served to restrict efforts to relieve suffering. Until the eighteenth century, Europeans commonly thought illnesses were a punishment or warning from God and that suffering was to be accepted (Lessard, 1991).

Other factors are also certain to have had an impact on dying and death in early Canada. One was the gender imbalance in the colonies. Almost all of the early explorers and settlers were men, as were the mainly Scottish fur traders arriving to work in Hudson's Bay Company posts (Brown, 1980). These young men had a high risk of death through misadventure and starvation during explorations to map the land and gather furs. Because their travels took them away from population centres, where health care was more available (Decker, 1997), it is not known how much assistance was provided to them when they were dying. In any case, male gender roles emphasized stoicism. This quality may have been enhanced through contact with First Nations cultures, which often considered pain and suffering an intrinsic aspect of living and which valued courage in the face of such challenges.

The demographic make-up of colonial Canada changed slowly. Precarious European settlements dominated by single men became home to an increasing number of women and children. Fur traders and other men had children with Aboriginal women, with Métis descendants the outcome. French settlement schemes brought unmarried women to New France to promote the development of new families. By the early nineteenth century, waves of British immigrants, many of them families with children, arrived to expand and develop new British North American colonies. The increasing presence of European women in Canada brought new patterns of dying and death. Maternal and child deaths were frequent, and these deaths served to further reduce the life expectancy of Europeans in early Canada.

As the number of European immigrants increased, the cultural values they brought with them also began to change the meanings attached to life and death. Christian religious views of life and death were in sharp contrast to the values common among First Nations (Dickason, 1984). For Aboriginal peoples, death was more likely to be a natural or unavoidable part of life, explained by their cosmology and given meaning by their spirituality. Death began to take on a new significance when viewed in the context of everlasting suffering in hell or eternal reward in heaven. Similarly, new meanings of dying and death were introduced, such as death being a punishment for sin, and suffering while dying as a means of securing a place in heaven (Lessard, 1991).

In addition to their religious values, the new immigrants brought with them a contemporary European emphasis on the individual (Morton, 1997). In traditional Aboriginal communities, the loss of an individual, while a serious occurrence, could be somewhat compensated for within the larger group. The individualism and self-reliance of pioneer life meant that death took on a different meaning, becoming more personally significant. Moreover, in practical terms, the death of either wife or husband in an isolated pioneer family could be disastrous for the survivors.

And death did come. The life of pioneer families was extremely difficult. Morton's (1997: 39) account of early life is particularly revealing: "For pioneers in a harsh and unfamiliar land, survival was a preoccupation, to be achieved only through relentless, back-breaking work.... Pioneers were described as being reduced to an unsmiling grimness by loneliness and labour. Women faced the terror of childbirth without even a neighbour to help. A single careless blow with an axe could cripple a man or leave him to die in the stench and agony of gangrene."

Life in colonial Canada could be difficult and dangerous, and the state could do little to make it safer. It was not until the late nineteenth century that public health measures were introduced by various levels of government, reflecting the public health movement that originated in Britain earlier in the century (Baumgart, 1992; Langham and Flagel, 1991; Leftwich, 1993). Long before hospital care became effective at saving lives, public health was rapidly extending life expectancy in Canada (Baumgart, 1992). Public health significantly reduced maternal and child death rates. Enhanced cleanliness, including sewage management, more effective quarantines, and better quality water and food reduced contact with infectious agents and raised the level of health among all Canadians. Public health measures significantly reduced many common infectious diseases including measles, cholera, scarlet fever, influenza, diphtheria, tetanus, tuberculosis, and typhoid. These illnesses had typically claimed the lives of younger persons, particularly children. By the turn of the century, campaigns for clean water and pasteurized milk were beginning to reduce the high death rates among children from gastro-intestinal diseases, particularly among the urban poor.

In summary, prior to the middle of the twentieth century, Europeans in Canada had a relatively low life expectancy, and many died from infectious diseases. Health care was largely ineffective and public health practices also tended to be inadequate, although they were beginning to change. Death came frequently, often claiming young people. Little could be done for the dying. Although health care was practiced in various forms in early Canada by both Aboriginal and European healers (Heagerty, 1940; Scalena, 2006), its success in preventing death was limited. Prior to the emergence of modern health care measures, death for both Aboriginal and non-Aboriginal people was a common outcome of illness or injury. The dying process would have also typically been shorter than it is today, because a severe illness or injury without specific and effective care often leads quickly to death.

DYING AND DEATH IN CANADA IN THE TWENTIETH AND TWENTY-FIRST CENTURIES

Up until the twentieth century, there were no dramatic gains in life expectancy in Canada. From the early 1900s on, gradual changes served to reduce the death rate and enhance the prospect of long life. These changes were mainly due to improvements in the standard of living and changes brought about by a concerted public health movement. These improvements benefitted some Canadians more than others. Aboriginal Canadians, for example, continued to suffer from a lower standard of living than their European counterparts (Corlett, 1935; Wilson, 1983), which then as now increased the incidence of health problems among First Nations and lead to a higher death rate and lower life expectancy (Adelson, 2005). Chief George Baker recounted how, when he was a child in the early 1900s, every member of a poor Aboriginal family he knew died of smallpox, and how during the epidemic no doctor came to the reservation (Wilson, 1983). By the 1970s, when health care advances had significantly reduced the incidence of death from acute conditions among the general population, pronounced differences continued to exist between Aboriginal and non-Aboriginal people in terms of health status, life expectancy, and rates of illness and injury causing sickness and death (Statistics Canada, 2006).

Modern health care treatments provided in hospitals by doctors and nurses, and the 1957 federal *Hospital Insurance and Diagnostic Services Act*, which initiated a universal health care system to serve Canadians, are commonly believed to be the most important factors explaining the dramatic increase in life expectancy in Canada in the later half of the twentieth century (Langham and Flagel, 1991; Leftwich, 1993). However, most of the reductions in the death rate and the resulting increases in life expectancy occurred prior to both the development of the Canadian health care system and the availability of the surgical and medical treatments that now greatly extend the lives of sick individuals. In 1770, the death rate in Canada was 37 per 1,000 persons, but this increased to more than 50 per 1,000 during epidemics (Heagerty, 1940). By 1926, the death rate had decreased to 13.5 deaths per 1,000 and by 1939 it had dropped even further to 10.4 (Heagerty, 1940). Today the death rate is between seven and eight deaths per 1,000 persons

(Statistics Canada, 2006). Although a substantial decline in Canadian mortality rates between 1931 and 1981 is reported (Blishen, 1991), a much greater decline occurred prior to the 1950s. This early twentieth-century decline in mortality rate is attributable largely to the public health movement's impact on life expectancy through disease prevention.

Public health measures had the effect of reducing the incidence and severity of most types of illnesses, infections, and other types of health problems. Millar (1995: 25) credits public health for improvements in longevity and increases in life expectancy, citing "public health programs in the areas of infectious disease control, maternal and child health, chronic disease prevention, environmental health, nutrition education, and injury prevention." Public health measures at the beginning of the twentieth century included sewage management, milk pasteurization, and the sanitation of drinking water (McGinnis, 1985). Other public health initiatives included the promotion of cleanliness in the home and community, and the enactment of legislation to ensure the safety of food, drugs, and health products. In general, the public health movement led to increased community and personal standards for cleanliness and health.

In addition to continuing efforts to improve sanitation, hygiene, and food safety, public health efforts after World War I began to include immunization programs. Immunizations create resistance to infectious pathogens. In the past, resistance usually developed through surviving a bout of illness, but, of course, many did not survive serious illnesses such as smallpox and diphtheria. Mass immunizations were able to greatly reduce the death rate from infectious diseases (Harding le Riche, 1979). For instance, diphtheria was one of the leading causes of childhood death until its vaccine became available in 1930. Mass immunizations for diphtheria, as well as smallpox, whooping cough, and tetanus, were administered in Canada in the 1940s (Grant, 1946). Some significant vaccines were developed even more recently, such as those in the 1950s to prevent poliomyelitis (polio) and the new vaccine for HPV (human papilloma virus), a common cause of cervical cancer in women.

It is important to note that epidemics continued during and even after what could be considered the heyday of public health, that is, the period immediately preceding the introduction and subsequent widespread use of antibiotics in the 1940s. The influenza epidemic of 1918-20, the polio epidemic of the 1950s, and other less well-known episodes claimed tens of thousands of lives in Canada. Indeed, the influenza epidemic following World War I killed between 50,000 and 70,000 Canadians (Buckley, 1988; MacDougall, 1994). The federal Department of Health was established in 1919 as a direct result of this epidemic (McGinnis, 1985). One reason why this epidemic was studied, reported on, and acted upon was the fear that it induced. Death from this strain of influenza was particularly gruesome — the victim drowned slowly from fluid buildup in the lungs. It also tended to strike young adults in the prime of life.

Changes in the historical rate of death from tuberculosis (TB) present a more positive assessment of the impact of public health measures across Canada. The incidence of tuberculosis, which had become by the late 1800s the most common cause of death in Canada, was very much reduced by the 1920s through public health measures. This abatement occurred fully 20 years before antibiotics began to be used widely to treat infections, including those arising from the TB bacillus (Zilm and Warbinek, 1995).

As early as the 1930s, immunizations and other public health measures had reduced infectious diseases as the leading cause of death in Canada. Throughout the remainder of the century and into the twenty-first century, the cause of death shifted from infectious disease to chronic disease, that is, to illnesses that are incurable and typically progressive, and that usually have increasingly debilitating effects.

Health care did not become important for effecting cures until after World War II. For instance, although Canadians Frederick Banting and Charles Best developed insulin in the 1920s, its successful use in conjunction with a dietary and exercise regimen for the treatment of diabetes was not perfected until after the 1940s (Winterfeldt, 1991). Antibiotics such as penicillin and the sulfonamides were also not in widespread use until after World War II. Furthermore, even though the X-ray machine and laboratory testing of blood and other bodily fluids were developed around the beginning of the twentieth century, these advancements in diagnostic capacity did not immediately lead to improvements in health. Most parts of Canada had neither a reliable laboratory nor an X-ray machine until after the 1940s, when the federal government began to directly fund hospital construction and modernization (Agnew, 1974). Major surgery such as heart surgery, vascular surgery, and kidney transplants did not begin in Canada until the 1960s (Audette, 1964; Hayter, 1968). Intensive care units and coronary care units, along with the drugs and other technologies common to them, also did not become available until after 1960. The modern method of closed-chest cardiopulmonary resuscitation (CPR) was first developed in 1960 (Kouwenhoven et al., 1960) and quickly reduced the likelihood of death following cardiac arrest. Tremendous breakthroughs in knowledge and the subsequent progress in diagnostic capacity and in surgical and non-surgical procedures for treating illnesses had a marked effect on society. Faith in health care and physicians increased rapidly, justified to a degree as the efficacy of health care grew quickly and substantially.

These and other health care developments overshadowed the earlier and ongoing successes of public health measures. In comparison to public health programs, which promoted population health and sought to prevent the development of illnesses that could cause widespread disability and death, modern health care comprised an immediate and dramatic way of saving lives. An illness-based and cure-oriented care perspective quickly began to prevail in the Canadian health care system (Ajemian, 1992), with efforts focused on treating illnesses and preventing death rather than preventing illnesses or providing hospice palliative care to the terminally ill.

This shift from prevention to treatment was reinforced by the increasing role of hospitals, which do not exist to prevent illnesses so much as to diagnose and treat them (Ajemian, 1992). Until the 1940s, health promotion and health care were most often carried out in homes by family members, assisted at times by visiting nurses or physicians. Thereafter, health care began to shift increasingly to hospitals (Bradley, 1958; McPherson, 1996; Wilinsky, 1943).

As we have seen, in colonial Canada, because of the ineffectiveness of health care at that time, hospitals had been thought of as places of death and were often shunned. Throughout the twentieth century, however, as the number of hospitals grew, the care of dying persons began to shift to this institution (Wilson *et al.*, 2001, 2002). For instance, in 1930, 40 per cent of deaths in Alberta occurred in the 90 hospitals operating at that time (source: archived Vital Statistics data for Alberta). By 1953, four years before hospital care was guaranteed to Canadians by federal law, half of all deaths in Canada took place in hospitals. In 1994, over three-quarters of all deaths in Canada were recorded as occurring in hospitals (Wilson *et al.*, 2001, 2002).

Not only was the location of death changing, so were its causes. The shift from acute to chronic illnesses has had a remarkable, although largely untold, effect on society. As a consequence, Canadians have tended to lose their fear of sudden as well as premature death. For example, pneumonia used to be feared as an illness that could bring a relatively quick death at any age. It could strike any person, and without good nursing care, or even despite good nursing care, death frequently occurred. After antibiotics began to be used, pneumonia quickly became an almost unheard-of cause of death, except in very old age or in cases of considerable disability.

The shift from acute to chronic illnesses also impacted nurses and physicians. Although the sick and dying have been nursed for centuries, the 1890 to 1940 era is significant in that nursing schools and medical schools opened across Canada to ensure enough well-educated nurses and physicians for public demand (McPherson, 1996). Licensure that restricted the practice of health care to educated physicians and nurses was also enacted during this time (Scalena, 2006). Although medical schools were university based, most early nursing schools were hospital based, with student nurses a source of reliable, high quality, as well as cheap labour (McPherson, 1996). Upon graduation, nurses typically provided private care in the home (McPherson, 1996). Often, they cared for the chronically ill and the dying. Yet, by 1943, only 2,000 of all 16,000 registered nurses in Canada were working in private practice (Canadian Nurses Association, 1964). Dire working conditions and either unemployment or underemployment had forced private duty nurses to seek more secure and also more familiar work in hospitals (McPherson, 1996). Almost every town and city across Canada had a hospital by the 1920s (Agnew, 1974). Ongoing demand for skilled nursing care, in hospitals predominantly, and the need to keep pace with rapid hospital-based care developments continued to impact nursing throughout much of the twentieth century. Today, however, only 60 per cent of nurses are employed in hospitals, while the remainder work primarily in community-based settings such as public health and home care offices (Canadian Nurses Association, 2006), indicating another change in employment site.

It is important to note that nursing the sick and dying became less significant for nurses in the excitement generated by health care developments during the latter half of the twentieth century (Langham and Flagel, 1991; Leftwich, 1993). Furthermore, with nursing and medicine both shifting their focus to preserving life, it is not surprising that there was little progress made in the area of hospice palliative care. Hospice palliative care — the art and science of caring for and comforting the dying — was not formally emphasized in Canada until 1975, when two Canadian hospitals opened inpatient units dedicated to the non-curative care of dying persons (Ajemian, 1990).

Although dying and death were frequent topics in health literature until the 1940s, there was little mention of either in the health literature from 1950 to 1990, nor was there much discussion about providing supportive care to dying persons (Wilson et al., 2001, 2002). One issue that did generate concern in these years was aging. Starting in the mid-1940s, numerous reports highlighted the growing number of older persons in Canada and the need to provide appropriate care for this distinct population (Canadian Nurses Association, 1964; Hall, 1947; Miller, 1960).

Most chronic illnesses, although they usually have their origins in early or mid-life, typically do not become symptomatic until later life. Most also worsen with aging. Heart and lung diseases, for instance, are often progressively debilitating in nature and not amenable to a complete cure. Lungs, once significantly scarred from smoking or recurrent lung infections, cannot be regenerated. Furthermore, atherosclerosis — that is, hardening of the arteries — develops over a period of many years and is not fully dissipated by life-saving surgery, which opens (sometimes temporarily) a few blocked arteries in the heart, neck, or legs. Although surgery, drug therapies, and other medical treatments have proven to be very successful for saving lives, they have also extended the length of terminal illnesses and also the final or end-stage dying process (Millar and Hill, 1995). In the second half of the twentieth century, death shifted from being an inevitable and generally quick event to a much less certain outcome of diagnostic testing and therapeutic treatment. In short, death began to be delayed through health care, even though the underlying disease remained.

In the mid-1970s, a concerted attempt to reduce the incidence and also the impact of unhealthy lifestyles began, largely because it became evident that unrelieved stress, inactivity, obesity, unhealthy dietary habits, and the use of tobacco products or excessive alcohol intake lead to serious health problems (Lalonde, 1978). The wellness or health promotion movement has since helped reduce the incidence of illness and death from acquired illnesses and from accidents. For instance, seat belt legislation in the 1970s and 1980s greatly reduced the incidence of accidental vehicular deaths (Hauser, 1974; MacKillop, 1978). More recently, the environmental movement is drawing attention to the unhealthy consequences of pollution and mismanagement of the environment in which we live. The implications of global warming are becoming increasingly apparent. While health care may be needed for the illnesses that are an expected outcome of global warming, the solutions to climate change are not within its realm.

Public perceptions of health care, despite being bolstered considerably in the middle of the twentieth century by many significant diagnostic and treatment advances, began to change as the end of the twentieth century neared. Not only did the irreversibility of aging, particularly in light of an aging Canadian population, become more evident, but so too did the limitations of modern health care treatments (Millar and Hill, 1995). For all our progress, human beings have escaped neither death nor disability. The optimism generated by the wonder of modern scientific health care has dissipated considerably. Canadians once again have become more conscious of the inevitability of death. Hospice palliative care is now once again an expected duty of all health care professionals, although now it has also become a respected specialization for the nurses and physicians who dedicate themselves to the compassionate care of the dying.

SUMMARY

In summary, for Aboriginal peoples in Canada before the arrival of the Europeans, death was common, visible, often came early in life, and was thus a familiar circumstance. Life expectancy was modest, although some Aboriginal persons reached advanced old age. Death followed a similar pattern for the Europeans who came to Canada from 1500 to 1900. However, the consequences of the European presence were disastrous for Aboriginal peoples, who were decimated by epidemics and by the destruction of their economies and ways of life. By the end of the nineteenth century, the public health movement and an increasing standard of living were benefitting the European immigrants. As a consequence, death rates declined and life expectancy increased.

Throughout the twentieth century, the public health movement continued to produce significant gains in health status. However, the development of health care knowledge and health care technologies, coupled with universal access to health care for Canadians, led to further and often spectacular gains in the saving of lives. The welcome and ongoing successes of modern health care substantially eclipsed the public health movement in public consciousness. In the twentieth century, the causes of death shifted from infectious diseases and other acute illnesses to chronic disease. The timing of death also shifted increasingly to later life. The care of the dying was transferred from family members to health care professionals, with dying and death moved from the family, home, and community to the hospital. Death, which had been common and familiar, became unfamiliar, remote, invisible, and expected only in old age.

CHAPTER 2
DYING AND DEATH IN CANADA TODAY

This chapter examines contemporary patterns of dying and death in Canada. It explores who experiences what terminal conditions, when, and under what circumstances. Circumstances include the length and course of the dying process, and the timing and location of death. The chapter begins with a discussion of current causes of death and then examines death by age, sex, and other variables.

CAUSES OF DYING AND DEATH

Two of every three deaths in Canada among all 218,062 that occurred in the year 2000 were from one of two primary causes (see Table 2.1) — circulatory disease (35.0 per cent of the total) or cancer (29.4 per cent of the total). Two much less common but still relatively frequent causes of death in 2000 were respiratory disease (8.1 per cent of all deaths), of which chronic obstructive lung disorders were the most common, and external causes including accidental injuries such as falls or vehicular accidents, unintentional poisoning, suicide, and homicide (6.1 per cent of all deaths). Four additional causes of death among many others are also notable for their frequency: nervous system or sense organ disease (4.4 per cent of all deaths), of which Alzheimer's disease and other degenerative or atrophic brain diseases were the most common; endocrine, nutrition or metabolic disease (3.9 per cent of all deaths), of which diabetes mellitus was the most common; digestive disease (3.7 per cent of all deaths), of which liver failure was the most common; and mental disorders (2.7 per cent of all deaths), of which dementia was the most common. Old age, although it has many obvious impacts on health, is not listed as a cause of death.

Although circulatory disease is clearly the most commonly recorded cause of death in Canada (Campbell *et al.*, 2006), it could be argued that deaths from cancer are actually more prevalent. This argument is supported by an understanding of how circulatory diseases are reported. In this case, deaths from all possible diseases

Table 2.1: Causes of Death in Canada in 2000

RANK	CAUSE	NUMBER OF DECEDENTS	PERCENTAGE OF TOTAL
1	Circulatory (cardiovascular, cerebrovascular)	76,426	35.0%
2	Neoplasms (cancer)	64,111	29.4%
3	Respiratory (lung)	17,745	8.1%
4	External (accidents, injury, and suicide)	13,249	6.1%
5	Nervous System	9,522	4.4%
6	Endocrine, Nutrition, Metabolic	8,558	3.9%
7	Digestive (liver, intestines)	8,148	3.7%
8	Mental Disorders	5,991	2.7%
9	Genitourinary	4,137	1.9%
10	Infectious and Parasitic Diseases	3,111	1.4%
11	All others combined	7,064	3.2%
	Total	218,062	100%*

*Percentages do not add to 100.0% due to rounding.

of the heart are combined with diseases involving blood vessels in all other locations of the body (such as the brain) into one broad category for reporting purposes. Circulatory disease thus consists of an often lethal set of conditions including heart attack, heart failure, stroke, peripheral vascular diseases affecting the veins and arteries of the legs, blood clots in veins that travel as emboli to other areas such as the lungs, and many other different types of life-threatening conditions. If the 15,576 deaths in 2000 that were recorded as having been from cerebrovascular (brain) disorders were separated from the other 60,650 deaths reported as circulatory disease, then cancer with 64,111 deaths would be the most common cause of death in Canada.

There are a number of reasons why heart and other circulatory diseases combined continues to be reported as the leading cause of death in Canada. One of the most prevalent stems from the fact that determining the primary or most important cause of death is still a somewhat inexact science. Autopsies are not often done to verify cause of death; generally, they are carried out only if foul play is suspected or if a patient dies soon after a surgical or diagnostic procedure. In 2002, only 8 per cent of decedents were subject to autopsy (Statistics Canada, 2002b). It is therefore not possible to say with complete accuracy what caused the death of every one of the more than 200,000 persons who die in Canada each year. For instance, someone who is well and dies suddenly could have died from a heart attack, a heart rhythm disturbance (arrhythmia), a stroke (brain bleed), a pulmonary emboli (one or more blood clots travelled to the lungs), or many other less common causes. Most of these causes, however, are vascular in nature, and so it is not unusual that the most probable cardiovascular or circulatory disorder is listed as the primary cause of death. Indeed, a number of studies have established that circulatory disease is often assigned by "default" when there is uncertainty about the cause of death (D'Amico et al., 1999; Lloyd-Jones et al., 1998; Iribarren et al., 1998; Myers and Farquhar, 1998). In another case, a person may have had cancer slowed but not eradicated by ongoing treatment. If this person died suddenly from a heart attack, stroke, a reaction to a drug, or another possible condition, what should be listed as the primary cause of death? In this case, according to Statistics Canada criteria, cancer should be listed as the primary cause of death, as it is the condition that primarily contributed to death or to the conditions favourable for death. Given these issues, it is unlikely that all of the 70,000 physicians and other persons who are authorized to complete death certificates in Canada will list the correct cause of death.

Selecting and recording a correct primary cause of death is important. The reported incidence of a disorder, particularly if it causes illness, disability, or premature death, is a significant indicator of the level of effort and resources that will be devoted to combat it. It is said that more money has been devoted to research-ing the treatment of heart disease, which is often listed as Canada's number one health issue, than has been committed to all other illnesses combined. Tremendous advancements in emergency and post-emergency cardiovascular care have resulted from this massive, targeted effort (Campbell *et al.*, 2006). These advancements have helped reduce deaths from heart disease and many other circulatory diseases (Manuel *et al.*, 2003). Furthermore, in some 150 instances now each year across Canada, hearts are transplanted when they cannot be repaired — another indica-tion of the success of the concerted effort to eliminate death from heart disease (Canadian Institute for Health Information, 2006). Nevertheless, the motivational slogan "cancer can be beaten" and cancer's rising predominance in causing signifi-cant illness, disability, and death result in more effort being expended to battle it (Canadian Cancer Society/National Cancer Institute of Canada, 2007).

Unfortunately, heart attack (death of heart tissue usually from blocked arter-ies feeding the heart muscle) continues to be one of the most common sudden lethal diseases, along with cardiac arrhythmias or altered heart functioning due to heartbeat irregularities (Campbell *et al.*, 2006). Strokes and motor vehicle or workplace accidents are two other common causes of sudden death. Sudden deaths are very difficult for families, who have no opportunity to have the meaningful last conversations that often take place in less rapid dying processes. Most deaths from heart attacks and other circulatory diseases occur in mid to late life. These diseases are typically acquired after birth, and they usually are progressive in nature, with few symptoms until the disease is quite advanced. At this stage, they are incurable and thus considered "chronic." This is not to say that cardiovascular diseases are untreatable; rather, most cannot be entirely eliminated or reversed once they have become symptomatic (Manuel *et al.*, 2003). Furthermore, the risk factors for acquir-ing heart and other cardiovascular diseases (such as smoking, inactivity, and a diet that is high in saturated fats or trans fats) are often associated with long-standing personal habits or lifestyle choices (Tanuseputro *et al.*, 2003).

Like circulatory disease, cancer tends to be diagnosed in mid to later life. A recent report indicated that 44 per cent of all new cases of cancer and 60 per cent of cancer deaths occur among persons aged 70 or older (Canadian Cancer Society/National Cancer Institute of Canada, 2007). There are many different sites of cancer, but lung cancer is by far the most common lethal cancer, followed by colorectal cancer (cancer in the bowels or intestines) and breast cancer (Canadian Cancer Society/National Cancer Institute of Canada, 2007). Other cancers are much less common causes of death (each accounts for 5 per cent or less of cancer deaths), in part because some types of cancer are rare and some are more amenable to treatment. Although cancer can cause death quickly, it is more typically a chronic illness as its cause, impact, progression, and treatment are all usually long term (Canadian Cancer Society/National Cancer Institute of Canada, 2007).

The process of dying, including the symptoms of illness and the speed at which death occurs, varies in relation to the disease. A terminal illness may progress rapidly to death or may be present for weeks, months, or even years during which it may abate or worsen. Dying processes are also influenced by the person's age; the number and type of concurrent health problems (or co-morbidities) they have; their will power, personal strength, and support network; and the treatments used to combat the disease or manage the symptoms arising from the disease and its treatment (Chochinov *et al.*, 1999).

Heart diseases are associated with variable dying processes. A person who experiences a heart attack or arrhythmia, for instance, may die immediately, with little or no warning. It is also possible that this person may be resuscitated from cardiac arrest. If resuscitated quickly and without incident, the individual may experience few, if any, lasting effects. On the other hand, the survivor may remain critically ill, needing a mechanical ventilator, for instance, to breathe and sustain life. During this illness episode, the person may or may not be conscious. Numerous medications will be needed to sustain life, along with the many other technologies and treatments that are first available in hospital intensive care or coronary care units and then in other places. Complete recovery or partial recovery may result from this aggressive treatment, but death may also occur in one or many days. Death is almost inevitable if a critical mass (40 per cent or more) of heart tissue has been irrevocably damaged (and no heart transplant occurs), or if the brain and other vital organs have been severely damaged by a lack of oxygen during an episode of restricted or interrupted blood flow to them.   death of heart tissue

Another example of variation in cardiac dying processes is presented by a common heart disease that is called chronic or congestive heart failure, or simply heart failure (Lee *et al.*, 2004). Only about 6 per cent of all deaths from circulatory disease are recorded as having occurred from congestive heart failure, yet most people who survive one or more heart attacks will develop heart failure because the heart has been affected by the death of some of its tissue. Persons diagnosed with heart failure usually live for at least five years, but with a progressively weaker heart. New drug therapies are increasingly extending life expectancy and also wellness for people living with heart failure. Sudden death, if it occurs, generally comes as a result of a fatal disturbance in the heart rhythm. The dying process, however, is usually much more gradual in cases of congestive heart failure. Signs of heart failure are present when the heart is not strong enough to pump blood to other organs and tissues, resulting in their reduced functioning and overall weakness. These signs also result from the backlog or congestion of blood in the lungs and other parts of the body that deliver blood to a heart that can no longer accept and pump all blood returned to it. This backlog results most commonly in leg edema or swelling (which is often seen and described as "fat" ankles) and shortness of breath from lung congestion (i.e., pulmonary edema). Acute air hunger can result, with restlessness or agitation and also blue or unoxygenated skin. Persons suffering from end-stage heart failure may or may not be conscious during the final hours or days of life. The mental and physical states of these patients, as well as the length of the dying process, are often dependent upon the treatments employed to extend life or provide comfort when dying. Oxygen is commonly used during acute episodes of heart failure to reduce the work of breathing and raise the oxygen level within the bloodstream, thereby improving the condition of the heart and other bodily tissues. If the heart continues to fail, however, and oxygen continues to be used, then the dying process can be lengthened by a few hours or even days.

The dying process is also quite variable in cancer deaths, but sudden death from cancer is rare. Although death may occur relatively quickly over a few days or weeks, it normally does not come for a few months, if not years, after a diagnosis has been made. During that time, the diagnosed person is likely to have variable states of health, ranging from good to poor. In 1994, Johansen *et al.* reported that frequent hospitalizations followed a diagnosis of cancer and that the highest re-admission rates to hospital were among persons diagnosed with cancer. Similarly, the 1994-95 National Population Health Survey (NPHS) established a relationship between cancer and hospitalization, as "nearly four out of every ten persons who reported they had cancer had spent at least one night in hospital during the 12 months before the NPHS" (Wilkins and Park, 1997: 30). Today, with health care advances allowing most diagnostic tests and health care treatments to be conducted on an ambulatory or outpatient as opposed to inpatient basis, persons diagnosed with cancer are much less frequently hospitalized. Visits lasting a few hours to hospitals, clinics, or physician offices for tests and treatments are now the norm. Much of the ongoing supportive care that cancer victims receive is thus provided in the home now, with family and friends largely responsible for the transportation needs that arise from the usual six month or more regimen of cancer treatment. Home-based care could also continue throughout the entire end-stage dying process, as persons diagnosed with cancer are among the most likely to say that they wish to die at home (Baillargeon, 2003; Higginson and Sen-Gupta, 2000). The suffering associated with cancer both throughout the active treatment process and the end-stage dying process is often considerable, however, which is why specialized hospice palliative care is most often provided to persons with cancer (Carstairs, 2000). Nevertheless, this suffering, coupled with a range of other factors, may make it difficult, if not impossible, to die at home.

Symptoms during the dying process depend a great deal on the location and extent of the cancer. They are often associated with the specific afflicted organ and the bodily processes that are affected by the cancerous growth or growths. Common symptoms include pain, fatigue, weakness, nausea and vomiting, anorexia (loss of appetite and reduced oral intake), weight loss, and breathing problems (Edmonds *et al.*, 2001). Symptoms tend to worsen as death nears.

Some symptoms are due to the treatments used to cure or slow cancer. Chemotherapy, surgery, and radiation are the most common cancer treatments. They may be undertaken early in the course of an illness to eradicate or slow the course of cancer, or later, even when it is evident that the end-stage dying process has begun. In some cases, treatment is aimed at reducing the size of a cancerous tumour to lessen the symptoms that result from blocked blood or lymph flow, or from pressure on surrounding tissues and nerves. One of the chief side effects of chemotherapy is nausea and vomiting; a common problem following surgery is pain. Analgesics, which combat pain, can cause constipation and other unwelcome side effects such as sedation. Symptoms arising from cancer treatments can thus be mistaken for symptoms of the disease.

CAUSES OF DEATH BY AGE

The most common registered causes of death vary considerably by age group. The 2000 Statistics Canada mortality data show that perinatal insults to health sustained before birth or in the first week of life (51 per cent) and congenital disorders that are present at birth (25 per cent) were the two most common categories of cause of death for the 1,736 infants under the age of one who died that year. External causes (accidents, injuries, and suicide) were the most common category for persons 1 to 39 years of age, accounting for just over half of all deaths in this age group (54 per cent), followed by cancer (16 per cent). Among decedents aged 40 to 49, external causes were the second most common cause of death (18 per cent), with cancer the most common cause (35 per cent). From age 50 to 79, cancer remained the most common cause of death (40 per cent), followed by circulatory diseases (30 per cent) and respiratory diseases (7 per cent). Circulatory disorders were the most common cause of death in decedents aged 80 and older (44 per cent), followed by cancer

(18 per cent) and respiratory diseases (11 per cent). It is also notable that this oldest age group had the highest incidence of "unclassified" disorders causing death than any other age group, as well as the highest rates of death from infections, diseases of the blood and blood-forming organs, endocrine or metabolic disorders, mental disorders, nervous system disorders, digestive system disorders, genitourinary disorders, and musculoskeletal disorders. In short, the oldest are much more diverse with regard to cause of death than decedents in younger age groups.

Focusing on the main or primary causes of death tends to overshadow life-threatening disorders that are not common causes of death at any age. Two such disorders are diabetes mellitus (which is recorded as only accounting for 3 per cent of all deaths in the year 2000) and chronic alcohol abuse. Recent technological advances that allow direct blood-sugar testing have almost eliminated death from diabetic coma (too much sugar in the blood) or insulin reaction (too little sugar in the blood). Nevertheless, diabetes is still a major contributor to high blood pressure (hypertension), heart disease and heart attack, stroke, kidney failure, blindness, and a large number of other illnesses. These illnesses are more life threatening than the original disease. Similarly, liver failure from prolonged excessive alcohol intake is another illness that has become a rare cause of death in Canada (accounting for less than 1 per cent of all deaths in 2000). Alcoholism, however, usually leads to a number of other serious diseases, such as heart disease, bleeding esophageal or stomach ulcers, stomach cancer, and pancreatitis. Although chronic liver failure and also acute alcohol excess can be fatal, it is more likely that these other diseases will end life.

It is also important to recognize that most deaths today do not result from a single cause. Instead, the majority of deaths result from a combination of the accumulated impact of various health insults that have occurred throughout the years, the direct and indirect effects of more than one illness or disease, and the effects of aging (Wilkins and Park, 1997). As such, focusing only on the primary cause of death does not provide much insight into the more normal consortium of death causes, nor does it indicate much about the dying process.

THE DYING PROCESS

Most illnesses, particularly those that are chronic or incurable, do not result in death immediately after diagnosis. Instead, a period of decline or even improvement in health follows. The trajectory of life during this period is dependent upon many factors, one of which is the availability of effective health care treatments. Most diseases, once correctly diagnosed, can be managed or stabilized through surgery, medication, a change of living habits, and/or a change of diet. It is not surprising, then, that experts warn that terminal illnesses — that is, those that will eventually cause death — can last for as long as 15 years (Allard *et al.*, 1995; Eastaugh, 1996; Kurti and O'Dowd, 1995). Whereas a quick death may have occurred in the past, a much longer end-of-life period is now possible. During a long terminal illness, a person is unlikely to consider him or herself to be dying; yet other persons, including family and health care providers, may think of them as gravely ill or even dying. This dichotomy in perceptions can bring about some difficult decision-making.

As the terminal phase of life progresses, the person's health may be relatively stable with only a slow decline over time. The terms "holding their own" or "losing ground" are often used in response to queries about the health of those who are terminally ill. Another trajectory that is common, particularly among persons with dementia and those at an advanced age, is that of a long and progressive "dwindling" (Lynn, 2001). This is often marked by sudden illness episodes, during which death may occur, but often with a recovery that does not return the individual to their pre-crisis health state. For this reason, this trajectory could be characterized as "bouncing on the bottom." All of these terminal illness trajectories are lengthy. Considerable work has gone into estimating the length of life remaining for terminally ill persons, with some prognostication tools now considered about 80 per cent accurate for persons with cancer (Harrold *et al.*, 2005).

In contrast, the final end-stage or active dying process — when death becomes immediate and inevitable — typically proceeds quickly and with much more certainty, with death occurring in minutes or at most a few days. This shift to the active dying process generally occurs whenever a major and irreversible change in health occurs. As approximately 80 to 85 per cent of terminally ill persons are able to walk about until the last few hours or days of life, the change to where a person becomes bedfast before death is very pronounced (Wilson, 2002).

Most final dying processes are recognized as such by close family members and friends, who see a critical change in the condition of the terminally ill person (Kerr and Kurtz, 1999). Health care workers, particularly those who have come to know the dying person or have witnessed numerous deaths, are also likely to recognize impending death. Unconsciousness may be the most commonly recognized signal of impending death, but becoming bedridden and/or developing a lack of interest in food and refusing food may also indicate that death is approaching (Allard *et al.*, 1995).

Although brain death and other definitions of death are still evolving (Hornby *et al.*, 2006), death is commonly considered the end of cognitive (brain) and physical (heart and respiratory) functioning; it is also considered the culmination of all end-stage dying processes. For example, a massive head injury or major stroke can result in almost instantaneous death. A heart attack that stops the heart from beating can cause death in as little as four to ten minutes. A more typical death takes place now after an end-stage dying process that lasts one to four days, with unconsciousness and irregular, laboured breathing signalling an irreversible decline prior to the cessation of heart, lung, and brain functioning (Kerr and Kurtz, 1999; Wilson, 2002).

FACTORS AFFECTING THE DYING PROCESS

Many factors can affect the dying process. As we saw in Chapter 1, deaths take place more often in hospital now than in any other location — a place where oxygen, intravenous fluids, and other life-saving or life-prolonging technologies are readily available for use. Deaths in nursing homes are increasing, however, because of population aging and other social changes that are resulting in an increased number of single seniors needing help from formal rather than family sources. Many of the same technologies that exist in hospitals to save or extend lives can be found in nursing homes. In a western Canadian study of deaths in nursing homes and hospitals, 97 per cent of the patients who died had at least one continuous life-saving technology in use at the time of death (Wilson, 1997). There is considerable ongoing controversy over the use of these technologies near death, which may explain why a recent Quebec study found considerable variance in their use (Feldman et al., 2004). It can be argued that these technologies comfort the dying person or, alternatively, that they comfort the family and other caregivers, particularly by allowing them to feel that they are "doing something" to ease the person's dying (Wilson, 1997). In contrast, it can be argued that they lengthen the dying process and possibly the suffering that is associated with dying. As there are no firm guidelines yet as to the use or nonuse of these technologies, each dying process should be considered unique and, therefore, one in which the benefits and drawbacks of each technology should be considered. This issue of how best to comfort dying persons is not confined to hospitals and nursing homes; these same technologies can be transported to the home, which means that the final dying process can be extended in any care setting.

As mentioned previously, there is often considerable uncertainty about the main or primary cause of death. Furthermore, death is often the outcome of a number of concurrent illnesses or health conditions, coupled with the influence of aging.

Thus, the practice of recording a single disease as the cause of death means that some illnesses, most often those involving the heart, appear to be more prevalent and more serious than they really are, while other illnesses do not appear to be as significant as they really are. The consequence of this practice is serious. If the method of assigning a single cause of death is not considered when population mortality data and other data are examined, then faulty health care and social sector planning follow. Of considerable concern is that efforts and funds are spent primarily on eradicating and treating certain diseases as opposed to developing and providing support for dying persons and their families. Indeed, minimal assistance is currently available in Canada for families, although they provide the majority of the end-of-life care needed by dying family members. Minimal assistance from government home care programs, for instance, is available even in wealthy provinces. An Alberta study found that only 20 per cent of dying persons had received home care in the last year of life (Wilson, Truman, *et al.*, 2005, 2007). Other current forms of assistance, such as paid leave from work for one family member, are also minimal. The Employment Insurance Compassionate Care Benefits program is limited to 50-60 per cent salary replacement and a period of six weeks during the last 26 estimated weeks of life (Service Canada, 2007). As such, considerable concern exists with regard to fostering and ensuring a "good" death (Smith, 2000; Williams *et al.*, 2006). The concept of a good death is oriented to ensuring that the dying process is as optimal as possible for all involved persons.

Despite advances in determining the length of life remaining for persons who are terminally ill from cancer, it can be difficult to determine when a person is in their last half year of life, as chronic health conditions which threaten life may exist for years prior to death. Most Canadians aged 12 and older report having at least one chronic health condition, with more than one condition common among older persons (Health Canada, 2002). The most frequent self-reported health problems by seniors are arthritis or rheumatism, high blood pressure, allergies, back problems, chronic heart problems, cataracts, and diabetes (Health Canada, 2002). The incidence and severity of both chronic and acute health problems tends to vary considerably among seniors, however, with some seniors much healthier than others. In response to questions in the 1996-97 National Population Health Survey, only 6 per cent of seniors who did not live in a nursing home reported "poor" health. Yet, an earlier survey found 39 per cent saying their activity was somewhat restricted by their health (Lindsay, 1999). Furthermore, this earlier survey found that one-half of all home-care recipients reported only fair or poor health (Wilkins and Park, 1998). These recipients of government-sponsored home care were typically of advanced age, female, had two or more health conditions (commonly cancer or stroke), had been hospitalized for eight or more days during the past year, and lived alone (Wilkins and Park, 1998).

Not surprisingly, the prevalence of health problems in institutionalized seniors is even higher. One report indicated that 58 per cent of seniors living in nursing homes who could rate their own health, rated it as only fair or poor, while one-quarter reported suffering from the effects of a stroke, and half from bowel or bladder incontinence (Tully and Mohl, 1995). Moreover, virtually all reported at least one chronic health condition, 80 per cent reported activity limitations, and 72 per cent reported needing assistance with personal care (Lindsay, 1999). Advanced Alzheimer's disease and other senilities causing considerable confusion and physical disability are common reasons for the institutionalization of seniors.

Chronic health conditions indirectly influence both dying and death. For instance, arthritis and many of the other health limitations that older people ex-perience serve to impede mobility. A number of problems can result from limited mobility, which can reduce not only physical activity and exercise tolerance but also the ability to obtain and prepare food and to engage in social activities. Although all of these can have serious health consequences, in the end, heart disease will be the most likely primary cause of death to be listed on the death certificate, par-ticularly if the deceased was obese. This situation raises the proverbial "chicken or egg" argument of what came first. Death certificates and other health records generally emphasize what came last and fail to recognize the factors that contribute to death and affect the dying process.

Hospital utilization is at times used to describe the prevalence and seriousness of health problems, both chronic and acute, with utilization rates and figures often related to age. Health Canada's (2002) report entitled *Canada's Aging Population* indicated that seniors aged 75 and older had roughly double the risk of being hos-pitalized in the 1996-97 year than seniors aged 65 to 74, who in turn had a roughly double risk of being hospitalized than persons aged 45 to 64. This information on the risk of being hospitalized was based on self-reports, a less accurate measure than actual hospital utilization data. Unfortunately, few reports on hospital utilization in Canada exist, and most currently available reports use hospital data from the years 1960-90, which means they do not reflect the recent major shift to ambula-tory care from inpatient care. For instance, the Public Health Agency of Canada's (2007) online information about the leading causes of death and the leading causes of hospitalization reports 1996-97 data despite much change over the past ten years. A recent, and as yet unpublished, study of the people who used two representative urban Canadian hospitals from 1995-96 to 2005-06 (Wilson, 2006) found the vast majority of persons admitted to hospital for inpatient and other types of health care services were under the age of 65 (see Table 2.2). Seniors, however, had a longer length of stay in hospital when admitted to hospital, as compared to younger persons (four days versus nine days), which illustrates the fact that the illnesses affecting older individuals tend to differ from those of middle-aged and younger persons (Public Health Agency of Canada, 2007; Rosenberg and Moore, 1997; Stokes and Lindsay, 1996). A report published in 1996 by Stokes and Lindsay outlined national hospital data findings for the years 1982-93; it revealed that heart disease was responsible for the highest hospitalization rates among seniors, followed by strokes, chronic respiratory diseases, falls, pneumonia, hernia, prostate cancer, lung cancer, intestinal diseases, gallbladder diseases, bladder and kidney cancers, diabetes mellitus, kidney diseases, and colorectal cancers. In 1996-97, circulatory diseases and cancer were the two most common causes of hospitalization for Canadians of all ages combined, and also for seniors aged 65 and older (Public Health Agency of Canada, 2007). These life-threatening disorders are serious in and of themselves, but when combined with other co-morbidities (additional illnesses) and additional social factors such as not having someone at home who can provide assistance if discharged early, they illustrate why seniors tend to have a longer length of hospital stay than younger persons. Chee *et al.'s* (2004) study of hospitalizations in Canada involving coronary artery bypass graft surgery showed advanced age (75 or older) was the sole factor that could account for an 11 per cent higher cost of care among some patients having this type of surgery. One additional reason why seniors have a longer length of hospital stay is that they may be actively dying, and, for compassionate reasons, they will be kept in hospital until that process is complete.

Table 2.2: Age of Patients Admitted for Care by Hospital Service Area

HOSPITAL SERVICE AREA	0-64 YEARS OF AGE	65+ YEARS OF AGE
Inpatient	81.1%	18.9%
Emergency Department	85.7%	14.3%
Daysurgery	90.8%	9.2%
Outpatient	78.5%	21.5%

Complete hospital utilization data for the years 1995-96 through 2005-06 provided for analysis by Caritas Health Group-Edmonton. The researcher would like to acknowledge Caritas Health Group for permitting the research study that derived this information, and both Caritas and Capital Health for providing the administrative data for this study. The interpretations and conclusions contained herein are those of the researcher (Donna Wilson), and do not necessarily represent the views of Caritas. Caritas does not express an opinion in relation to this study or its findings.

AGE AT DEATH

As Figure 2.1 illustrates, the majority of deaths in Canada occur in old age. More specifically, in the year 2000, 77.7 per cent of all Canadians who died were 65 years of age or older. The fact that death in Canada now typically comes in old age is also illustrated by the finding that persons aged 85 and older comprise 27.4 per cent of the total. It is also highly remarkable that 2 per cent of all decedents were aged 97 or older and 2 per cent were aged 22 or younger. Nearly half of all deaths among this younger group of decedents were children under the age of one year. As was discussed in Chapter 1, childhood deaths have become increasingly uncommon. Death has clearly shifted to old age.

Age at death has a major impact on how death is perceived. If a young person dies, it is often unexpected and normally considered tragic. In contrast, the death of an old person, particularly someone very old, is much more common and also more likely to be expected and accepted, or at least anticipated to some degree. This does not mean that the death of an older person is not mourned; it simply means that death at an advanced age is a more normal occurrence now than death at a younger age.

Figure 2.1: Age at Death in Canada in 2000

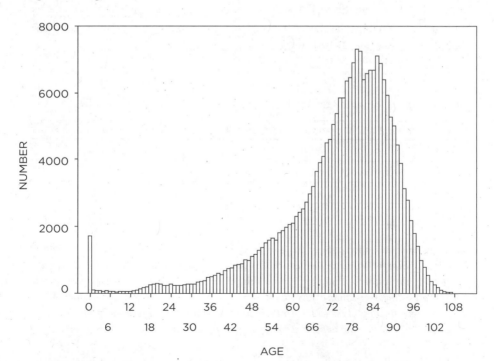

AGE

It is also remarkable that in 2000, while the average age at death was 73.5 years among the approximately 218,000 Canadians who died that year, 1,516 (0.7 per cent) were 100 years of age or older. These 1,516 individuals overcame many barriers to a long life and as such could be considered "hardy" survivors. Ongoing public health improvements, continuing social and economic progress, and advances in health care are likely to continue to reduce barriers to a long life. Barring a world war, global economic collapse, or the emergence of new untreatable illnesses, it is highly likely that more and more Canadians will reach the advanced old age of 85 or more.

Population aging has led to some interesting conjectures on maximum life expectancy. Some experts believe there is a biological limit to life, that is, that humans have a fixed life-span (of perhaps 120 or even 125 years) beyond which life cannot be extended (Fries, 1980). Human life expectancy increased markedly over the twentieth century (Simmons-Tropea and Osborn, 1987), meaning that a much higher proportion of persons were living longer into advanced old age. This trend is expected to become even more pronounced as the baby-boom generation ages. This large and influential cohort, born in the years 1946 through 1966, will begin reaching the retirement age of 65 in 2011 and will thereafter contribute significantly to the pattern of dying and death in Canada well into the twenty-first century. The baby-boom generation has benefitted much from many social and health care advances throughout their life time, and so their deaths are expected to further emphasize the century-long trend toward death in old age.

Senescence is the term used to refer to "wearing out" of body parts as a result of aging, with Hall reporting in 1922 that senescence occurred over the last half of life. More recent information suggests that senescence begins much earlier in life and is slowly progressive over a life time. With more people reaching old age, senescence is becoming a major factor in both the quality and quantity of their lives. Senescence tends to be overlooked, though, as a "cause" of death or even as a cause of the many health limitations that can lead to death. For instance, even when a death occurs in a centenarian, a disease or illness and not senescence or "old age" is always registered on the death certificate as a cause of death. Chappell (1992) labelled this phenomenon the "medicalization" of death. She considers dying to be a normal physiological event at the end of a long life (see also Fries, 1980). As we have seen, the practice of labelling every death as an outcome of a potentially treatable disease or health condition is problematic. If it appears that people are dying from unsuccessfully treated illnesses, then it is much more likely that health care efforts will focus on finding cures than on finding ways to make dying people *disease four?*

more comfortable. This issue is increasingly a concern now that many people are living well into their eighties and beyond

By the age of 85 or increasingly by age 90, considerable senescence in the form of physical frailty is usually evident (Rosenberg and Moore, 1997; Lindsay, 1999). For this reason, persons aged 85 and older are often referred to as the "oldest old" or the "frail elderly." This population group is one of the fastest-growing segments of the Canadian population. For instance, between the years 1991 and 2001, persons aged 80 and over increased 41 per cent to approximately 932,000 persons (Statistics Canada, 2002b). By 2011, that number is expected to increase to 1.3 million (Statistics Canada, 2002b). This age group is significant, because despite being hardy survivors, the frail elderly become unduly ill if they experience a common cold, flu, or another illness that would not be life threatening at an earlier age. The World Health Organization (1989) recognized this health state as a loss of physiologic adaptability with aging.

While Canadians in general are living longer than earlier generations, women typically live considerably longer than men (see Figure 2.2). In 2000, the average age of male decedents was 70.4 as compared to 76.7 for female decedents (a difference of 6.3 years). Other statistics for that year serve to emphasize that death comes earlier to males, such as the median ages of 74 and 80 for males and females

Figure 2.2: Age at Death, by Sex, 2000

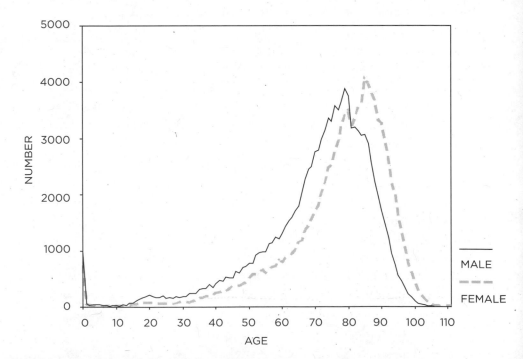

respectively, and 79 as the most frequently occurring age at death among males as compared to 85 for females. This is not to say that males all die younger — one man who died in 2000 lived to be 109, although one woman lived to be 111 years of age. This gender difference is further illustrated by the fact that among all decedents in the year 2000, 82.8 per cent of all of the females who died and 72.8 per cent of all of the males who died had reached the age of 65 before death occurred. This longevity of females compared to males is further accentuated by an analysis of deaths among the oldest old. Nearly twice as many women as men had reached the age of 85 or more at the time of their deaths (20,911 males compared to 38,365 females). The difference between males and females is even greater among those who die at age 100 or older. Nearly five times more women than men lived to be 100 years of age or older before their lives ended (272 males compared to 1,224 females).

This sex difference in life expectancy has been evident for some time (Millar, 1995); consequently, life expectancy is calculated separately for males and females. According to Statistics Canada (2007), the life expectancy for girl babies is 81 years and for boy babies it is 75 years. The sex differential in life expectancy is not static, and while it grew in the past 50 years, this gap has begun to decrease (Millar, 1995; Nault, 1997). This narrowing of the sex differential in life expectancy may result from factors negatively affecting the health of women. One such factor is an increase in smoking among women (Ellison et al., 1999). Another is the increased stress and reduced health maintenance activities among women as a result of the "double shift" phenomenon; that is, women who work outside the home still fulfill most of the responsibilities of maintaining the home and family (Valentine, 1994).

There is some ongoing speculation, however, over why women typically live longer than men and why men have higher death rates than women at most ages. The 2000 Statistics Canada mortality data revealed more male babies than female babies died under the age of one year (984 compared to 751). This sex difference continued throughout childhood. Of all children aged one to 18 who died in the year 2000, 848 were boys and 516 girls. This difference continued throughout adulthood, except for the oldest-old age group where the number of female deaths exceeded the number of male deaths, with this difference simply a reflection of the fact that women have come to outnumber men in the oldest years due to their higher rates of survival in earlier years. Obviously, there are a number of ways in which sex influences age at death and thus all aspects of dying and death.

Not only are males more likely to die at younger ages than females, but Table 2.3 shows that the causes of death also differ somewhat between the two sexes. In 2000, males and females died most often of circulatory disease, cancer, and respiratory disease, although sex-based differences in these proportions are apparent.

info on why woman live longer.

Table 2.3: Leading Causes of Death in 2000 on the Basis of Gender

CAUSE OF DEATH	PERCENTAGE AND RANK AMONG MALE DECEDENTS (N=111,742)		PERCENTAGE AND RANK AMONG FEMALE DECEDENTS (N=106,320)	
Circulatory	34.1%	(Rank 1)	36.1%	(Rank 1)
Cancer	30.5%	(Rank 2)	28.2%	(Rank 2)
Respiratory	8.4%	(Rank 3)	7.9%	(Rank 3)
External (accidents, etc.)	7.9%	(Rank 4)	4.2%	(Rank 5)
Digestive	3.7%	(Rank 5)	3.8%	(Rank 7)
Endocrine	3.7%	(Rank 6)	4.2%	(Rank 6)
Nervous System	3.5%	(Rank 7)	5.3%	(Rank 4)

Differences in cause of death are more apparent when the less common causes of death are compared. In particular, males are nearly twice as likely to die of injuries, accidents, and suicide (i.e., external causes). In contrast, females die more often of nervous system disorders and endocrine disorders than males do. These two latter disorders largely reflect the greater age of females at death.

In summary, males are more likely to die at all ages than females. The higher death rate for males is associated with a substantial difference in the life expectancy between males and females. Nevertheless, this sex differential in life expectancy may continue to diminish as the lifestyles and social roles of males and females become increasingly similar.

PREMATURE DYING AND DEATH

In Canada and elsewhere, death has been defined as "premature" if it occurs before the age of 75 (Statistics Canada, 1991). The age of 75 is also commonly used to calculate potential years of life lost (PYLL), an estimation of the additional years a person might have lived had premature death not intervened. Cancer deaths typically result in the highest PYLL. Although the concept of a premature death can help distinguish early from late death, using age 75 as a marker disregards gender differences in life expectancy. It may be more appropriate, for example, to consider a male death premature if it takes place before the age of 70.4 (the average age at death for males) or perhaps 74 (the median age at death), and a female death premature if it takes place before the age of 76.7 (the average age of death for females) or 80 (the median age). Although this may seem an unimportant distinction, treatment decisions are frequently based on age. If a person is thought to be dying prematurely, then aggressive cure-oriented treatment is more likely to occur.

Using age 75 as a benchmark also disregards more individualized health factors. For instance, many of the infants under the age of one who died in 2000 were born with serious congenital deformities and illnesses that were not compatible with life outside the womb. Some people are also born with less serious but still life-threatening conditions, such as cystic fibrosis. Health care has done much to improve and extend life for persons with cystic fibrosis, but few if any persons living with this disease can expect to reach age 75. In the 1940s, most individuals with cystic fibrosis died in infancy. By the 1970s, with health care and other advances, the majority could expect to live into their twenties. Even today, death from cystic fibrosis usually occurs by age 40; therefore, death from cystic fibrosis at age 40 is not entirely premature. *relative nature of premature death*

Another example of the importance of individual factors in aging relates to acquired variations in health among individuals. Some experience negative health consequences from smoking or other risky personal lifestyles, while others have more positive health consequences from regular exercise and other health-promoting habits (Shields and Martel, 2006). Such individual behaviours, along with the environment in which a person lives and works, do much to influence health, and in turn, life expectancy (Shields and Martel, 2006). These individual differences in health are not acknowledged when age 75 is used to differentiate premature from non-premature death.

In summary, most deaths occur in old age. Deaths in childhood and even in middle age have become increasingly uncommon and are thus often unexpected. Although there are some issues with this definition, deaths occurring before age 75 are often characterized as premature. These changes have not gone unnoticed; death is now much more expected in old age.

OTHER INFLUENCES ON DYING AND DEATH IN CANADA

Indicators of social class such as income, education, housing, and occupation have clearly and repeatedly been associated with rates of death and therefore life expectancy (Canadian Institute for Health Information, 2004; Epp, 1986). For example, Statistics Canada (1997: 5) indicated that "socio-economic status affected people's chances of survival as well as of becoming ill. Being in the lowest household income groups in 1994/95 was predictive of death before age 75, even after controlling for sex, chronic diseases, and smoking." Asada and Kephart's

(2007) recent Canadian study of equity in health services utilization revealed that the poor and those with lower educational levels had less contact with family physicians and physician specialists. The implications of this issue arise over a lack of early attention for health problems that could progress to life threatening conditions needing hospital-based interventions. Some research has shown that poor people in Canada are higher users of hospitals. For instance, the National Population Health Survey of 1994-95 showed an inverse relationship between income and hospitalization; in short, the poor were more likely to be hospitalized than the rich (Wilkins and Park, 1997). Income level is often directly linked with education level, with higher incomes and more income security associated with higher education. All such factors impact upon health (Canadian Institute for Health Information, 2004). Finally, occupation is also directly associated with varying exposure to health risks. Aronsen *et al.*'s (1999: 270) study of mortality in Canada's work force illustrated "excess" mortality from selected diseases among certain occupational groups, for example, "a high rate of laryngeal cancer deaths among male metal fitters, lung cancer deaths among female waiters, and ischemic heart disease deaths among female inspectors and foremen and male taxi drivers and chauffeurs."

Ethnicity is another factor that can contribute to longer or shorter life expectancy and therefore to rates of death. For example, accidents are among the leading causes of death for Aboriginal peoples in Canada (Canadian Institute for Health Information, 2004). Sheth *et al.* (1999) found that cardiovascular and cancer mortality varied among Canadians of European, South Asian, and Chinese origin. Chen *et al.* (1996) were among the first to find that immigrants to Canada had a longer life expectancy than native-born Canadians. The "healthy immigrant effect" (i.e., people of ill health are less likely to immigrate to another country) was thought to bring about this difference. Despite the healthy immigrant effect, research has since found members of visible minority groups use general physician and specialist services less often than other Canadians, and their use of hospitals and cancer screening services are also markedly less (Quan *et al.*, 2006), factors which could shorten life. In addition to differences in income and education levels, ethnic differentials in illness and death rates may result from genetic differences, as well as cultural factors such as diet and lifestyle. Language is another issue. John-Baptiste *et al.*'s (2004) study involving three hospitals in Ontario showed patients with limited English-language proficiency had considerably longer hospital stays.

As noted above, Aboriginal peoples in Canada continue to have lower life expectancy and higher rates of death than non-Aboriginal peoples (Canadian

Institute for Health Information, 2004). This is true despite increases in Aboriginal life expectancy, largely through a decrease in infant mortality and in death rates from respiratory conditions, digestive disorders, and infectious diseases (Canadian Institute for Health Information, 2004). Nevertheless, Aboriginal peoples in Canada continue to have higher rates of infectious diseases, such as tuberculosis, meningitis, and HIV. Furthermore, they also have higher death rates from suicide, homicide and other violence, and accidents including motor vehicles, poisonings, and residential fires (Canadian Institute for Health Information, 2004). Trovato (2001) suggested that this unenviable health state is the result of geographic isolation, poverty, and social psychological marginalization leading to high rates of social disorganization, alcoholism, and other forms of substance abuse.

Despite higher death rates in the Aboriginal population compared to the non-Aboriginal population, a trend towards the convergence of Aboriginal and non-Aboriginal death rates suggests that there will be continuing decreases in acute or sudden causes of death and increases in death rates from circulatory disease and cancer among Aboriginal peoples. Nevertheless, Aboriginal persons who get circulatory disease or cancer currently have lower survival rates than non-Aboriginal persons (Canadian Institute for Health Information, 2004). Aboriginal persons also have a high rate of diabetes and associated problems such as chronic kidney failure (Canadian Institute for Health Information, 2004). The lower life expectancy and considerable burden of illness among Aboriginal people was the impetus for the Canadian Institutes for Health Research establishment in June 2000 of an Institute of Aboriginal Peoples' Health (IAPH). This Institute was formed to foster a research agenda in the area of Aboriginal health and promote innovative research to improve the health of Aboriginal people in Canada.

Canada is a land of climatic variation, with extremes of hot and cold weather occurring throughout the yearly cycle. More deaths occur in Canada in February and March than in other months. In fact, approximately twice as many deaths take place in those two months than during August and September, when the lowest incidence of death occurs (Trudeau, 1997). Similarly, a more recent study on the seasonal incidence of deaths and hospitalization associated with congestive heart failure in Canada showed that both hospitalization and death occur much more often in January than September, the month with the lowest rates (Feldman et al., 2004). There are several possible explanations for this seasonal variation in death rates and hospitalization rates, such as variation in patterns of exercise and socialization, as well as an increased incidence in the winter of flu, colds, and pneumonia, falls on ice, road accidents, and overexertion from shovelling snow. In short, the weather affects our health and thus death rates.

LOCATION OF DEATH

As outlined in Chapter 1, there was a pronounced trend towards the hospitalization of death from the middle to near the end of the twentieth century. The percentage of deaths occurring across Canada in hospital reached a peak in 1994 and then began to decline (Wilson *et al.*, 1998). Although it is not certain that an ongoing trend toward death out of hospital will continue into the future, it is becoming evident that the final days of life are increasingly taking place either at home or in a nursing home (i.e., a long-term or continuing-care facility). This situation is at considerable odds with the prevailing view that terminally ill and dying persons are high users of hospitals. The importance of hospital utilization data analysis for addressing myths and other common beliefs is shown by a study of Alberta's inpatient hospital utilization and related data that found 19 to 24 per cent of all deaths in that province occurred each year in hospital emergency departments for the years 1992-93 through 1996-97, a smaller but still considerable percentage (10-15 per cent) died each year in long-term care facilities, and around 10 per cent each year died in all other locations, leaving just under half (48 per cent) of all deaths in the province during that five-year timeframe occurring after an admission to hospital had taken place (Wilson *et al.*, 1999). Furthermore, 17 to 20 per cent of all of the deaths each year occurred after only a single day's admission to hospital (Wilson *et al.*, 1999). This is not the only province where the current use of hospitals for dying and death purposes is much less than had been previously noted or previously thought to be the case (Menec *et al.*, 2007).

The location of death and the location of the end-of-life care near death are affected by many factors, one of which is the type of dying process. Persons experiencing long drawn-out dying processes who have developed considerable dependency are more likely to be living in a nursing home or another type of care facility prior to their death there, while those with relatively short dying processes are more likely to live at home prior to death at home or in hospital.

While dying at home has its appeal, it also raises certain issues. One major issue, given limited formal home care support — the equivalent of one hour of assistance each day over the last three months of life (Wilson *et al.*, 2007) — is that there must be a family willing and able to care for the dying person in the home. When there is such a family, it helps if there are several family members willing and able to provide care, especially female family members, as informal caregivers are largely the female members of that family, generally the spouse or the daughter, who provide most of the care (Greaves *et al.*, 2002; Status of Women, 2003). This work often involves much physical and emotional work over long hours, and this work

caregiver burn out

is now noted for its negative effects on the health of these caregivers (Greaves *et al.*, 2002; Hawranik and Strain, 2000; Status of Women, 2003).

Much concern has been raised to date about informal caregiver burden, and it is important to point out the need for much more formal home care to support   *plus $* dying and death in the home, as well as for the ongoing care of disabled persons at home. At the same time, it is unfortunate that the many benefits of informal family caregiving have been largely overlooked. Research is only now beginning to point out the tremendous benefit to all persons involved in the shared caring that occurs between caregivers and care recipients (Koop and Strang, 2003). That this mutual caregiving benefit occurs over the final days of life, a unique and special time when a once-in-a-life-time process occurs, is an added dimension that needs much more attention. This attention may help to dispel the considerable fear that   *movie* exists over informal caregiver burden and other difficulties associated with provid- *2 weeks* ing end-of-life care at home.

In Britain, considerable formal home care provision and other developments have enabled the majority of end-of-life care in the past 10 to 15 years to take place in the home, and, although most deaths still occur in hospital, these hospital stays are typically only one to three days in length (Boyd, 1993; Eastaugh, 1996). As early as 1990, Duffy *et al.* (1990) indicated that a pediatric palliative care program in Toronto was assisting parents who wanted to keep their dying children home as long as possible, thus reducing both the length of the final hospital stay and also the incidence of hospital deaths. Other early Canadian research indicates that out-patient or in-home palliative care programs can help shift death successfully out of hospital (Farncombe, 1991; Gardner-Nix *et al.*, 1995; Howarth and Willison, 1995; Levy *et al.*, 1990; McWhinney *et al.*, 1995). It is now believed possible that most,   *is this a good thing?* if not all, of the care needs of dying persons can be managed outside of hospitals. While a small proportion of persons (5-10 per cent) experience difficult dying pro-cesses, such that they require specialized hospice palliative care (Carstairs, 2000), the majority of persons who die have a relatively short phase of dependency near death and also have fairly basic care needs near the end of life (Wilson, 2002).

Although much dialogue is occurring about dying and death in the home, a considerable number of deaths actually take place in nursing homes and other long-term care facilities. Statistics Canada data for the year 2000 shows 3.3 per cent of all deaths in Canada that year occurred in long-term care facilities. As some deaths of nursing-home residents will have occurred in hospital after transfer there, this figure hides the fact that end-of-life care will typically have previously been provided over many days or months in the long-term care facility. As this institutionalized care is often long term, the nursing home becomes the patient's

but not considering children's families wishes

home. The Canadian Healthcare Association reports annually on the number of long-term care beds and acute care hospital beds across Canada, with long-term care beds consistently higher in number by 20 per cent or more than acute care hospital beds. Given the considerable and rising public demand for hospital services, as illustrated by long wait lists, a concerted effort is being made to reduce unnecessary hospitalizations and to shorten hospitalizations. Nursing homes and other long-term care facilities have developed considerable expertise in the care of dependent seniors, and some are becoming recognized for their provision of expert or specialized hospice palliative care. Transferring a dying person from a long-term care facility to receive end-of-life care in hospital is therefore not usually required. Furthermore, sending a dying resident of a nursing home to hospital means this person moves from a familiar environment and familiar caregivers to an unfamiliar environment, one which is primarily concerned with acute cure-oriented care. Considerable discomfort during and after this move is of concern. Another hazard is that the peace and reflection that normally occurs at the deathbed in the vigil that is customary during the final hours or days of life can be lost in the rush to transfer and treat what may appear to unfamiliar health care professionals as a potentially reversible trajectory to death. All of these factors indicate that transfers of dying persons from nursing homes to hospitals is minimal and declining. Transfers of terminally ill and dying persons from hospitals to nursing homes instead can be increasingly expected; indeed, this is already becoming the case for some forward-thinking hospitals. In addition, some hospitals have established subacute care facilities, where persons who no longer need or desire acute curative care, but still need some ongoing care, can be transferred (Wilson, 2006).

Some other factors affect the chances of dying in hospital. Deaths from accidents, injury, and suicide are much less likely to occur in hospitals. In contrast, the highest rate of hospitalized death is for congenital disorders that are present and often noticed at the time of birth. In 2000, 95 per cent of all deaths of infants under the age of one year from congenital disorders occurred in hospital. Deaths from congenital disorders will either occur in hospital after a hospital birth or later in childhood, often after repeated hospitalizations.

The amount of time that dying people spend in the hospital varies, but hospitalizations that end in death have tended to be lengthy. For instance, in 1990, Levy *et al.* reported that the average stay for dying children at the Toronto Hospital for Sick Children was 29 days. This end-stage stay appears to be declining in length, however, and for many different reasons. In Alberta, from 1992-93 to 1996-97 when hospital bed numbers were reduced considerably as a cost-cutting measure, the average length of hospital stay prior to death in hospital declined from 28 to 15 days

(Wilson *et al.*, 1999). Regardless, these hospital stays were between two and three times longer than the average stay for all other patients. Other studies have also illustrated longer lengths of stay (Alberta Health, 1992-97; Randhawa and Riley, 1995; Statistics Canada, 1998). Frequent hospitalizations prior to death are another concern. Approximately half of all persons who had an inpatient hospital death in Alberta in the year 1996-97 had three or more hospitalizations in the five years before they died (Wilson *et al.*, 1999). This same study, however, as indicated earlier, established that only 48 per cent of all deaths in the province occurred after an admission to hospital and that approximately one in five deaths in hospital occurred after only one day there. Thus, this information should dispel some concerns over the high use of hospitals by terminally ill and dying persons.

Although a lack of home-based caregivers could be a major factor contributing to dying and death in the hospital (McWhinney *et al.*, 1995; Rosenberg and Moore, 1997), the 2000 Statistics Canada mortality data show married persons are more likely to die in hospital than persons who are not married. Similarly, males, who are more likely to have female family members, who are the prime candidates for providing home-based end-of-life care, are still more likely than females to die in hospital.

Other variables, some known and others unknown, also appear to influence location of death. One such variable is the province or territory: considerable variation is evident in location of death across provinces and territories. In 2000, the Northwest Territories and Nunavut together had the lowest percentage of deaths in hospital (45.0 per cent of all deaths), followed by Saskatchewan (55.7 per cent) and Prince Edward Island (57.2 per cent). Nova Scotia and British Columbia had the highest recorded rates of hospital deaths (both over 80 per cent). Although death location recording problems may account for some of this variance, other largely unknown factors are also indicated.

SUMMARY

Today, having moved well into the twenty-first century, dying and death in Canada typically come in old age and usually through chronic health problems such as circulatory disease and cancer. Death occurring early in life is unexpected, and deaths before the age of 75 are labelled premature. However, the process of dying and the event of death typically come later in life for females than males. This sex differential in life expectancy is not fixed; it could converge if it is not already converging, largely if the health of women suffers as a result of lifestyle issues, such as smoking and the double-shift phenomenon. There also continues to be a differential in the health status and life expectancy among Canada's social classes and cultural groups, with the poor and less educated being at greatest risk for poor health and thus premature death. Finally, although most deaths are recorded as taking place in the hospital, it is becoming evident that hospitals are not the predominant place of end-of-life care, nor perhaps should they be. What is certain, as a consequence of both a growing and aging population, is that an increase in the number of Canadian deaths can be expected each year.

PART II
THE SOCIAL AND CULTURAL RESPONSE TO DYING AND DEATH

CHAPTER 3
DYING AND DEATH IN THE CONTEXT OF CANADIAN SOCIAL INSTITUTIONS

Death is a normal physiological event that occurs at the end of every life. As described in Chapter 2, the process of dying may be short, culminating in a sudden and unexpected death, but more often it lasts a number of days, weeks, or even months, with death a more expected or at least anticipated event. Nevertheless, dying and death have many different meanings and implications for individuals, as well as for Canadian society. Current views of dying and death, along with current practices related to these phenomena, are extensively influenced by the social institutions — family, religion, the health care system, the legal system, and the funeral industry — that have developed over many years. Each is undergoing changes that have consequences for dying and death. This chapter provides an overview of how these social institutions affect dying and death in Canada. Topics such as hospice palliative or non-curative health care, euthanasia, assisted suicide, the right to die, quality of life, sanctity of life, prolongation of life, withdrawal and withholding of life support, and advance directives or living wills are contentious issues discussed in this chapter.

THE FAMILY

Family life provides the experiences and the broader context that shape our personal understandings of dying and death. Although the death of a friend may be distressing, the loss of a family member through death is usually a major life event. Each person is affected variably, however, by the dying and death of family members, as death in the family can occur at any point in a lifetime and the circumstances of each death can vary considerably. One such circumstance is when the dying process profoundly changes the dying person, such that the loss actually precedes their death. For example, deaths due to Alzheimer's disease often represent two deaths, the death of the person as they have been known and then the physiological death of the body.

Much of what we understand and come to expect about dying and death is gained during our formative years. The reactions of family members to the deaths of grandparents, family friends, or even family pets teach children much about dying and death. In some cases, children are sheltered: they may not be taken to visit dying persons or to funeral and memorial services. In such circumstances, they may learn to respond to dying and death with avoidance, revulsion, despair, anger, or fear. In other cases where children are more involved in the dying and death experience, they are more likely to develop positive perspectives and coping skills (Webb, 1997; Colman, 1997).

Family members often provide a great deal of support to dying family members and to each other. Yet not all families are able to support dying, grieving, or bereaved family members. Dying and death experiences are often stressful and can strain family relationships. In some cases, these relationships are already strained, with dying and death bringing difficult memories forward and bringing together family members who have perhaps not met by mutual consent for many years. Moreover, and often largely from lack of experience, some families may simply not know how to cope with the situation. Reduced experience with dying and death has made it more difficult for families to develop collective stances, positive role models, and comfortable traditions to help them cope. Smaller nuclear families and increased longevity have tended to reduce the number of deaths that individual Canadians experience. In the 1960s and 1970s, Canadian families used to bury a family member

Chronology of death experiences

every eight to ten years on average; by the 1990s, it was once every 15 to 18 years (Flynn, 1993). Deaths in hospital, and thus outside the home, as well as non-contact between family members because of physical or emotional distance have also contributed to dying and death becoming unfamiliar concepts. In this context, Webb (1997: xvii) reported "most of adulthood passes without personal contact with dying." Anderson (1980) was among the first to point out that it is in middle age that children have to come to terms with the "finitude" of their parents, a central task of mid-life. He coined the term "middle-aged orphan," which is meant to indicate the significance of parents passing away. Their passage allows increased autonomy for the child but may also be a potential crisis, as death seems closer now that their buffer (the last surviving parent) to old age and eventual death is gone.

Much has been made in recent years about the disintegrating family. Although some aspects of family have changed, from the traditional view of family consisting of a married mother and father and one or more children, families are still present and still clearly influential in Canadian society. The Vanier Institute of the Family in Ontario (2007) defines a family as "any combination of two or more persons who are bound together over time by ties of mutual consent, birth and/or adoption or placement and who, together, assume responsibilities for variant combinations of some of the following: physical maintenance and care of group members; addition of new members through procreation or adoption; socialization of children; social control of members; production, consumption, distribution of goods and services; and affective nurturance — love." Despite continuing high levels of divorce and an increasing incidence of single or never married persons in Canada, remarriages, common-law marriages, and gay/lesbian marriages (either sanctioned by the state or not) are continuing to ensure that individuals are part of a family. Long-term friendships, particularly among persons who never married, could also constitute a family. In some cases, these changes have meant that individuals have much larger extended families, as may be the case of a child whose parents have divorced and remarried. This child could have four persons now who fulfill the role of parent as well as eight persons whom they consider as grandparents and many additional aunts, uncles, and cousins.

Regardless of how large a family is, considerable geographic mobility and thus physical distance between family members plus the normal living arrangements in which elderly parents and their children live separately, have combined with the mid to late twentieth-century trend which placed death primarily in hospital to make it unlikely that individual Canadians have had much experience in providing hands-on care to dying family members (Charlton and Dovey, 1995; Wilson et al., 1998). Hospitalization is still a reality during most serious bouts of illness, along with institutionalization in a long-term care facility whenever there is a long decline leading to death. In these settings, nurses have taken on many of the responsibilities that family members and friends used to have when home deaths were the norm (Wilson *et al.*, 1998). Even if dying and death take place at home now, palliative home nursing care and information on how to care for a dying person are still needed (Kerr and Kurtz, 1999; Wilkins and Park, 1998).

It is possible that this distance between dying persons and family members is in the process of change. A decline in hospital deaths, discussed in Chapter 2, may mean that an increasing number of deaths are occurring at home. Indeed, in 1994, McWhinney and Stewart forecasted an increase in family involvement in both dying and death: "during the next few decades, the increasing prevalence of cancer and other chronic disease and the reduced number of [hospital] beds are likely to increase the number of home deaths. Even when patients die in hospital, their length of stay is likely to be reduced, so that a longer portion of their terminal illness will be spent at home" (240). Another major socio-demographic factor that could reduce the distance between dying persons and their family members is an outcome of the fact that death is increasingly occurring at an advanced age, with retired children potentially having both the time and the emotional or physical capacity to assist their parents through their dying days. This assistance could continue even if institutionalization in a nursing home occurs. As a consequence of these changes, dying and death for many families could increasingly become "up close and personal," instead of something delegated to health care professionals (Donnelly, Michael, and Donnelly, 2006).

For the present, however, few families plan for a home death or even for home-based end-of-life care; consequently, the deaths of family members are highly unlikely to take place either in the home of the deceased person or any other family member's home (Charlton and Dovey, 1995; Flynn, 1993; Payne *et al.*, 2007). Death is also difficult to forecast, even when there is an awareness of impending death, so family members may not be present at the time of death in a hospital or nursing home. As a result, many Canadians never actually witness a death. Contact with death may be limited to attending a funeral or memorial service. In many cases, the casket (if there is one) is closed, and other constraints such as short viewing hours mean there is limited opportunity to see the deceased person. Caring for the body and even planning for the care of the body after death are normally done by persons other than family members. In short, few families perform the required duties that arise after death has occurred.

In a few cases, decisions are made at or near the time of death to enable organ or tissue donation. Although individual Canadians can arrange before death to donate all or select organs and tissues for transplantation, families have the right to determine if the harvesting of any organs and tissues will occur. Many different body organs and tissues, including skin and bone, can be harvested. These decisions about organ and tissue donation, as well as the rituals, ceremonies, and customs that follow death vary depending on the cultural origins of the family of the deceased person, the relationship of the deceased person to other members of the family, and changing social concepts of what is acceptable. A concerted effort is being made at present to increase the low number of organ and tissue donations in Canada. Over 4,000 Canadians are on waiting lists for transplants, and many die while waiting, despite the transplantation of hearts and other tissues having become a relatively routine surgery and also a highly successful one with regard to long-term health (The Organ Donation and Transplant Association of Canada, 2007). With age and health limits impacting the number of organs and tissues that can be harvested, the families of younger persons who have suddenly died are typically the ones making decisions about donation. Although this decision-making comes at a very difficult time, research is beginning to show that donor families are comforted by the feeling that their loved one's death was not in vain (Health Canada, 2001).

Following death, a funeral home or transfer service (where the body is taken directly to a cemetery or crematorium) is almost always given the responsibility of taking the body and performing death care (Kerr and Kurtz, 1999). Yet, as little as 70 years ago, around the time of the Great Depression, Canadian families commonly used their own vehicles to transport the deceased, cleaned and dressed the dead body, built coffins, used their own homes as places where family and friends could view the body, performed burials, and arranged for deaths to be registered (Colman, 1997; Ontario Coalition of Senior Citizens' Organizations, 1995). Although these activities are not prohibited today, few families carry them out. Instead, families have become much more reliant upon various other social institutions to manage death. It is therefore important to consider the influences of these social institutions.

RELIGION

For centuries, religion has played a major role in both dying and death. The concept of a life after death is common to many societies. Religion has also provided meaning for the dying process; for example, in the past, suffering was considered important for salvation and death was considered an avenue to eternal life (Lessard,

7

1991). Religion also established familiar and comforting patterns of human behaviour and thus provided direction during difficult times. Religious representatives are often still called to the deathbed to support the dying person and the grieving family, and last rites remain an important religious ritual for both dying and grieving Catholics.

In the twentieth century, the influence of religion on dying and death declined considerably, in part because scientific developments increasingly saved lives (Stingl, cited in Wilson et al., 1998). In the past, health care could do little to prevent death, but ongoing scientific advances have radically changed this situation. These developments quickly led to the rising significance of hospitals and physicians in Canadian society. The increased success and prominence of health care tended to overshadow religious conventions regarding dying and death. Furthermore, the rising significance of science during the twentieth century was accompanied by a decline in participation in organized religion (Bibby and Brinkerhoff, 1994).

Science is not the only area that has affected the role of religion in dying and death. The modern funeral industry, for example, has also constricted the role of religion. Flynn (1993) observed: "most religious groups have stepped back and allowed the funeral director to define the social customs of the burial rite.... Religious leaders have not recognized the need to set clear guidelines on funeral rites, and have not educated their clergy on the financial issues surrounding death and rituals" (6-7). It is also important to note that secularization has also led to funeral professionals taking over the roles that clergy once had (Emke, 2002).

This is not to say that the institution of religion, and religious roles and traditions in relation to dying and death, are now irrelevant in Canadian society. Some dying persons and grieving families still involve a spiritual leader in decisions over the use of life support or its discontinuation (Wilson, 1993). Furthermore, priests, ministers, rabbis, imams, and other spiritual leaders still commonly preside over funerals and memorial services, which are frequently provided in places of worship. Churches often have visitation teams to support dying persons, and large hospitals commonly employ clergy to ensure that dying individuals and their families receive assistance if needed or desired. Many religious-based groups offer bereavement support to help families after a family member's death. In short, religion still has significance for individuals, but it is clearly more significant for some people than others.

Religion also influences dying and death at a societal level. Religious groups have provided leadership and advice on social and health policy related to dying and death. A notable example of this occurred in 1984 and then again in 1995 when the Catholic Health Association of Canada, along with the Canadian Nurses

Association, Canadian Medical Association, Canadian Bar Association, and the Canadian Hospital Association, developed guidelines on health care decision-making for terminally ill persons (Joint Statement on Terminal Illness, 1984; Joint Statement on Resuscitation Interventions, 1995). These guidelines addressed ethical issues arising out of technological developments that increased health care workers' ability to resuscitate patients. The initial 1984 guidelines stated that, although resuscitation interventions are often life saving, health care professionals often feel uncertain when deciding to resuscitate a patient for whom such an intervention would not appear to be beneficial in that it would "prolong the dying process rather than extend life" (24). Furthermore, these guidelines indicated that: "palliative care to alleviate the mental and physical discomfort of the patient should be provided at all times" (24). In 1991, the Catholic Health Association of Canada developed additional written guidelines to further assist difficult health care decision-making in life-and-death situations. Among other topics, these ethics guidelines oppose assisted suicide and euthanasia.

THE HEALTH CARE SYSTEM

Although all health care workers are expected to be prepared to deal effectively with dying and death, there is considerable and long-standing concern that they are not adequately prepared to care for dying persons or their grieving families (Brazil et al., 2006; Goodridge et al., 2005; Hall et al., 2006; Kristjanson and Balneaves, 1995; Scott, 1992). Recent surveys of medical and nursing school curriculums show that education on specialized hospice palliative care is increasingly being sought and that basic programs contain content on dying, death, and supportive care (Hall et al., 2006; Oneschuk et al., 2002). Although thanatology education is now routinely provided in nursing and medical programs, this does not ensure that these health care professionals, the ones who must actually provide care for terminally ill or dying persons and their families, feel confident in dealing with dying and death (Brockopp et al., 1991). In addition, many paraprofessionals and health care assistants are involved in the care of dying persons, whether this care takes place in homes, hospitals, or nursing homes (Hall et al., 2002; Goodridge et al., 2005). These persons may not have even the basic thanatology education that nurses and physicians have (Brazil et al., 2006).

Ambulance workers, physicians, nurses, and untrained or minimally trained assistants are the health care workers most likely to provide care to dying persons. Nevertheless, death is not an everyday event in ambulances, hospital nursing units, and continuing-care centres. Death is also a rare occurrence in certain health care specialties, such as pediatrics and obstetrics (Brockopp *et al.*, 1991).

Of all health care employees, nurses provide the most direct, hands-on care to dying persons. Through their work, nurses often gain different perspectives on patient and family needs and preferences than do physicians and other persons who spend less time with the patient (Beaton and Degner, 1990; Lindsay, 1991; Rodney and Starzomski, 1993). Nurses often become advocates for the patient and/or family (Van Weel, 1995). Although nurses are the most likely health care professionals to be present during the dying process and at the time of death, their personal comfort with dying and death understandably varies (Brockopp *et al.*, 1991). This comfort or discomfort reflects, in part, whether or not the nurse believes that the amount and type of patient care is appropriate to the situation (Ericksen *et al.* 1995; Rodney, 1994). A recent study found that 95 per cent of Canadian nurses working in intensive care units felt that futile care was often provided, with family members and physicians said to be responsible for this type of care (Palda *et al.*, 2005). Futile care is thought to be provided largely as a consequence of denial of the impending death by families and physicians (Zimmermann, 2004) and to give family members time to accept the inevitable (Harvey, 1997). This futility, coupled with the frequency of death among intensive care patients, and the commonness of withholding and withdrawing treatment there, could explain why the majority of nurses and respiratory technicians working in Canadian intensive care units are now "comfortable" with withdrawing life support (Rocker *et al.*, 2005). Nurses working in other areas may not be as comfortable.

Professional detachment may buffer the personal impact of caring for seriously ill and dying persons (Beaton and Degner, 1990; Marquis, 1993). This detachment could help explain why 50 per cent of continuing-care residents at a Quebec facility believed staff were indifferent to the death of residents (Lavigne-Pley and Levesque, 1992). Similarly, Wilson (1997) found nurses and physicians working in a large Canadian hospital frequently could not recall details about patients who had died recently under their care. In contrast, nurses and physicians working in a continuing-care facility and in two small rural hospitals were much more likely to recall details about the patient, the dying process, and the patient's family. This difference appeared to be related to the size and type of health care institution. Health care workers in large acute care hospitals, such as nurses, physician specialists, and physicians in training, usually have very little contact with patients and their families. Contact is frequently limited to one hospital stay, with no additional connection outside the hospital. In contrast, small hospitals are most often situated in rural communities or less densely populated urban communities where there is a much greater chance of ongoing contact between health care workers and community residents, both in hospital over one or more admissions and outside of the hospital. For residents in continuing-care facilities, long lengths of stay usually allow relationships to develop between health care workers and residents (Wells, 1990). In some cases, relationships between health care workers and families also develop, especially when continuing-care residents are unable to communicate. Dementia, other conditions such as stroke that impair speech or cognition, and serious health problems are common among continuing-care residents (Burke *et al.*, 1997; Hill *et al.*, 1996; Lindsay, 1999; Ostbye and Crosse, 1994), and family members tend to assume responsibility for communicating with health care workers. In other cases, when the family does not live nearby or does not visit frequently, health care workers develop a relationship with the resident and not the family (Rutman, 1992).

Although individual health care workers vary in their personal perspectives on dying and death, the context in which health care is provided has a powerful impact on dying and death. Medical programs, in particular, have been criticized for focusing on training physicians to preserve life (Bulkin and Lukashok, 1991). For physicians, death may be perceived as a failure of medical care. Similarly, hospitals are primarily oriented to saving lives (Willison, 2006). The majority of health system funding, approximately 60 per cent, is used for hospital and physician services and thus largely for the diagnosis and treatment of illness (Canadian Institute for Health Information, 2005, 2006). The nature of the Canadian health care system, whereby access to hospitals and medical care is ensured for all Canadians, has led to a situation whereby all Canadians can receive a wide variety of treatments to support and extend life (Romanow, 2002). Indeed, treatment normally continues until "nothing further can be done to preserve life" (Wilson, 1997: 36). Public and health care professional concern about death taking place in hospital, where dying is managed by physicians, has been evident for quite some time now as it became evident that hospitals are basically oriented towards resisting death, not easing dying (Wilson *et al.*, 1998).

There are some indications that health care approaches to dying and death have changed in recent years and are continuing to change. Despite the ready ability to use cardiopulmonary resuscitation (CPR) and more advanced life-saving technologies to preserve life, since the mid-1970s hospitals and continuing-care facilities in Canada have developed policies that allow decisions about withholding CPR to be DNR made in advance of death (Choudhry *et al.*, 1994; McPhail *et al.*, 1981; Rasooly *et al.*, 1994; Wilson, 1996). In cases where such a decision is made, CPR is not performed when the heart stops beating or when breathing ceases. In the mid 1990s, Wilson

(1997) found less than 3 per cent of all adults who died in four Canadian hospitals or continuing-care facilities had CPR performed at the time of death. In 97 per cent of cases, a decision had been made, often shortly before death, not to initiate CPR. Similarly, a large study of end-of-life care in the United States found that almost half of no-CPR orders were written on patient charts within two days of death. This study also found one-third of American patients did not want CPR, yet more than half of their doctors did not know their end-of-life care preferences (Webb, 1997). More recently, in Canada, DNR or do-not-resuscitate orders are increasingly being written at any point in a hospitalization, including at or near the beginning of the hospital stay. They are also being written on a large proportion of charts on which the recorded health information demonstrates both long-term ill health and a consensual decision that DNR is appropriate given the circumstances. Written DNR orders are often clarified by such statements as: no intubation, no transfer to an intensive care unit, et cetera. More patients are also arriving in hospital with written living wills or advance directives that indicate their wishes about life support. Most patients, as well as their families, however, are still unprepared for this major decision. One Canadian study found this unpreparedness was largely a consequence of not having enough health care knowledge to comfortably make this and other related decisions (Heyland et al., 2006).

Although increasingly planned for, hospital deaths are largely hidden from conscious consideration. Many hospitals carry out a practice whereby deceased persons are only removed from their rooms when the doors to other rooms are closed and in specially designed stretchers that conceal the body. Long-term or continuing-care facilities can also downplay the occurrence of death among residents by transferring dying residents to a special room designed to permit family visitation but which also effectively shields the dying person from the view of others. All such actions reduce the effect of death on other residents and patients, as death is still an uncomfortable topic for many people. Increasing comfort, however, with the topic of hospice palliative care is evident, as nurses and physicians are increasingly seeking to specialize in it, and both patients and families are increasingly asking that it be provided.

The Canadian Hospice Palliative Care Association (2007) defines hospice palliative care as "care that aims to relieve suffering and improve the quality of living and dying." This aim is not oriented to lengthening life, although this may occur in some cases. This philosophy contrasts sharply with the dominant orientation in health care, which is curative and life saving. Instead of emphasizing cure and the extension of life, hospice palliative care emphasizes the management of symptoms, making the dying person as comfortable as possible, and other actions designed to improve the quality of life while dying. Hospice palliative care is one of the most interdisciplinary and team-based of health care services as it involves nurses, physicians, and many other professionals and paraprofessionals who work together in various settings and across settings (MacLean and Kelley, 2001). Hospice palliative care is more holistic than curative care, as it emphasizes the physical, psychological, and social needs of the dying person. In addition, hospice palliative care addresses the needs of the family of the dying person.

The first palliative care units in Canada opened in 1975 in Montreal and Winnipeg hospitals. By 1985, approximately 300 hospital-based palliative care programs and 1,000 hospital beds were devoted to palliative care across Canada (Ajemian, 1990). Although such growth may seem impressive, there were at that time around 135,000 acute care hospital beds in some 2,000 hospitals across the country (Canadian Healthcare Association, 2007). Only a very small percentage of hospital beds and hospital services then and now are exclusively devoted to hospice palliative care. Considerable growth in non-hospital settings has occurred since then, with free-standing hospices, palliative day programs, and home care agencies now offering hospice palliative care across Canada. Most home care programs provide home nursing care and other home-based services to support the dying person at home. Some offer respite care, so family members can sleep, go to work, or leave the house for a few hours. Hospice palliative day care, where the dying person goes to a care centre during the day, is another option (Wilson, Truman, et al., 2005). These options may allow a wage-earning family caregiver to keep working. In addition, the dying person may stay occasionally for a weekend at a care centre or stay for a few days in a hospital or continuing-care facility to relieve the family of caregiving or to accommodate family travel or other family activities (Symons, 1992). Early research comparing hospital-based and community-based care programs found both types of programs benefit dying persons and their families (Downe-Wamboldt, 1985).

Although now increasingly diversified in terms of setting, the initiation of hospice palliative care in acute care hospitals created a competition for funding between curative and non-curative care. In some cases, palliative care units were closed following hospital-funding cutbacks (Priest, 1987). Issues of funding also plague non-hospital programs given that hospice palliative home care clients are only a small proportion of total home care clients (Wilson, Kinch, et al., 2005; Wilson, Truman, et al., 2007). As a consequence, hospices and day programs must fundraise to support their day-to-day operations, and limited expansion of hospice palliative care programming is evident in most regions of Canada.

Regardless, hospitals, health care professionals, and also families are increasingly recognizing and responding to terminal illnesses and active dying. Terminally ill and dying people are often offered home-based hospice palliative care, with this option originating in Vancouver in 1974 (Malkin, 1976). Discharge from hospital may now involve a transfer to a palliative care program in a continuing-care facility, such as a nursing home, another option that has developed over the past 20 years (Fry and Schuman, 1986). Hospitals are also discharging to subacute units, as nursing home beds are not always available and home care may not be an appropriate care option (Wilson, 2006). Hospices — that is, freestanding facilities offering inpatient and other forms of hospice palliative care — are another option. Toronto's first hospice was established in 1979 (Hailstone, 1979), while Casey House, a hospice for people dying from AIDS, opened in 1998 (Murrant and Strathdee, 1992). In the early 1990s, Vancouver established the first children's hospice in North America (Eng and Davies, 1992). A limited number of other hospices have opened since then. More support of terminally ill persons and their families is thus somewhat evident, but there are also gaps.

As the Canadian population continues to age, and the number of persons dying each year continues to increase, new developments in the organization and delivery of hospice palliative care can be expected. An array of different programs is likely to develop, as the needs for, and possible options for, programs within one community can be quite different from another. For example, small remote or rural communities and large urban communities are likely to develop different hospice palliative care programs. Moreover, the care needs of people who are dying can vary considerably. Hopefully, funding for these programs will not be as much of an issue as it has been. Canadian social values have traditionally emphasized rescuing people from death and thus preserving life, so diverting money from programs that save lives to hospice palliative programs that facilitate dying has been difficult to accept or enact. Additional health care funding that is specifically directed for hospice palliative care programs and services may be needed instead.

Dying people can use a considerable amount of resources. Hospital care is approximately ten times more expensive than care in a continuing-care facility, and care in the home is usually half the cost of care in such a facility (Noseworthy, 1997). One further fiscal, as well as ethical, issue associated with hospital-based end-of-life care is the technological approach to care in hospitals. On admission, patients routinely have a number of blood tests, X-rays, and other diagnostic tests done at considerable expense. Aggressive treatments are also common (Wilson, 1997). Even when it becomes obvious that death is unavoidable and immediate, diagnostic tests and treatments may occur and may continue until death. In addition, dying persons may be given high levels of oxygen to ease breathing, intravenous fluids to maintain hydration or deliver painkillers, powerful antibiotics to reduce chest congestion, and other medications to strengthen the heart or other systems (Wilson, 1997). As a result of these interventions, dying typically lasts longer. Although many of these procedures cause pain and irritation to the dying person, health care professionals and the public continue to be reluctant to adopt a non-interventionist approach during the dying process. Apparently, few trust nature to produce a good death. Interventionist care is occurring despite calls for over 20 years for a more natural death, one in which pain medication alone is used to ease suffering (Murray, 1981; Pannuti and Tanneberger, 1992; Turner *et al.*, 1996).

It is increasingly clear, however, that a curative orientation is both ineffective and inappropriate for patients who are dying. Nevertheless, a terminally ill person may want to be kept alive to see a child graduate, get married, or have a baby, for example. To achieve this, the dying person may accept antibiotics to combat a life-threatening infection, tube feeding to prevent physical wasting, or surgery to slow the progression of a disease rather than accept hospice palliative care.

Because death is so final, is viewed with such aversion in a youth-oriented and success-oriented society, and is so painful on a personal level, the decision, by the patient or the family or both, to shift from curative care to hospice palliative care is often delayed (Davies and Steele, 1996). While people are becoming more accepting of hospice palliative care, some dying persons and family members today are still tremendously reluctant to acknowledge that a cure or remission is no longer possible. Often this reluctance is expressed by a dying parent's child who has not seen their parent for a number of years and so has not come to an understanding that their parent is irrevocably dying. This situation is so common it has been labelled the "California daughter syndrome." This refers to a child who moved far away from his or her parents and has had little direct contact over the years, returning only when a parent is facing death, and is thus unprepared for the parent's dying. This child may be very much at odds with the other children in the family who have come over time to accept the certainty of impending death. Parents are also often reluctant to accept death for their terminally ill children. Davies and Steele (1996), two British Columbia nurses, found that the parents of most dying children never consider their children to be dying, even when a shift in their treatment from cure-oriented to hospice palliative care has been decided upon. Phillips (1992) was among the first to report a need to refocus our approach so that it does not appear that hospice palliative care begins when treatment ends; instead, there should be a gradual and overlapping shift from curative care to hospice palliative care. More recently, the routine integration of hospice palliative care throughout an active treatment regimen is encouraged whenever advanced ill health or advanced frailty with old age is evident.

In summary, dying and death are associated extensively with health care institutions, particularly hospitals. In these settings, health care workers such as nurses and doctors provide most of the care for the dying. Although care is too often oriented towards extending life and aggressively easing suffering through technological means, hospitals are increasingly withholding CPR and other life supports in recognition of impending death. Both hospital-based and community-based hospice palliative care programs offer alternatives to the dying.

LEGAL SYSTEM

The law is also highly influential with respect to dying and death in Canadian society. Civil and criminal law, and other legal guidelines, have developed in Canada in response to advances in health care and changes in society. Today, most large health care facilities, as well as government departments of health, retain lawyers to provide ongoing legal advice. An organizational policy that addresses a life-or-death issue is likely to be formalized only after legal advice has been received. Legal advice is also frequently sought whenever there are questions about the adequacy of patient care, such as in the case of an unexpected patient death or when a medical error has jeopardized life. The 2006-07 trial of four physicians who faced criminal charges arising from Canada's tainted-blood scandal of the 1980s and 1990s is but one illustration of the role of law with regard to health care, particularly when unfortunate and perhaps preventable cases of dying and death are involved.

The Criminal Code of Canada has a substantial impact on dying and death. It defines both murder and assisted suicide as criminally indictable offences. Although it would seem obvious that murder is a serious offence, mitigating circumstances influence how judges and juries view the crime and assign punishment. Each year, cases of "mercy killing" are identified in news stories that often only briefly outline the circumstances of each case. For instance, an 88-year-old man in Winnipeg, Mr. Jaworski, was charged with second-degree murder after he stabbed his ill, hospitalized wife to death; he was given three years probation in 2006. Apparently, according to the news story, he had been afraid his wife would have further treatment, despite considerable suffering from her treatment to date and her various illnesses. This sentence was given after he had already spent 17 months in jail, however ("Senior sentenced for wife's death," 2006). Previously, a mother in Ontario who attempted to kill her disabled six-year-old child by giving her an overdose of medication through her feeding tube was found guilty of attempted murder but was not sentenced to jail ("No jail time," 1999). Instead, she was given a two-year sentence to be served in the community. Crimes motivated by familial love are often treated differently from other crimes. *should they be?*.

It is not illegal to take your own life in Canada, but it is illegal to knowingly assist another person who is trying to commit suicide (Kerr and Kurtz, 1999), and it is illegal to intentionally cause another's death. The prohibition against assisted suicide and causing death may have unintended and undesirable consequences. For example, families may withhold strong painkillers from a dying family member for fear of being prosecuted for hastening death. In the past, physicians were concerned that pain relief could lead to prosecution if it was thought that death was hastened (Bresnahan, 1993; Mount and Flander, 1996; Wood and Martin, 1995). This concern has been relieved considerably in Canada by the 1984 Joint Statement on Terminal Illness regarding health care decision-making for terminally ill persons (mentioned earlier in this chapter), the 1995 revision of the Joint Statement (CMA Policy Summary, 1995), and then the publication of the goals of palliative care in Canada (Canadian Palliative Care Association, 1997). All of these statements indicate that effective care of dying persons is of paramount concern and that, although death may be hastened by comfort-oriented care as compared to curative care, the intent to relieve suffering is most important.

Physicians and also health facility administrators have also been concerned that they might be prosecuted for hastening death by withholding or withdrawing treatment from the dying (Wood and Martin, 1995). For the most part, this concern has become outdated because of significant legal cases such as the Karen Ann Quinlan case in the United States. The parents of Karen Ann Quinlan won the legal right in 1976 to have their comatose daughter's "life support" (the ventilator) removed. Her case became a springboard for end-of-life law in the United States and other countries (Webb, 1997).

Most deaths in Canada occur now after one or more treatments have either been withheld or withdrawn (Cook *et al.*, 1995; Faber-Langendoen and Bartels, 1992; Smith, 1995; Webb, 1997). In Canada, in 1984, the Joint Statement on Terminal Illness supported the withholding and withdrawal of treatments if these treatments did not benefit the terminally ill or dying person. The revised statement in 1995 focused on withholding CPR but also noted that "a decision not to initiate CPR does not imply the withholding or withdrawing of any other treatment or intervention. A person who will not receive CPR should receive all other appropriate treatments, including palliative care, for his or her physical, mental, and spiritual comfort" (CMA Policy Summary, 1995: 1652C). Few if any physicians, health care administrators, or other health care workers in Canada have been charged for withdrawing or withholding care from dying persons.

Case law developments have clarified rights and responsibilities on an individual level and set precedents for larger, societal-level rights and responsibilities. Although American case law and other developments arising out of sensational cases, such as the Karen Ann Quinlan case and the more recent Terri Schiavo case involving the withdrawal of tube feeding which was sought by her husband and opposed by her parents (Mikos and Wilson, 2003), are of interest and have some effect on Canadian society, Canadian case law differs both in historical sequence and outcomes. One of the first such precedent-setting cases in Canada was in 1992, when an Ontario physician was found guilty of assault and battery for insisting that blood be given to a woman of the Jehovah's Witnesses faith (*Malette v. Schulman*, 1992). The physician knew that the injured woman had signed a card indicating she did not want to receive blood. The ruling in favour of the plaintiff, whose life was likely preserved by the transfusion, identified personal autonomy in health care decision-making as legally binding and morally compelling. In this and subsequent cases, the physician's judgement as to what is beneficial for the patient was not considered the key factor in decision-making. Instead, what the patient considered to be acceptable or appropriate treatment was deemed more important.

The Malette decision, which supported the withholding of life-sustaining treatment at the patient's request, was quickly followed by another major legal precedent, this time in regard to withdrawing treatment. In this case, a judge was asked to grant a request by a young woman, Nancy B, who lived in a Montreal-area continuing-care facility and wanted to have her life-supporting ventilator removed. After it had been determined that she was fully aware of the consequences of her decision to stop this life-supporting technology, her request was granted, and Nancy B died (Campion, 1994; Sneiderman, 1993). Still more recently, a mother in British Columbia was not prosecuted for allowing her ten-year-old daughter to die after the mother refused tube feeding for her and other medical treatments ("No charges," 1999). The daughter had been suffering from Rett syndrome, a rare and fatal neurological disease. It was thought that the daughter understood this choice and its ramifications.

Thus, while criminal law in Canada continues to prohibit euthanasia and assisted suicide, a dying person who is mentally competent has the right to refuse treatment, which may be withheld or withdrawn even though death results. Under these circumstances, withholding or withdrawing treatment is not defined as euthanasia or assisted suicide, and, therefore, does not trigger prosecution under the law.

Withdrawal and withholding of treatment is important to consider, as most terminally ill persons can have their lives extended by health care therapies. Furthermore, persons in comas, near-comas, or persistent vegetative states (PVS) can be kept alive for years and even for decades. For example, Karen Ann Quinlan was kept alive for ten years, with tube feeding, after her American parents won the legal right to have her "life support" equipment removed (Webb, 1997).

Right-to-die groups, such as the Hemlock Society in the United States and Dying with Dignity in Canada, have raised questions about the appropriate time to withdraw and withhold life-supporting treatments. The Hemlock Society was founded in the United States in 1980 by Derek Humphry, who wrote a best-selling book *Final Exit* in 1991; it evolved into the Compassion and Choices group in 2003. On the other side of the debate, right-to-life groups, including groups who represent disabled persons and the unborn, such as the Campaign Life Coalition in Canada and the National Right to Life organization in the United States, are becoming more organized and vocal about their concern that life is too easily ended.

Much of the debate over the use of life support to prolong life and over the withholding or withdrawing of life support, hinges on questions of human rights, most notably on informed consent. In the past, physicians made many, if not all, health care decisions (Webb, 1997). Since the 1970s, greater awareness of the need for personal autonomy, punctuated by significant case law developments, has brought about a remarkable change in health care decision-making (Ott and Nieswiadomy, 1991). Today, competent persons can make their own health care decisions.

Physicians and other persons still tend to influence many treatment and non-treatment decisions, however. Physicians may even unilaterally make decisions; indeed, some people still want the physician to make the difficult "life and death" decisions (Storch and Dossetor, 1994). Alternatively, some patients choose to refuse or to demand treatment against physician advice. Nevertheless, health care professionals in Canada are not obliged either to offer or to provide futile care (CMA Policy Summary, 1995; Joint Statement, 1984). Futility, however, is an issue for future legal and other developments, as it is not clearly evident what futile health care is.

Living wills or advance directives allow competent persons to indicate their preferences for care before care is actually needed and in anticipation of circumstances where the person might not be able to make decisions. In other words, living will laws that have now been enacted in every Canadian province enforce the right of persons to direct their own health care even after they become mentally incompetent. Living wills are commonly called advance directives and at times are also referred to as personal directives, representation agreements, health care directives, power of attorney for personal care, mandates, directives, or authorizations (Kerr and Kurtz, 1999). Although living will statutes vary across Canada, most allow one or more substitute decision-makers to be named and allow instructions about health care to be left for these decision-makers, as well as other possible health care decision-makers such as nurses and physicians. The instructions in the living will must be followed or sanctions can be brought against those who do not abide by them, providing that the instructions are legal. Thus, living wills can direct that treatment be withheld or withdrawn but cannot result in euthanasia or assisted suicide even if the person clearly states that a hastened death is desirable in certain situations for them. Living will instructions are supposed to take precedence over the preferences of family members and health care professionals. Even though living wills are still relatively uncommon, there is an advantage to them, as "there is a good chance that the instructions in a living will will be followed" (Kerr and Kurtz, 1999: 19).

Living wills are designed for the intention of ensuring that care preferences are carried out if individuals lose the ability to direct their own care. Unfortunately, many patients and their families are not certain what should be done or not done in cases of serious illness and potential death. One recent study found that, despite serious long-standing illnesses, patients and families did not know what to do about CPR if the heart or breathing stopped (Heyland *et al.*, 2006). CPR, which has the potential to revive a person after death has technically occurred, is one of the most straightforward decisions. Other decisions, such as those that can hasten death — for example, stopping renal or kidney dialysis — are much more difficult. Another major problem is that most, if not all, dying persons lose consciousness near death and so lose the ability to direct their care at a time when decisions often need to be made (Wilson, 1997). Other persons are then in the position of having to make decisions, and these decisions may be difficult as written instructions in living wills or verbalized instructions are often general in nature — such as the person saying that they do not want their life to be extended. Another major issue is that there can be differences of opinion among family members, as illustrated by the much-publicized case of Terri Schiavo's husband who requested the withdrawal of her feeding tube while her parents opposed this withdrawal (Mikos and Wilson, 2003). Unfortunately, few people actually make a living will (Landry *et al.*, 1997). Even people whose death is imminent often do not have living wills (Heffner *et al.*, 1996; Teno *et al.*, 1997). One study in British Columbia, undertaken at a time when there was no life-extending treatment for HIV, found only half of all persons suffering from AIDS (the serious illness that occurs when the HIV infection has progressed) had a living will (Osgood, 1994).

Withdrawing or withholding care from the dying should not be confused with euthanasia or assisted suicide. Several legal commissions in Canada, including the Supreme Court of Canada, have upheld a ban on euthanasia and assisted suicide.

In the early 1980s, several law reform commissions recommended against legal-izing euthanasia (Curran and Hyg, 1984). Notably, in 1994 the Supreme Court of Canada was asked to consider Sue Rodriguez's request for assistance in ending her life. Rodriguez's situation is discussed in more detail in Chapter 5. The major point here is that the Supreme Court, in a five to four ruling, upheld the prohibition against assisted suicide for terminally ill persons. Following this ruling, a Senate Committee was set up to study the issue of euthanasia and assisted suicide (Blouin, 1995). The subsequent report of the Senate Committee on Euthanasia and Assisted Suicide (Senate of Canada, 1995) contained a number of recommendations, one of which was that palliative care should become more accessible to dying Canadians. The Committee assumed or felt that dying persons would not request euthanasia or assisted suicide if their symptoms were managed and they were comfortable. It has not been established, however, that access to or experience with hospice palliative care necessarily deters people from asking for assisted suicide or euthanasia. A subsequent Senate Committee report followed in 2000, with the Chair, Senator Carstairs, continuing to be concerned about the plight of dying persons. Her work led to the Compassionate Care Benefits program (Anonymous, 2004).

It is also important to point out that despite losing her case, Sue Rodriguez was helped to die at her home in British Columbia. Her death is an example of voluntary euthanasia or assisted suicide. No one was ever charged with this "crime." The circumstances surrounding her death can be contrasted with non-voluntary euthanasia, as illustrated by another controversial Canadian court case. Robert Latimer, a Saskatchewan farmer, was found guilty of murder after he confessed to using carbon monoxide in 1993 to kill his severely disabled daughter, Tracy, who was mentally incapable of consenting. While some considered his actions to be a "mercy killing" to save Tracy from further surgery and also from daily suffering, others felt he did not have the right to make this ultimate decision for his daughter. Yet, even if Tracy had been able to give consent and had done so, Latimer's act of euthanasia would still have been against the law. After serving seven years of a ten-year jail sentence, Latimer was released in 2008 on day parole.

Another example of non-voluntary euthanasia involves a physician in Toronto who was found guilty of giving inappropriate medication prescriptions to two people who had AIDS. The prescribed medications were intended to hasten death, with the physician alone making these decisions (Foot, 1997). A perhaps more per-plexing case involves Dr. Nancy Morrison, a physician in Halifax, who was charged in 1997 with first-degree murder for hastening the death of a dying intensive care patient. The patient, who had had extensive treatment for esophageal cancer over a period of eight months in hospital, had just been granted his pre-stated request to be taken off life support. After his life support was terminated, he did not die and instead continued to struggle to breathe. Dr. Morrison is thought to have ended his life a number of hours later with an intravenous injection of a substance known to cause death. The charges against her were later withdrawn, but only after a considerable amount of time and effort to evaluate the evidence and the context of the case (Hamilton, 1997; Robb, 1998).

It is not known how often assisted suicide or euthanasia occurs in Canada. Some data is available for the Netherlands where 3 per cent of deaths have been found to result from euthanasia (Van der Maas *et al.*, 1996). The Northern Territory of Australia legalized euthanasia between July 1996 and March 1997, during which time four persons were euthanized (Kissane *et al.*, 1998). In the state of Oregon in the first year following the legalization in 1997 of assisted suicide by prescription medications to end life, 15 people died after self-administering lethal prescriptions obtained from a doctor (Chin *et al.*, 1999). The 2006 annual report indicates that 257 persons have died to date under the terms of that law (Death with Dignity Annual Report, 2007). In June 1990, Dr. Jack Kevorkian helped Janet Adkins, a 55-year-old Portland music teacher and Alzheimer's victim, die (Webb, 1997). During the 1990s, Kevorkian helped many more patients to die by assisted suicide, with each person voluntarily taking his or her own life, using the aids he provided. This method protected Kevorkian from conviction until he deliberately ended the life of a disabled person who was not able to carry out his own suicide. Kevorkian was subsequently convicted of murder and served eight years in prison before being released on June 1, 2007. Despite or perhaps because of these developments, considerable interest around the world in euthanasia is evident (Burkhardt *et al.*, 2006). This interest may result from the increasing awareness of the futility of health care for preventing death and rising concern about suffering during a long dying process. Quill and Kisma (2006) recently asked what might become an important question: "How much suffering is enough?" (10).

In summary, in Canada, a competent person can request that life support be withheld or withdrawn, even if this hastens death. Similarly, a dying person who has become incompetent may have expressed his or her wishes in a written advance care directive, which can then justify the withholding or withdrawing of treatment. Nevertheless, a person cannot ask any other person for active euthanasia or assisted suicide, both of which are illegal in Canada.

THE FUNERAL INDUSTRY

The final stage of the dying process is an important time when most families want to be together with their dying family member. Following death, families typically also gather to demonstrate respect for the deceased person and to provide support to each other. Funeral and memorial services do much to assist those who grieve by providing an opportunity to reflect upon the life of the person who has died and to publicly and collectively acknowledge the person's death.

One of the most profound changes in the death industry is that more cremations are taking place. Over half of all deaths in Canada now involve cremation (Cremation Association of North American, 2007). Cremation occurs when a very hot fire is used to reduce the body and usually the coffin to only a few kilograms of ash (Colman, 1997). Cremations have long been performed by certain religious or cultural groups (Nault and Ford, 1994). In contrast, other religious and cultural groups consider it to be disrespectful to the deceased person (The Canadian Encyclopedia, 2007b). Some people choose cremation because they are disturbed by the thought of the body decaying in the ground after burial (Flynn, 1993; Kerr and Kurtz, 1999).

Cremations have become common in Canada for a variety of other practical reasons. One very significant reason is reduced cost. The average funeral in Canada costs between $5,000 and $10,000 (Roberts, 1997). There are charges for every service received, including transporting the body, preparing the body for burial (which may or may not include embalming), providing the casket in which the body is buried and the burial (i.e., cemetery) plot or tomb (i.e., crypt) in a mausoleum, and conducting the funeral service (Industry Canada, 2007). Cremations and memorial services typically cost less than half what a funeral costs (Flynn, 1993; Industry Canada, 2007).

Cremation also allows for flexibility. Funerals usually take place soon after death — in some cases within one day, as is expected in certain cultural groups, but most often within three or four days. Families typically are widely dispersed geographically, and gathering family members together quickly for a funeral can be difficult. Not only is the cost of travel on short notice very high (despite special travel discounts, such as a reduction on airline ticket costs for close family members when flying to a funeral), but also childcare may have to be arranged, leaves of absence from work or study obtained, and many other personal circumstances attended to during the time of bereavement. Cremation allows for flexibility, as the urn containing the ashes of the deceased person can be easily transported to any location. A memorial service can thus take place at any location and also at any time convenient to the family. There is less urgency, as well, in taking the ashes to their final resting place or in scattering the remains, in comparison to a body, which must either be buried within a few days of death, kept "on ice" until a later burial, or embalmed.

Embalming is a semi-surgical process that replaces body fluids with liquid chemicals (such as formaldehyde and methyl or wood alcohol) to disinfect and also preserve the body. Embalming is not required unless the body is to be shipped across national or international borders or transported by public carrier (The Canadian Encyclopedia, 2007b). Bodies that have been embalmed and buried have been exhumed 20 years later and found relatively unchanged.

The funeral industry itself is an important social institution. The funeral or death industry provides many persons with an income through employment or through investment. Caskets and urns have to be made; bodies need to be prepared for embalming, burial, or cremation; funeral parlours and crematoria have to be built and kept in good repair; and cemeteries and mausoleums have to be developed and maintained. In addition, other businesses benefit, as notices of death and funeral notices are usually published, flowers sent, donations made to charities, and travel undertaken to attend the funeral or memorial service. Flynn (1993) considers this industry to be virtually recession proof. Indeed, fewer than 5 per cent of deaths in Canada do not involve a funeral or memorial service (The Canadian Encyclopedia, 2007b).

It should also not be surprising that the death industry in Canada is a large and highly profitable business. In North America, approximately $9 to $10 billion a year were grossed in the early 1990s by businesses that provided death-related services (Flynn, 1993). One of the most noteworthy facts about the death industry is that the local, family-owned funeral home was largely replaced during the 1980s and 1990s by huge corporations with billions of dollars in assets (Flynn, 1993; Kennedy and Milner, 1999). Today, only a small number of large corporations supply most of the North American "death market" (Roberts, 1997). Service Corporation International (SCI), located in Houston, Texas, is the largest. In the early 1990s, SCI had 758 funeral homes and 184 cemeteries/crematoria internationally (Flynn, 1993). Their 2006 annual report stated that they had over 2,000 funeral homes and crematoria in North America, a cash flow of US$324.2 million from their operations, and a US$50 million increase over the previous year (Service Corporation International, 2007). They are listed on the New York Stock Exchange.

Loewen Group Incorporated, based in Vancouver, British Columbia, was Canada's largest funeral company and the second largest funeral business conglomerate worldwide (Flynn, 1993). Created in 1985, the company was worth

US$4.3 billion by the fall of 1996 (Hasselback *et al.*, 1999). By 1998, their holdings included 1,172 funeral homes and 628 cemeteries in North America and Britain (Kennedy and Milner, 1999; Waldie and Kennedy, 1999). A year later, Loewen filed for bankruptcy protection. Too rapid expansion was blamed. Another factor may have been competition from firms that had begun to sell "wholesale" caskets and "no-frills" funeral services, thereby reducing demand for expensive, full-service burial (Bourette and Milner, 1999; Waldie and Kennedy, 1999).

High prices, together with effective marketing to promote end-of-life services, have made the death industry profitable (Roberts, 1997). Flynn (1993) has expressed concern with the ethics of the industry: "the funeral industry has learned to use religious customs against the consumer for financial exploitation. How else does one explain the fast-paced rise in profit for an industry that used to be service based and is now profit driven? ... Funeral practitioners have failed miserably to provide an open and honest line of communication to customers so they can make a knowledgeable decision on a purchase. All these factors create an industry in which a clientele is rushing out to make major purchases without adequate knowledge and very little experience — a salesperson's dream" (6-7). *and no time*

According to Flynn (1993), "one-stop shopping," whereby families use one service provider to make all funeral arrangements, coupled with an increased range of services, have led to spiralling funeral costs. The amount of disposable income available to the family impacts which ceremonies are held and which customs are followed. In a time of intense difficulty and pressure, families must choose between a traditional, full-service funeral or an "alternate" funeral for which there is no standard format (Roberts, 1997). In addition, families must choose how elaborate the service and the casket or urn will be (The Canadian Encyclopedia, 2007b). The latter is a concern, as there is a 100 to 400 per cent mark-up on these items (Flynn, 1993). Some other common decisions that need to be made include whether to have a closed or open coffin; whether to permit visitation or calling at the funeral home to see the body; whether to hold a funeral with the casket present or hold a memorial service at a later time; and also whether the body will be buried, cremated, or entombed in a mausoleum. Given all these considerations, it is prudent to pre-plan a funeral to lower costs and ensure that important rituals and customs are upheld (Industry Canada, 2007). Various associations assist dying persons and their families in planning the funeral, in preparing for death, and in times of bereavement (see Appendix).

In summary, the funeral industry is big business, offering a wide range of services to the family and friends of the deceased. Funeral arrangements can and should be made in advance. When this has not been done, the family of the deceased must make many decisions quickly at a time when decision-making tends to be difficult. In such circumstances, the bereaved may pay more than they need to, may purchase more services than they can afford, or may find they have a funeral that does not meet their needs and expectations. Cremation has become common in Canada, in part because it costs less than a traditional burial, and it allows for greater flexibility in planning this important event.

SUMMARY

While dying and death typically take place in the context of the family and the health care system, the course of dying and death is also shaped by religious, legal, and funeral considerations. As social institutions have changed over time, so also have dying and death changed. In particular, although the hospital continues to have a major role in dying and death, the primary location of dying and death is shifting from the hospital to continuing-care facilities, the home, and other locations. Similarly, although health care professionals may be primary caregivers for the dying, the family is increasing their involvement and participation in decisions and actual caregiving. The shift to a more normalized dying process outside the traditional cure-oriented hospital setting is occurring in large measure because of three major developments. The first is increased awareness of the limits of health care for curing illnesses and extending life. The second is the long-standing concern about inadequate and inappropriate care in hospital, as characterized by attempts to cure illness, prolong life, and deny death. Third is that hospice palliative care has become well established in Canada, with this and other end-of-life care shifting the emphasis of care to that of a "good" death. Other social changes, such as secularization, mean religion tends to play a lesser role in dying and death than in the past. Legal developments have legitimized the advance care directive or living will and, in some countries outside Canada, active euthanasia and assisted suicide. The funeral has moved from the home, church, and community to the profit-driven funeral industry, where death processing has been professionalized and corporatized, if not bureaucratized. These social changes have implications for the meaning of dying and death for individuals, families, and society as a whole.

CHAPTER 4
DYING AND DEATH IN THE CONTEXT OF CANADIAN CULTURE

This chapter explores cultural constructions of the meaning of dying and death and the resulting social responses to dying and death in Canada. Cultural constructions are evident in various forms, such as literature, television, movies, the daily news, Internet sites, everyday language, and folklore, as well as in the processes of medicalization, professionalization, and bureaucratization. Socio-cultural responses to dying and death include making sense of death by means of shared discourses, distinguishing between different types of death, stigmatizing dying and death, and observing social rituals accompanying death. Each of these topics is described and discussed below. Finally, this chapter examines ethnic variations in these cultural constructions and social responses.

It has been argued that Canadian culture, along with that of other western societies, became a death-denying culture in the twentieth century (Becker, 1973;

Ariès, 1974, 1981). Nevertheless, the reality of dying and death cannot be completely denied — dying and death do come to each in turn. In a death-denying culture, reactions to dying and death vacillate between denial and awareness, fear and fascination (Joseph, 1994: 1), and detachment and morbid obsession. Among these, fascination with death is evident in cultural forms such as literature and television. This fascination has lead several notable Canadian authors to explore the processes of dying and the mysteries of death.

SELECTED WORKS OF LITERATURE

Margaret Laurence is one of the most enduring icons of Canadian literature. Laurence published *The Stone Angel* in 1964. The book begins with 90-year-old Hagar Shipley's reminiscences of the stone angel standing over her mother's grave in the cemetery above the fictional town of Manawaka, Manitoba, which was patterned after Neepawa, Manitoba, where Laurence herself was born. Through Hagar's memories, descriptions, and reflections, the reader is given a series of impressions about attitudes towards dying and death in Canada in the late nineteenth and early twentieth centuries.

Hagar remembers not only the stone angel, other commemorative stonework, and the inscriptions in the cemetery but how strange and even amusing these things could be to a young girl. As an old woman, she recalls lives lived and largely forgotten, and observes the tendency for weeds to overgrow the cemetery, a metaphor for how time obscures the memories of the dead. The young Hagar sneaked into Simmons's Funeral Parlour with some other children to look at Hannah Pearl's pale stillborn baby in a white satin box. Told by her brother Matt that Mr. Simmons, the owner of the funeral parlour, drank embalming fluid, Hagar avoided the man, thinking of him as a ghoul. In these accounts, Laurence illustrates the paradoxical fascination and at the same time revulsion that people manifest with regards to death and all that is associated with it.

Throughout the novel, Hagar mentions deceased ancestors, including her mother, who died when Hagar was born, and her teenage brother, four years her senior, who caught pneumonia and died in an upstairs bedroom asking for his long-dead mother. The death from consumption (tuberculosis) of a schoolmate's mother is also recalled as are the deaths of non-humans as well: the pathetic death of a fighting cock and the gruesome euthanization of some newborn chicks. As she reflects on her youthful emotions, she wonders why she could not then intervene to kill the chicks more humanely nor comfort her dying brother. In her youth, she recoiled and distanced herself from dying and death, both human and non-human.

Even the lily of the valley, either as a flower or as the name for the eau de cologne she wears, reminds Hagar of death. As she reflects back in her old age, her memories often focus on death, as if past deaths are a harbinger of her own. When the minister asks if she has many friends, she observes that most of them are dead. Her parents are also long dead, as are her two brothers. Her husband and one of her two sons are dead as well. Hagar knows that her own death is near. She also knows that others, her son and daughter-in-law, her doctor and the nursing staff in the hospital where she spends her final days, are waiting, anticipating, expecting her demise. Though no one speaks directly to Hagar of her impending death, she guesses the meaning of their whispered conversations.

Through this book, Laurence portrays death as both strange and familiar. While death is common and inevitable, it is also mysterious and repulsive. Laurence portrays death as something to be avoided and resisted as much as possible through cognitive, emotional, and behavioural distancing and denial. Nevertheless, she also shows it to be intimately personal and inevitable. Finally, Laurence describes the drama of mutual pretence (Glaser and Strauss, 1965) that has often accompanied dying. In this drama, everybody involved knows that death is imminent and yet nobody speaks openly or directly about it. The dying person is also discouraged from speaking of her own dying and imminent death.

Another literary great, W.O. Mitchell, described death in the context of early twentieth-century prairie culture. His book *Who Has Seen the Wind*, which was published in 1947, begins with a quote from Psalms: "As for man, his days are as grass: as a flower of the field, so he flourisheth. For the wind passeth over it, and it is gone; and the place thereof shall know it no more." Mitchell then provides the reader with an explanation of the meaning of the story he is about to tell. The wind, he says, is a symbol of God, and the story to be told is about the mysteries of the cycle of life from birth to death.

Mitchell's classic tells the story of young Brian O'Connal, who grows up in a small town in Saskatchewan in the 1930s. Brian's family consists of his mother, father, grandmother, and a baby brother. The story begins when Brian is four years of age. His baby brother is very sick, and it is feared that he will die. Although the baby recovers, his near death sets an ominous tone for the book. Mitchell seems to be telling the reader that life begins and continues in the shadow of death; the possibility of death at any moment and its ultimate inevitability raise fundamental questions about the meaning of life.

A baby pigeon that Brian brings home is not as lucky as Brian's brother. When the pigeon dies, it is Brian's first experience with the demise of a being that had meant something to him. Several years later, when Brian is about eight years of age, his beloved dog is run over by a horse-drawn wagon. Brian sadly buries his dog under the prairie sod and grieves.

As the story unfolds, Brian approaches ten years of age. His grandmother is now 80 years old and knows her death is near. At the same time, Brian's father gets sick and becomes jaundiced. Once again the ominous tone moves from background to foreground, and the reader is left to anxiously wonder who will live and who will die. In the summer of Brian's tenth year, his father dies. He is laid out in a coffin at home in the living room with blinds drawn against the light. Friends and neighbours come by with flowers, tears, and sympathy, everyone observing that the deceased was a fine man. Brian's mother is quiet, stunned; his grandmother sits, looking frail.

The minister conducts the funeral in the living room. Afterwards, Brian is sad, filled with longing, but he doesn't know what to do. He wants to cry because he feels it is the right thing to do. But, although he loved his dad, the tears are not there. He goes out to the prairie. As he thinks in his ten-year-old way of the endless cycle of the seasons, the endless cycle of birth and death, he realizes that his father is gone forever. He thinks of the irony that, although people are forever being born, at death the individual is forever gone. When he thinks of his mother grieving the loss of her husband, he cries, but his tears are for the living as much as for the dead.

Following the funeral, Brian thinks often of his father and frequently dreams that he is still alive. As time passes, he feels guilty that he thinks of his father less often. The family visits the cemetery frequently, and during these visits Brian tries to think of his father. He grows closer to his mother, brother, and grandmother.

The story ends with the death of Brian's grandmother. Brian has reached the age of 12 and his grandmother has lived 82 years. Her death is not as shocking as the death of Brian's father, who had died prematurely, in the prime of his life — his death was unexpected, shocking, tragic. The grandmother's death is expected, legitimate, bittersweet. Her long life and the frailty preceding her death justify her passing. In her own — that is, Mitchell's — words, her time had come. This is not to say that her death is without pain, and Brian grieves her passing.

The story of Brian's childhood is thus punctuated with accounts of death and youthful attempts to make sense of life and death. Brian remembers the deaths of the baby pigeon, a gopher, his dog, a two-headed calf, his father, and his grandmother. He recalls the stench of a rotting cow. He reflects on his dead ancestors from whom his own life has come. Brian will continue to live, hunger, love, and wonder about the sense of it all.

Who Has Seen the Wind explores the mysteries of life and death. The book suggests that death is omnipresent and yet ominous; mysterious, unwelcome, disturbing, distressing, and inevitable. All who live die: this observation is inescapable and yet hard to accept and even harder to understand. Mitchell suggests that if answers are to be found, they are ethereal, like the wind.

Mitchell describes the society's cultural and ritual ways of dealing with death, including churches, theology, philosophy, funerals and flowers, cemeteries and gravestone epitaphs, and sympathetic, if trite, sentiments expressed to the bereaved. In the end, though, the novelist suggests that individuals must come to terms with life and death on their own, in their own way, and in their own time.

Both novels — Laurence's *The Stone Angel* and Mitchell's *Who Has Seen the Wind* — are about the culture and experience of life and death in small-town and rural settings in the first half of the twentieth century. The urban experience of death in the second half of the twentieth century and in the early twenty-first century continues to reflect many of these earlier cultural orientations.

LANGUAGE

The printed program at a funeral service for a colleague who died says "In Loving Memory Of" and then states his name. Under the heading "Born," his date and place of birth are listed. Under the heading "Passed Away," the date when and the place where he passed away are listed. The word "death" does not appear in the program. It is as if people are born, but do not die. People simply pass away. Nor was this colleague buried. According to the program, the funeral service was followed by an "interment," not a burial.

Death cannot be completely denied, even in an allegedly death-denying culture, although convention can distance us from it. While one could speak directly, using terms such as dying, dead, death, and burial, the conventional language of death is often indirect and euphemistic. Speaking directly seems too harsh, too cold, even cruel. The direct language refers to a harsh reality, a reality that is known but that people prefer to soften rather than to acknowledge explicitly.

According to *Webster's Dictionary*, a euphemism refers to "the use of a word or phrase that is less expressive or direct but considered less distasteful, less offensive … than another." In Canadian culture, common practice indicates that it is less distasteful and less offensive to use euphemisms than to speak directly of death and related topics. Williamson *et al.* (1980: 434-35) present an extensive list of euphemisms for dying, death, and burial. The dead person is often referred to as the departed or the deceased; the coffin is often called the casket. When a person dies, it may be said that the deceased has passed on, passed over, laid their burden down, gone to a well-earned rest, been called home, or gone to heaven. Instead of saying the person has been buried, it might be said that the person was laid to rest. The corpse may be referred to as the body or the remains; an impersonal "the" is used instead of the personal pronoun "his" or "her." This depersonalization of the dead body disassociates the memory of the living from the evidence of death.

While the euphemisms for death tend to be tasteful, inoffensive, and sentimental, and serve to soften a harsh reality, there are other euphemisms that are, at best, humourous and, at worst, vulgar. While euphemisms can obscure the starkness of an uncomfortable reality, humour presents an alternative way of dealing with what makes us uncomfortable. Making light of something that terrifies us is one way of whistling in the dark, of convincing ourselves that we can manage our fears. Humourous terms for death include "bit the dust," "kicked the bucket," "pushing up daisies," "your goose is cooked," "he croaked," and so on. Other slang includes "cold meat" for corpse, "bone box" for coffin, "bone orchard" or "marble city" for cemetery, and "planted" or "deep sixed" for buried. In summary, by either distancing from, or making light of death, various euphemisms facilitate coping with the strong emotions that tend to accompany death.

FOLKLORE, POPULAR CULTURE, AND CONTEMPORARY MEDIA

Folklore embodies beliefs, customs, myths, legends, folk tales, stories, rumours, jokes, and sayings that are anonymously produced, collectively shared, and communicated verbally in both oral and written forms (Clifton, 1991). Note that folklore tends to reflect popular culture. As such, some may judge the following stories and jokes to be in poor taste. Cultural constructions regarding death range from sensitive to insensitive, respectful to disrespectful, and tasteful to tasteless.

The following story has apparently been circulating on the Internet. Its origins are unknown.

A few years ago in California there was a raging brush fire. Once the fire was extinguished, the firefighters began the process of clean-up. In the middle of where the fire had been burning, they found a dead man wearing a scuba tank and wet suit. At first the firefighters were baffled as to why a man would be out in the middle of the countryside wearing full scuba gear. Upon further examination, it was determined that the man died from impact with the ground and not the fire. As best anyone can determine, this man was scuba diving off the coast of California and was accidentally picked up by one of the fire-fighting aircraft when it was refilling its water tanks offshore.

Not only are the origins of this story unknown, there are several versions, and it is not known if there is any truth to any of the accounts. Stories that are not true but nevertheless circulate widely and are told as if they are true are called "urban legends" (Kendall et al., 2000: 648-49). Urban legends usually deal with topics that are particularly sensational from a culture's point of view, such as death or the threat of death. While the tale told above is ironic and amusing, folklore such as this also has the potential to define and instruct. If there is a message in this story, it is that death may come unbidden, unexpected, like a macabre prank played on an unsuspecting victim.

The above story illustrates a notion that is common in Western oral culture, namely, that death will find you "when your number is up." A certain fatalism or notion of inescapable bad luck is evident. Another story concerns a middle-aged man whose car was blown off the road and into a river during a windstorm. As the car sank beneath the water, the man broke a window, climbed out, and swam to shore, where a tree blew over and killed him. If there is a message in this story, it is that death cannot be avoided "when your time is up."

The following two urban legends were heard in Winnipeg several decades ago. Both stories concerned medical students enrolled in the University of Manitoba's medical school, and both were told by persons who swore they were true. According to the first story, some of the students from the medical school had taken an arm severed from a cadaver that they were dissecting in the course of their studies. They dressed the arm in a shirt sleeve, pasted a dollar bill to the hand, and boarded a bus. In those days, bus drivers gave change for a dollar bill (and there were still dollar bills), but as the bus driver reached out to take the money, he pulled the whole arm off, had a heart attack, and died on the spot. Oh!,

It is very unlikely that this prank ever actually took place. Indeed, it appears to be one of a number of similar stories that have circulated widely and been described as "cadaver stories" (Hafferty, 1988). If there is a culturally mediated discomfort with the topic of death, there is a virtual taboo against contact with dead bodies. Medical students must not only break this taboo, they must learn to control their emotional revulsion about doing so. Cadaver stories are a vehicle by which medical students can acknowledge the problem of death and at the same time claim to have transcended their difficulties with death. In these stories, the students are usually portrayed as pranksters in control of their fears, while the victims of the pranks are portrayed as lay persons who are shocked and horrified. The underlying message is that death is horrifying, although exceptional people such as doctors can and must learn to overcome, or at least manage, their horror.

The next urban legend contains a twist on the usual cadaver story. A medical student had been dissecting a corpse, starting at its feet. The body was covered with a sheet, and each part was uncovered in turn. Finally, the head was un-covered, and the student realized that he had been dissecting his own recently deceased father.

In the first story about medical students, the students showed their emotional control by allegedly playing pranks on people who are easily shocked by death. In the second story, fate plays a trick on the medical student, reaffirming the horror of death. Although medical students can gain some control through strategies such as emotional distancing and depersonalization, the horror is still there and can overtake a person suddenly. The message of this story is that death is horrible and there is no escaping that horror, especially when death takes a person you love.

Legends, new and old, centring around death, are widespread in Western folk-lore. Consider, for example, ghost stories and tales of haunted houses. Canada has its own deathly legends. The South Nahanni River in the southwest corner of the Northwest Territories is a place of such legend. The back cover of *Dangerous River*, R.M. Patterson's (1989, originally 1954) account of his time on the Nahanni says, "The Nahanni River follows its treacherous course between Yukon Territory and the mighty Mackenzie River. One section is dominated by Deadmen Valley, so-called because of the hair-raising legends about the fate of those brave enough to enter — and unfortunate enough never to return." In 1927, Patterson made his way by canoe from Alberta north to the Nahanni. He was told by many whom he met on his way about canyons with sheer walls thousands of feet high and treacherous currents. He was told that not many people went into that country and came back to tell about it.

> There was gold in there somewhere … Deadmen Valley was tucked away in there some place … A valley between two canyons where the McLeods were murdered for their gold in 1906. No man ever knew what happened to them, but they were found — at least their skeletons were — tied to trees, with the heads missing. And enough men had disappeared in there since then that it was considered best by men of sense to leave the Nahanni country alone. (Patterson, 1989: 6)

Patterson was also told of the wild Mountain Men — "Indians" who "lorded it over the wild uplands of the Yukon Mackenzie divide and made short work of any man, white or Indian, who ventured into their country" (7). Whether the alleged murderers were the mysterious Mountain Men or not, story after story told of the gruesome end that so many had come to in the Nahanni country.

In 1946, stories about the "Headless Valley," — that is, Deadmen Valley — appeared in the *Toronto Star* and *Chicago Tribune*. According to Hartling (1993: 94), the stories were "a blockbuster. Nahanni became synonymous with unearthly phenomena. Stories sprang up in support of the reputation: tales of hidden tropical forests, murder, head hunters, hot springs, canyons, waterfalls, and gold. Much of the reputation was based on fantasy, but an eager readership ate it up." A year later, Pierre Berton, then a young reporter for the *Vancouver Sun*, led an expedition into the Nahanni. His reports fanned a national interest in the old legends. These stories resonate even today in the place names of the region: Deadmen Valley, the Headless (mountain) Range, the Funeral (mountain) Range, Sunblood Mountain, Broken Skull River, Hell's Gate, Hell Roaring Creek, and Headless Creek. In 1970, Prime Minister Pierre Elliott Trudeau visited the Nahanni, and in 1971 it became a national park (Hartling, 1993: 99).

The stories of the Nahanni are part of Canadian folklore. They not only reflect the fear and fascination that people have with death, but they foster that very fear and fascination. While death for ourselves and our loved ones is usually unwelcome, bitter, and tragic, and while we often distance ourselves from the possibility or actuality of such death, death in general remains a topic of great interest. Finally, these stories serve as cautionary tales warning people to be careful lest tragedy befall them.

The invention of the Internet provided a new medium for the circulation of folklore and popular culture. Since the early 1990s, stories about accidental deaths have been posted on Internet websites and have circulated as e-mail. Wendy Northcutt has operated her website www.DarwinAwards.com since 1994 and has listed candidates annually since that date for the Darwin Award of the Year. According to Northcutt's website, Darwin Awards are "named in honor of Charles Darwin, the father of evolution, [and] commemorate those who improve our gene pool by removing themselves from it." These stories, circulated as humour, feature persons portrayed as "idiots," who in an unfortunate and often stupendous lapse in judgement bring about their own deaths. Readers smugly enjoy a laugh at the expense of the deceased but at the same time are reminded that they too are only a misstep away from a similar fate. Starting in 2000, Northcutt has written a series of best-selling Darwin Awards books, and in 2006 a Darwin Awards film was premiered at Sundance.

The contemporary media, including television and newspapers, for example, not only reveal social constructions of dying and death but also play a role in creating, disseminating, and maintaining those constructions. The news media report daily in great detail about death by crime, accident, disaster, and war. Visual images of death are frequent on television, in the newspapers, and in news magazines.

The role that the news media is thought to play in shaping collective definitions and motivating social responses to death is illustrated by the following controversy. In late April 2006, the recently elected Conservative government led by Prime Minister Stephen Harper announced that media coverage of soldiers' bodies being returned to Canada following their deaths in Afghanistan would be banned (where Canadian soldiers had been deployed since 2002). The rationale offered for the media ban was respect for the privacy of the grieving relatives of deceased soldiers. Furthermore, the government announced that the flag on the Parliament Buildings in Ottawa would not be lowered to half mast on the return of each individual soldier, but it would be lowered once a year on Remembrance Day to commemorate all military personnel who have been killed in wartime conflict. This practice, the government claimed, would be more consistent and equitable, treating all deceased military combatants, past, present, and future, with the same respect. Considerable controversy erupted. Opponents argued that media coverage was important to acknowledge and honour the deceased soldiers and their families. They also argued that the Harper government was attempting to muzzle the media and manage public opinion regarding the war by downplaying military deaths and eliminating disturbing and potentially opinion-shaping images from the evening news. It was alleged that the government feared that images of soldiers returning to Canada in coffins might lead to a decline in public support for Canada's involvement in Afghanistan, a commitment that the Conservative government intended to maintain. A month later, after considerable and sustained public outcry, Harper lifted the ban and announced that media coverage would be left to the discretion of individual families.

The deaths of individuals can have important social significance. The deaths of Canadian soldiers, for example, may be used by both proponents and opponents of a war as symbols mobilized to win support for their separate positions. Other deaths may also hold cultural significance. For example, Ramos and Gosine (2002) examined newspaper coverage of the death on May 27, 2000 of hockey legend Maurice ("the Rocket") Richard. English newspapers in Quebec and across Canada tended to emphasize Richard's greatness as a hockey legend while Quebec French newspapers tended to emphasize his place as a Quebec cultural and political sym-bol. That is, the Quebec French newspapers focused on Richard's iconic status and its relevance to the development of a Quebec national identity. Thus, while death has personal significance, death as reported by the news media can also have social, cultural, and political significance.

Recently, Nancarrow Clarke (2006) examined the portrayal of death in high-circulation English-language magazines available in Canada in the 1990s and early 2000s. She argued that portrayals of death reveal an underlying "frame" or discourse, namely, the optimistic notion that death is, can be, and should be under individual control (Nancarrow Clarke, 2006: 157, 162). She concluded that the emphasis in magazine articles on the power, success, and potential of modern medicine, along with the individual's right and ability to choose, presents an image of death as controllable and downplays the lack of control that most, especially the less privileged, have over death.

Nancarrow Clarke (2004) also examined the portrayal of sex-specific cancers — breast cancer, testicular cancer (which most often affects younger men), and prostate cancer (which most often affects older men) — in mass print English-language magazines in Canada from 1996 to 2001. She suggests that the mass media raises fears about these cancers in part by portraying them as threats not only to life but also (and perhaps more importantly) as threats to one's femininity or masculinity, that is, to a person's fundamental gendered identity. While media portrayals raise fears, at the same time they offer solutions such as early detection and medical treatment to alleviate those fears.

Popular culture such as television programming, movies, and novels (con-sider the success of horror-story writer Stephen King) regularly deal with death. It is ironic that, in an allegedly death-denying culture, contemporary television programming is often preoccupied with dying and death. Indeed, some prime-time dramatic series are centred on health care professionals and their struggles to save the lives of the sick or injured, while others are concerned with law enforcement officers and legal professionals who seek to bring justice for unjust deaths.

Perhaps dying and death make good dramatic fare because of the individual and collective fear they inspire. Dying and death get our attention and can provoke deep concern and great interest. While television often captivates viewers by capitalizing on fears of death, such programming tends to offer happy endings. In the hospital dramas, dying and death are usually managed successfully, or at least humanely, and in the crime dramas, the perpetrators of unjust deaths are typically brought to justice. In short, television programming raises fears of dying and death and then calms them. The message is that, despite the chaos of illness, accident, and crime, dying and death are manageable in a world that is, in the end, patterned, purposeful, and coherent.

THE SECULARIZATION, PROFESSIONALIZATION, MEDICALIZATION, AND BUREAUCRATIZATION OF DYING AND DEATH

As discussed in Chapter 3, religion has played an important role historically in making death meaningful and providing guidelines for dying persons, for their family and community, and for the management of the dead body. Increasingly, however, Canada is a secularized society; that is, the importance of religion as a central social institution has declined. Church and state are separated, and weekly attendance at church has declined substantially, especially since the mid-twentieth century. Increasingly, death is defined by secular rather than religious elements of society and culture. Doctors, nurses, philosophers, ethicists, psychologists, and lawyers, for example, have tended to replace theologians as definers of the meaning of death. Similarly, officials such as medical examiners, morgue attendants, and funeral-home directors supplement or replace religious officials such as priests, ministers, pastors, and rabbis.

In addition to the church, the family and the community used to play major roles in assisting the dying, managing the dead body, and supporting the bereaved. However, during the twentieth century, dying, death, and even grieving came to be managed increasingly by professionals such as doctors and nurses, medical examiners and coroners, funeral directors, and grief workers such as psychologists and social workers. Control of dying, death, and grieving shifted from persons one knew to strangers, and from laypersons to professionals, particularly medical professionals. Furthermore, medical professionals tended to define dying, death, and grieving as medical problems to be solved by medical therapeutic intervention. They fought dying with high technology, defined death in medical terms, and recommended the management of grieving through counselling and prescription drugs. Dying and death were removed from the context of normal life and placed instead in the context of health care institutions to be managed by professionals.

Cultural rules and practices develop to govern the process of dying as well as the individual and collective responses to death. In bureaucratic settings, these rules about dying and death are formally defined (Marshall, 1986). As noted in Chapter 2, dying and death typically take place in the hospital, an elaborate bureaucracy with diverse officials and formal rules. Control over dying persons is assumed by the bureaucracy, although the requirement for voluntary and informed consent leaves the dying person with some degree of control. Death is also bureaucratized. The dead body is certified and managed by various functionaries who work in the hospital, the medical examiner's office, and the funeral-home industry. These functionaries perform their services according to professional and governmental rules. Bureaucratization shifts control over dying and death away from the dying person, the family, and community, and towards officials who are strangers and who operate according to the bureaucratic culture rather than the individual's relevant subculture.

Kaufert and O'Neil (1991) reported on interactions between health care professionals and Aboriginal Canadians (Cree, Ojibway, and Inuit) in Winnipeg hospitals. In the hospital, health care professionals tend to take control of the dying patient. They impose predominantly Euro-Canadian, professional, and bureaucratic rules not only on the treatment of the dying person but also on the involvement of that person's family and friends. In addition, health care professionals apply bureaucratic rules regarding the processing of the body of the deceased. The Aboriginal community tends to find these rules inappropriate and inconsistent with their own cultural guidelines. Similarly, the health care workers tend to find Aboriginal cultural norms equally inappropriate. In short, neither group understands or accepts the other (see Stephenson, 1992, for a similar discussion involving Hutterites). This impasse is alleviated by Aboriginal interpreters who serve as language translators, cultural informants, mediators, and patient and community advocates.

Marshall (1986: 133; see also Marshall, 1980: 159; Frank, 1991) extends this argument to all Canadians. He argued that with the "bureaucratization of death and dying through such institutions as hospital death and the funeral industry," the family and community of dying persons and of the deceased have become marginal spectators of processes in which they have traditionally played central roles. Nevertheless, the grief experienced by the bereaved is not likely lessened by this marginalization, and indeed may be intensified.

Emke (2002) examined the secularization of funeral practices in Newfoundland. He argued that secularization is evident in the following: the rise and professionalization of the funeral director, who is increasingly taking over the role that the clergy used to play with respect to death and bereavement; the personalization of the funeral ritual with its emphasis on celebrating the life of the deceased in place of a focus on theological constructions of the soul and the next life; the increasing emphasis on the needs and preferences of the family members; and the emerging role that funeral professionals play as definers and protectors of funeral rituals as new rituals are substituted for old. As Emke put it: "what secularization has displaced, professionalization has offered to replace" (2002: 270).

Zimmermann (2004) argued that medical practitioners exert "disciplinary" power over the dying. For example, she conducted a discourse analysis of the usage of the term "denial" in the hospice and palliative care literature. She concluded that denial is a label imposed on the dying and/or their family members by medical practitioners when the dying and/or their family members are not in agreement with the medical practitioners who are managing the patient's dying. In other words, if the patient or patient's family disagrees with prognosis, treatment plan, etc., then the patient or patient's family is "in denial." The patient or patient's family is no longer in denial when they have come to accept the same point of view as the clinical practitioners. In short, medical, professional, and bureaucratic defini-tions of the situation have considerable power and influence over the layperson's response to dying and death.

The medicalization, professionalization, and bureaucratization of dying and death may seem hostile or indifferent to the dying person and his/her family. This is not always or necessarily the case. For example, Johnson *et al.* (2000) examined the construction and use of end-of-life narratives in an intensive care unit (ICU) in a hospital in Ontario. These narratives tended to be shaped patiently and gently by ICU staff in discussion with family members of dying patients. Through a consen-sus-building dialogue, the narratives were co-authored by the intensive care team members and the families of dying patients and served to facilitate decision-making regarding the withdrawal and withholding of life-supporting technology in order to allow death to occur. These narratives often had a similar structure and used similar metaphors. In other words, they became part of the ICU culture and one of the tools used by health care professionals in this hospital ICU to help families make end-of-life decisions for a dying family member. Despite the standardized nature of these narratives, they functioned therapeutically and provided comfort for both ICU team members and families of dying patients by defining the dying and death of the patient as inevitable, natural, dignified, and "good."

MAKING SENSE OF DEATH

Marshall (1986: 129; 1980) observed that humans construct meanings to make sense of the world and to facilitate functioning in the world. People everywhere have tried to make sense of death. While an individual's search for meaning is a highly personal endeavour, it is facilitated by systems of meaning that exist separate from the individual. These meaning systems are components of culture. Through processes of socialization, cultural meaning systems are often internalized by the individual without critical reflection. For example, a person may be raised with a particular religious belief that provides this individual with answers to questions of meaning, in particular, the meaning of life and death. Systems of meaning are also found outside religion, in philosophy, psychology, schools of thought regarding therapeutic grief counselling, and so on.

Yet, having a culturally based meaning system is no guarantee that death will be easily accepted. An individual may find that the circumstances of a particular death undermine their system of meaning. In such circumstances, the individual is suddenly forced to search for meaning and to make sense of the incomprehensible. If systems of meaning are socially constructed, they can be deconstructed. Sometimes, events in life do just this. Death, in particular, can be very destabilizing.

In contemporary Canadian culture, death is typically considered acceptable if, and only if, it comes at the end of a long life and ends a period of deterioration. Other deaths are not so easily accepted. Deaths by murder, suicide, and accident are typically seen as tragic and senseless, especially when these deaths are "premature." Braun (1992: 80–89; see also Chasteen and Madey, 2003) discusses the commonly shared beliefs, values, assumptions, and rules that make the death of a child problematic. She makes a number of observations: contemporary Western culture places a high intrinsic value on children; children may provide meaning and purpose for their parents' lives; there is an expectation that life will be long and good and that death will come only in old age; there is a belief that if life is lived responsibly and correctly, then things will turn out well; and, finally, in a death-denying society, the death of a child is a taboo topic, unthinkable, obscene, and unacknowledged. In a cultural context such as this, parents will lack a meaning structure through which they can make sense of the death of their child.

Furthermore, the death of a child may threaten any meaning structures that the parents do have. Marriages may end with the death of a child, since the marriage may no longer be meaningful or relevant to the grieving parents. The death of a child may also undermine the parents' faith in God. Parents who have believed all of their lives might find themselves asking: "If there is a God, and if God is good and all powerful, then why is our baby dead?" While human beings crave and create systems of meaning, these constructions can be fragile. In the face of death, most people find themselves searching for meaning. Some find meaning in the cultural constructions of their upbringing while others find themselves separated from their cultural moorings.

DIFFERENT TYPES OF DEATH

Death is not simply a biological event. It is also a social and cultural phenomenon. Indeed, from social and cultural points of view, there are different types of death. The most obvious type is "biological death," which is the death of the body. The death of the body is accompanied by "personal death" — that is, the death of the person. However, while the dead body decays, the dead person can seem to live on in the memories of survivors and may be believed to live on as a spirit or soul in a "life after death."

There are other types of death that may come to those who are not biologically dead. Sudnow (1967) wrote of persons who were treated as if they were physically dead when they were still alive: he called this "social death." Years ago, following a disaster at a coal mine in Nova Scotia, 12 men were trapped underground for six and a half days, and another six men were trapped for eight and a half days. Lucas (1968) records the following:

> On the fifth day a high-ranking official of the mining company publicly announced that there could be little hope that any man remained alive. The trapped miners although physiologically alive were socially dead. The wife of one of the trapped miners had ordered a coffin for her husband, had bought mourning clothes and prepared the house for his funeral. After rescue, the miner's comments on his social death were: "Well when I came home they talked about [how] they had my casket ready, and then the wife she got sympathy cards, and when you think about all that it hurts you. [They] had you dead when you wasn't dead, you know." (2-3)

Other examples of people who are likely to be treated as socially dead include persons who are comatose, in a persistent vegetative state, institutionalized, frail, or socially derelict. The comatose can also be said to have experienced "psychological death" in that they lack consciousness (Doka, 1995). Doka also writes of "psychosocial death," in which a person is significantly changed so that they no longer seem to be the person they once were. Examples of psychosocial death include mental illness, trauma to the brain through head injury or stroke, organic brain diseases such as Alzheimer's, drug or alcohol addiction, religious conversion, and even growing up. Parents may grieve when their offspring has suddenly, so it seems, become a young adult and is no longer the little child that was loved so dearly. Finally, relationships are also said to die, as when a marriage ends in divorce or children are given up for adoption or taken into foster care.

Legal death is yet another type of death. A person who is declared legally dead may or may not be biologically dead. In wartime, persons missing in action may never be proven to be deceased but may be presumed to be so and declared legally dead (Aiken, 2001: 8). Such a declaration allows for the settlement of the missing person's property and terminates that person's legal relationships. A declaration of legal death ends a marriage relationship and makes remarriage possible for the surviving spouse.

Doka (1995) argued that cultural definitions and rules recognize some deaths as legitimate while others are "disenfranchised." The biological death of a close family member such as a parent, grandparent, child, or sibling is typically recognized as legitimate, and the bereaved are offered social support such as time off work, flowers and cards, and attendance at the funeral service. The bereaved are allowed to grieve because the death is perceived as a legitimate death. The biological deaths of more distant relatives such as uncles, aunts, or cousins tend to receive less legitimization and therefore less social support. No support at all may be offered for the biological deaths of ex-spouses, gay or lesbian lovers, extramarital lovers, roommates, friends, colleagues, clients, and pets, all of which tend to be disenfranchised. Similarly, other deaths that tend to be disenfranchised include spontaneous and induced abortions. Disenfranchised deaths are seldom acknowledged, publicly mourned, or socially supported.

Non-biological deaths also tend to be disenfranchised. Social death, psychological death, psychosocial death, and the death of a relationship may all be illustrated by a person who reaches the later stages of Alzheimer's disease. On this point, a woman in a National Film Board of Canada video (McGowan and Bowen, 1990) speaks of her husband who has been institutionalized as a result of Alzheimer's: "I feel that it is like widowhood except (pause) you know you're grieving but, uh, but there isn't any ritual. I try not to have as my only conversation my husband's illness because … you really need to keep that part of your grieving to yourself." As Doka (1995: 272) said, "societies have sets of norms — in effect, grieving rules — that attempt to specify who, when, where, how, how long, and for whom people should grieve. Each society defines who has a legitimate right to grieve." The woman in the video does not yet have the right to grieve, despite all she has lost. Her husband is no longer the person he was, and their marriage, as it was, has come to an end. However, without a dead body, grief is disenfranchised.

DYING AND DEATH AS SOCIAL STIGMA

A culture is a set of definitions and beliefs about reality, rules about how to behave, and evaluations about what is good and bad. These beliefs, normative rules, and values tend to be widely shared and persist over time. Some things are quite arbitrarily defined and evaluated as either good or bad. Consider racism, where a whole category of people are defined as bad, inferior, and so on, on the basis of physiological characteristics such as skin colour.

Death is generally defined as bad, repulsive, contaminating, and threatening. Accordingly, an ideology of beliefs has developed to justify these evaluations, and normative guidelines have developed to manage death. There may be good reason to evaluate death negatively. First, the smell of death — that is, the smell of rotting flesh — is highly disagreeable. Moreover, rotting flesh is associated with disease and pestilence, contamination and contagion. Second, threats to life are generally feared and avoided. Finally, the death of a loved one tends to be one of life's most emotionally painful experiences.

Nevertheless, the negative evaluations of death go well beyond the obvious. In many cultural groups, death, the dead, and places of death such as graves and cemeteries are feared and negatively valued because of beliefs about the danger and malevolence of departed spirits and ghosts. Furthermore, death may be feared because of what might come after — religious constructions of everlasting torment in hell, for example. Even more curiously, people who are not dead but are merely associated with death may be negatively evaluated. Posner (1976) wrote that the widow, the orphan, the "hangman," the processors of the dead (such as the morgue attendant and undertaker), and the aged, all tend to be negatively valued. Yet, what offence does the widow or orphan or undertaker commit? None, except they have a relationship with the dead. The widow's husband is dead, the orphan's parents are dead, and the undertaker's clients are dead. What offence do the aged commit? None, except that their age is a harbinger and reminder of death. The cultural logic seems to be that if death is bad, then anybody and anything that is associated with death is also bad. Such treatment is an example of what Goffman (1963) referred to as a "courtesy stigma"; that is, a person is stigmatized because of a stigma attached to someone with whom they are associated. Because death is stigmatized, almost anyone and anything associated with death is also stigmatized. The contamination is not literal, it is cultural (Posner, 1976).

SOCIAL RITUALS ACCOMPANYING DYING AND DEATH

Major changes in an individual's life and social status tend to be publicly acknowledged and celebrated in rituals known as rites of passage. Examples of rites of passage include the christening of a newborn baby, the bar mitzvah for a Jewish boy who has reached the age of 13, high school graduation, post-secondary graduation, marriage, retirement, and death. Regarding death, Posner (1976: 46) wrote:

> In a culture such as ours which abhors death, it is not surprising to find that we attempt to deny it or at least repress the emotional responses which accompany such occasions. It is appropriate to conclude that funeral rituals represent a rather clever attempt to deal with a paradoxical situation. On the one hand, death must be denied, covered or played down at all costs. On the other hand, the occurrence of death must be tactfully disclosed so that members do not inadvertently touch upon contaminating topics.

Funeral rituals acknowledge the death of a member of the community, acknowledge the grief of those who have lost a loved one, and provide guidelines for the public display of emotion. These guidelines describe what emotions should be shown, and where and when they should be shown. Furthermore, funeral rituals provide guidelines as to how to proceed with the disposal of the dead body and how members of the community are to provide support to the bereaved. As Posner notes, funeral rituals have a dual and paradoxical function: they simultaneously allow for the display of emotion and control emotional displays. In addition, funeral rituals simultaneously acknowledge disruption of the normal social order and provide a mechanism for re-establishing social normality. (For a discussion of the funeral industry in Canada, see Chapter 3.)

Post-death rituals in Canada typically acknowledge both the deceased and the mourners. In many funeral services, a eulogy — a selective and idealized reconstruction of the life of the deceased — is given. Furthermore, the grief of the mourners is discussed openly. Support is offered in the form of attendance at the funeral service, flowers, sympathy cards, donations to charities or research organizations, and verbal expressions of sympathy. In addition to the eulogy, a formal speech is often given at the funeral service that constitutes a message for the living about the meaning of life and the meaning of death. Burial or cremation typically follows the funeral service. Alternatively, a memorial service may follow a burial or cremation. At the conclusion of the formal funerary rituals, community members return to their normal lives, and the bereaved are expected to return to public normality shortly thereafter.

CULTURAL CONSTRUCTIONS OF DYING AND DEATH

Culture influences personal beliefs, subjective perceptions, and the meanings that an individual assigns to dying and death. Furthermore, post-death rituals vary from one culture to another. In a multicultural society such as Canada, made up of many ethnic and religious groups, there are considerable variations in cultural definitions and guidelines regarding dying, death, and grieving. The balance of this chapter examines these definitions and guidelines among several different groups in contemporary Canada.

Coast Salish

Aboriginal or First Nations persons comprise many groups and thus potentially many different expressions of cultural constructions of dying and death. The Coast Salish are an Aboriginal people living on the west coast of Canada. Joseph (1994) studied their cultural values and rituals regarding dying and death. Salish people combine traditional beliefs with Catholic and other Euro-Canadian beliefs, past with present. Furthermore, beliefs vary from one individual to another among the Salish as they do in any other community. Joseph noted that in traditional Salish culture there is a belief in the continuity of life from this world to the spirit world and in the connection between these two realms. The deceased lives on in the spirit world and is taken care of there. It is believed that the living and the deceased can communicate through rituals and in dreams, and that the spirits visit the living from time to time. These beliefs do not lessen the pain of grief, but do facilitate healing.

In her study of the Salish, Joseph records the recollections of two sisters concerning the death of their father some eight years earlier following a series of strokes. The two sisters were members of the Squamish Nation living on a reserve in North Vancouver. Joseph notes that, while one sister relied on a Christian church and prayer to deal with her grief, the other sister relied on traditional Salish cultural rituals, going to the Longhouse to engage in socially supported ritualized emotional expression for the purpose of healing. Other social rituals included use of water, cedar, and devil's club (a shrub) for purification, as well as the grieving circle, smudging, pipe ceremony, and burning (to send selected items to the deceased). The sister who relied on Salish traditions also received ministrations from a medicine man.

The dying of the elder in Joseph's study was described as a time for family gathering. As is customary, on the third day after the elder's death, a wake was held, where the body of the deceased was viewed. On the fourth day, a funeral at the church was followed by a graveside service. The church service combined elements of both Catholic and Salish tradition. Not long afterward, the family had a burning to send their loved one clothes and other items that they thought he would need in the spirit world.

While culture can shape and assist grieving and mourning, the sisters selected different cultural elements. Both exercised faith, although faith in different cultural elements. It is an oversimplification to assume that culture is necessarily a mono-lithic homogenizing force. Instead, there is a diversity of cultural elements from which individuals select (Molzahn *et al.*, 2004, make the same point with respect to the diversity of Coast Salish values and beliefs about organ transplantation). In short, culture tends to shape but also permit a diversity of individual responses.

Cree

Preston and Preston (1991) noted that emotional restraint is the general rule among the Cree living in Quebec near James Bay. Cultural rules require a person to say goodbye when leaving on a journey lest death intervene unexpectedly. Similarly, it is considered important that goodbye be said to a person known to be dying and that the dying have an opportunity to say goodbye as well. Saying goodbye affirms relationships and completes them should death intervene.

When death comes for the Cree, it is to be met competently with composure and self-control by both the dying and the bereaved. The bereaved are informed promptly after death has occurred, and a brief intense emotional outpouring of grief is permitted at that time. Grief is shared by others and social support given. Grief is expressed periodically up to and including the burial, which is held without undue delay. It is expected that composure and self-reliance will be regained soon thereafter, and inner emotions held in check.

Dene

Ross Gray, a psychologist from Toronto, was sent by the government to consult with northern communities about suicide prevention (Gray, 1993). One of the communities he went to was Fort Simpson, near the Nahanni River area discussed earlier in this chapter. The majority of the people at Fort Simpson were Slavey Indians, who are one of several First Nations peoples collectively referred to as Dene. Gray found a cultural taboo against speaking publicly about loved ones who had committed suicide and about the strong feelings that such suicides generated. Nevertheless, many people informally sought out respected elders who had come for the consultation about suicide prevention. Gray also found that school children at the local school seemed to abandon the taboo and talk more readily about suicide than did adults.

Inuit

During his assignment as a consultant for suicide prevention, Gray also visited several predominantly Inuit communities, including Rankin Inlet, Baker Lake, and Coppermine. There, he observed among the Inuit "a natural leeriness of 'southern' professionals [who] come to enlighten northerners about the nature of reality" (1993: 206). Instead of simply listening to the "expert," the people preferred to tell their stories of loss and pain, each in turn, in detail, and in as much time as the stories took to tell. Gray had to give up his time-bound agenda. He wrote:

> Several people ... talk[ed] to us about the style of this consultation. They say it reminds them of the way things were in the past, when there would be much community discussion of issues, with decisions arising out of the discussions. More recently, consultations from government and others have tended to be top-down. Hierarchical notions of wisdom, with travelling experts dispatching information to needy recipients. People have become disconnected from their own wisdom. (1993: 210).

Muslim

Hebert (1998) observed that Islamic society, like Western society, is pluralistic and multicultural. Furthermore, in both Western and Islamic societies, individuals practise their religions with varying degrees of devotion and adherence to traditional beliefs. Nevertheless, it is possible to compare in a very general sense Western and Islamic orientations to death.

Hebert examined Western and Islamic cultural definitions and prescriptions regarding perinatal death, that is, death of a baby before or shortly after birth. In Western societies, Doka (1995) observed that fetal death is generally unacknowledged and grief following such a loss tends to be disenfranchised. Hebert wrote:

Consistent with the Muslim attitude toward life and death, the death of a fetus or neonate is not minimized as it tends to be in the West, nor does it carry with it the same onus evident in Western societies — that of being an illogical, unnatural, and incomprehensible event to be quickly forgotten as soon as possible. Rather, the loss is regarded as being just as significant and meaningful as the loss of someone later on in life and the fetus is treated with the utmost dignity and respect by all. (1998: par. 12)

Prayers in the case of Muslim infant deaths are said at the site of death, which may be the hospital. The baby is given a name. Autopsy, cremation, and embalming are prohibited by the Muslim faith. The family prefers to take the baby quickly for preparation for burial. This preparation may include ritual washing and shrouding. The burial takes place very soon after death, usually within 24 hours. Uncontrolled emotional outbursts are discouraged, as grieving parents are encouraged to accept the will of Allah. The official mourning period is three days, but unofficial mourning may go on for 40 days, with visits to the grave on Fridays, the Muslim Sabbath.

Hebert described a case involving a Muslim family and a perinatal death that occurred in a Montreal hospital. The mother had a miscarriage and lost her baby of 22 weeks gestational age. A bereavement support team including a social worker was called in. The following are excerpts from the case report:

A conflict ... was brewing. The nurses had offered the patient [the mother] an epidural, which her husband had refused outright, and [the nurses] were becoming increasingly frustrated with the men, their loud chatter in the hallway, and their seemingly controlling and unsympathetic attitude toward their patient ... The first successful intervention centred on the need to find a female physician. Once found, [the father] seemed to calm down. The mother was asked if she would like to hold the [dead] baby. [The father] refused for her, saying that it would be too painful. He, however, would hold the baby, which he did lovingly and tearfully ... He was horrified when offered a snippet of the baby's hair.... One family member declared that there should be no autopsy, that the body should be kept, unwashed, with the placenta, and that formalin [a preservative] should not be used ... The men's loud praying, once again, became disturbing to the staff ... and the social worker had to find an empty room in which they could continue their prayers. The nurses felt that [the father], because of the time he spent with the men, was unsupportive of his wife. To make matters worse, within an hour after the delivery, [the father] was asking to take the baby home. The nursing team became extremely upset ... On clarification, it was discovered that [the father wanted to take the baby] to the Islamic Centre for preparation for burial … Finally, after much negotiating and compromising, the baby was ready for transport. (1998: pars. 27-29)

These excerpts from the case report reveal the intense frustration felt by the hospital staff. The Western nurses were reluctant to set aside practices to which they were committed as modern women and also as mediated professionally and bureaucratically. Furthermore, while the nurses were sympathetic to the mother, they were extremely critical of the father and the other Muslim men. From the Western point of view, the men were authoritarian and overbearing, and the nurses felt that the mother was oppressed and abused.

While the case report does not portray the Muslim men sympathetically, the reader can extrapolate that the Muslim men also felt a great deal of frustration. They had to fight every step of the way in order to follow their cultural and religious practices. This case study reveals how difficult interactions can be when cultures collide.

Jewish

Fishbane (1989) studied the mourning rituals of persons affiliated with an orthodox Jewish synagogue located in a major Canadian city. At the funeral home and immediately before the funeral service for the deceased, a garment is torn by and for seven relatives: father, mother, brother, sister, son, daughter, and spouse. The practice for this synagogue is to have the women tear a black kerchief while the men tear a black tie. The tearing is done on the left side of the body for a deceased parent and on the right side for any one of the other relatives who might be the deceased. The torn garment is worn for a seven-day mourning period. From the time of death until the burial ceremony, the bereaved are not supposed to shave, cut their hair, bathe, work, go to parties, or engage in the usual daily religious observances. The official mourning period begins immediately following the burial ceremony that is supposed to be held within a day of death.

A funeral service takes place before burial. There is a requirement that a minimum of ten men be present. At this service, a eulogy is given and prayers are said. At the burial ceremony, a male survivor recites a special prayer. Those present then form two lines, and the mourners walk away from the grave through the two lines which close behind them.

The mourners are transported from the cemetery to the house of the deceased. Before entering the home, the mourners ritually wash their hands and remove their shoes. They are then served a meal of condolence, consisting of bread and eggs prepared by friends or neighbours. The mourners remain at home for seven days, during which time visitors come to offer their condolences, and a minimum of ten males come regularly to offer prayers. A number of prescriptions and proscriptions — to burn candles, cover mirrors, to not bathe or cohabit — are supposed to be observed, but may not in fact be followed. (Many of the members of this orthodox synagogue are not committed observant Jews.) The seven-day mourning period ends with a walk of some distance out-of-doors to signify rejoining the community. Additional rituals are traditionally observed for more extended periods following burial.

Chinese

Bowman and Singer (2001) interviewed 40 Chinese seniors in Toronto who had been born in Hong Kong or the People's Republic of China, had come to Canada between 1975 and 1986, and were assessed as relatively non-assimilated to Canadian culture. These relatively non-assimilated seniors were asked about their attitudes toward end-of-life decisions including, in particular, their views regarding advance directives. The seniors rejected the notion of the advance directive and gave the following reasons, which reflect their cultural values: it is important to maintain hope and a positive attitude and not focus on the negative; advance health care planning focuses on the negative and can have undesirable consequences; patients and their families are to rely on the advice of physicians; decision-making should be done collectively and should involve a consensus of family members rather than being imposed by the dying person who expresses his/her will in an advance directive or by a single proxy decision-maker named in an advance directive. The authors suggested that the views of these Chinese seniors living in Canada can be understood through the lens of Confucian, Taoist, and Buddhist traditions rather than from Western points of view.

Molzahn *et al.*, (2005), in a study done in the greater Vancouver area, interviewed 15 Chinese Canadians and also conducted four focus group interviews with an additional 24 Chinese Canadians about their values and beliefs regarding organ donation. These authors found that there was considerable diversity in beliefs, reflecting a mix of Confucian, Buddhist, Christian, and Taoist teachings, and that a mix of cultural, philosophical, and religious perspectives, more than formal religious dogma, influenced beliefs about organ donation. Because the Chinese have a tradition of not discussing matters relating to dying and death, organ donation was usually not discussed and therefore was less likely to be done.

Ethnic Viet and Lao Hmong

Schriever (1990) compared medical and religious belief systems related to dying for ethnic Viet and Lao Hmong refugees in Canada. Ethnic Viet refugees (not to be confused with ethnic Chinese refugees from Vietnam) arrived in Canada from Vietnam in the late 1970s. About the same time, Hmong refugees arrived from Laos. Both groups place a strong emphasis on family genealogy, that is, on one's ancestors.

Schriever (1990) also discusses the intricacies of the traditional Viet and Hmong beliefs and practices regarding dying, death, and mourning. She observes that it is not clear to what extent these refugee groups in Canada continue to maintain their traditional beliefs and practices and to what extent they have incorporated Western beliefs and practices. In a multicultural society, there is a tendency for one culture to borrow from another. This fusion of differing belief systems is known as syncretism. It follows that individual Viet and Hmong immigrants may be traditional, syncretic, or Westernized. Schriever encourages Western professionals involved in the process of dying to ascertain the belief system of their clients rather than proceeding on the basis of stereotypes or limited understanding.

Through her study, Schriever (1990) offers a number of suggestions for workers providing palliative care to dying Viet or Hmong patients. She recommends using bilingual and bicultural interpreters, including extended family in care, and not isolating the patient from the family. The worker should expect that the patient and family will use dual medical systems (traditional and Western) and should not assume that traditional remedies are inconsequential. The workers should not dismiss accounts of dreams or encounters with spirits as having no meaning or relevance and should be aware that emotional distress may be reported in physiological terms. It is important to note that the individual's surname is often placed first instead of last. Several gestures may be inappropriate. For example, it is rude to touch an adult's head, to show the bottoms of one's feet (shoes), to snap one's fingers, or to beckon with an upturned finger (fingers should be pointed down instead). Referring to the deceased by name may also be inappropriate. Invasive procedures such as drawing blood, surgery, and autopsy should be avoided. The workers should be prepared to facilitate dying at home, as this may be preferred to hospitalization. Finally, it is important to note that Western notions regarding grieving and emotional release may be inappropriate.

Western European and Euro-North American

Philippe Ariès (1974; 1981) surveyed portrayals of death in Western European culture from the Middle Ages to the present. He suggests that until the early Middle Ages (through the twelfth century), death was "tame," or omnipresent, familiar, and accepted as the natural order of things. Later, death became "wild" and it was increasingly feared and resisted. By the twentieth century, death had become dirty, ugly, shameful, hidden, and denied.

Alternatively, Stroebe *et al.* (1995) characterized nineteenth-century Western culture as romanticist. Romanticism emphasized the soul or spirit, love, and enduring commitment to intimate human relationships, even after the death of a loved one. Accordingly, "To grieve was to signal the significance of the relationship, and the depth of one's own spirit. Dissolving bonds with the deceased would not only define the relationship as superficial, but would deny as well one's own sense of profundity and self-worth" (1995: 237). From the romantic perspective, grief could legitimately last a lifetime. In contrast, Strobe *et al.* (1995) characterized twentieth-century Western culture as modernist. Modernism emphasizes efficiency, progress, and rationality rather than emotionality. From the modernist point of view, "bereaved persons need to break their ties with the deceased, ... form a new identity of which the departed person has no part, and reinvest in other relationships" (1995: 234). From the modernist perspective, grief is to be gotten over.

Postmodernism takes the view that romantic and modernist conceptualizations of death are products of cultural and historical processes; that is, they are socially constructed (Stroebe *et al.*, 1995; see also Marshall, 1986). Nevertheless, it is not clear that one perspective is more correct than the other or that one perspective has better therapeutic outcomes than the other. Each perspective defines death differently, and each prescribes different courses of action for the bereaved. What is defined as appropriate in one culture may be inappropriate in another. What "works" for the individual then often depends on that person's cultural frame of reference. It follows that the meaning of death for the individual and the individual's reaction to death must be understood in cultural context. It also follows that, when support or therapy is offered to an individual, the support must be tailored to the individual and must fit with that person's cultural point of view. In an increasingly heterogeneous society like Canada, death has different meanings for different subcultures, and reactions to death will vary depending on subcultural frames of reference.

SUMMARY

This chapter explores cultural constructions of the meaning of dying and death in Canada and resulting social responses. Canadian culture became a death-denying culture in the twentieth century, and reactions to dying and death vacillate between denial and awareness, fear and fascination, detachment and morbid obsession. While death cannot be completely denied, convention can distance us from it. Indeed, the conventional language of death is often indirect and euphemistic. Alternatively, humour presents a way of dealing with what makes us uncomfortable. By either distancing from or making light of death, various euphemisms, sayings, and stories facilitate coping with the strong emotions that it evokes.

While it is usually unwelcome, and while we often distance ourselves from its possibility or actuality, death in general remains a topic of great interest. The contemporary media, including television and newspapers, not only reveal social constructions of dying and death but also play a role in creating, disseminating, and maintaining those constructions. While media portrayals raise fears, at the same time they offer solutions to alleviate those fears. The message is that, despite the chaos of illness, accident, and crime, dying and death are manageable in a world that is, in the end, patterned, purposeful, and coherent. Nevertheless, having a culturally based meaning system is no guarantee that death will be easily accepted. Individuals may find that the circumstances of a particular death undermine their system of meaning. In such circumstances, they are suddenly forced to search for meaning and to make sense of the incomprehensible.

Death is increasingly defined by secular rather than religious elements of society and culture. Further, while the family and community used to play major roles in assisting the dying, managing the dead body, and supporting the bereaved, during the twentieth century, dying and death were removed from the context of normal life and placed instead in the context of health care institutions to be managed by professionals.

It follows that death is not simply a biological event; it is also a social and cultural phenomenon. From such points of view, there are different types of death, and each society defines who has a legitimate right to grieve. Death is generally defined as bad, repulsive, contaminating, and threatening; the cultural logic seems to be that if death is bad, then anybody and anything that is associated with death is also bad. In terms of social responses to death, funeral rituals acknowledge the death of a member of the community, acknowledge the grief of those who have lost a loved one, and provide guidelines for the public display of emotion. Funeral rituals have a dual and paradoxical function: they simultaneously allow for the display of emotion and control emotional displays. In addition, funeral rituals simultaneously acknowledge disruption of the normal social order and provide a mechanism for re-establishing social normality. In contemporary Canada, these definitions and guidelines differ among various ethnic and religious groups.

PART III
THE INDIVIDUAL RESPONSE TO DYING AND DEATH

CHAPTER 5
INDIVIDUAL PERSPECTIVES ON DYING AND DEATH

Death presents an existential problem for the living — as an individual becomes more and more aware of the inevitability of death, questions arise about the meaning and purpose of one's existence. How should one live, given that life ends in death? What is the meaning of life? What is the meaning of death? Furthermore, for dying persons and their family members who face imminent death, questions arise about how a person should die and how dying itself can be made meaningful.

EXPECTATIONS OF DYING AND DEATH

The possibility of dying can be assessed in both statistical and psychological terms. Statistically, babies born in Canada 100 years ago had a much higher likelihood of dying in infancy or early childhood than do babies born now (Gee, 1987: 269;

Marshall, 1986: 132; Morrison, 2004; Joseph *et al.*, 2005). Today, death typically comes in old age, and the death of a child is highly unlikely.

In psychological terms, very young children tend to have a limited awareness of the possibility of dying. At birth, a newborn child cries when it experiences cold, hunger, thirst, pain, and fear. Crying expresses the baby's discomfort and distress, and typically elicits caregiving responses from persons in the baby's social environment. In other words, the baby has an innate capacity for dealing with threats not only to its comfort and well-being but also to its very existence. Nevertheless, it may be some years before the young child can fully conceptualize dying and death (Aiken, 2001: 229-35).

Children and young adults give little thought to the possibility of dying. For young people, their own death is a distant possibility. Nevertheless, fear of death may underlie distancing from death. Thus, while young people may rarely think of death, they may fear dying when they do think about it. Because young people often perceive death to be removed from them, they can simultaneously fear death and put it out of their minds. In contrast, middle-aged and older persons, who because of their age are closer to death, are more likely to think about dying and death. Yet, older persons are less likely to fear death than are middle-aged or young adults (Novak and Campbell, 2006: 323; Aiken, 2001: 256-58). It appears that proximity to death in old age motivates one to think of death (Marshall, 1986), but not necessarily to fear it.

Claxton-Oldfield *et al.* (2005) asked young adults enrolled in introductory psychology courses in New Brunswick about their willingness to volunteer in a classroom, nursing home, food bank, and palliative care setting. While most expressed a willingness to volunteer in a classroom, food bank, and nursing home, they were much less likely to express a willingness to volunteer to work with dying persons in a palliative care setting. Male undergraduate students were even more likely than female undergraduate students to indicate that they would not be willing to become a palliative care volunteer. Both young men and young women feared that volunteering with the dying would be too demanding emotionally and too stressful, that they would not know what to do in a palliative care situation, and that they lacked either the skills or the inclination for this kind of volunteer work. This study suggests that many, though not all, undergraduate university students tend to distance themselves from dying and death.

Death has come to be unexpected, except in old age. Recently a colleague died at the age of 57. Even at that age, death seems inappropriate, premature, too early. When a child dies, it is incomprehensible and unacceptable (Martin, 1998). Some years ago, death was more expected. Consider a man and a woman born on the

Prairies in 1912 and 1922, respectively, who married in 1946, and who in the early 1950s bought three grave plots, two for themselves and one for a child they expected to lose to early death. Eight children and almost 60 years later, the extra grave is still unused. Earlier in our history, it seemed prudent to expect death at any time. Now Canadians generally do not expect death, except in advanced old age.

DYING TRAJECTORIES

In one sense, we all begin to die from the moment we are born. However, relatively healthy children, adolescents, and young adults do not think of themselves as being on a trajectory ending in death. Similarly, while awareness of one's mortality does tend to become more acute in middle age, the healthy middle-aged do not think of themselves as dying (Marshall, 1986: 137-38). The everyday phrase "over the hill" reflects the perception that one has reached the midpoint or zenith of one's life and has begun the inevitable decline into old age, illness, and, ultimately, death. Nevertheless, the concept of the dying trajectory is reserved for those who are perceived to have a disease or condition with an explicit terminal prognosis; that is, death is clearly anticipated as the end of the person's present circumstances.

The dying trajectory refers to the course that a person follows over time as they move through the dying process to death. Glaser and Strauss (1968; see also Kastenbaum, 2007: 117-23) noted that there are various dying trajectories. In unexpected deaths such as sudden infant death syndrome (SIDS), accidental death, homicide, suicide, or heart attack, the dying trajectory is precipitous and brief: death comes quickly. Alternatively, the dying trajectory may be long, as with Alzheimer's disease, for example, and may be complicated with remissions and relapses, as can be the case with cancer.

Patients who are undergoing a long dying trajectory often express their concerns about being or becoming a burden on others. McPherson et al. (2007) interviewed 15 patients in Ottawa who were receiving palliative care for advanced cancer. All but one of these patients were being cared for at home and in most cases the primary caregiver was the spouse of the terminally ill patient. These dying cancer patients expressed concerns about the physical, social, financial, and emotional burdens they felt they had created and might create in the future for their caregivers. This perception of being a burden resulted in feelings of guilt, regret, sadness, frustration, anger, loss, failure, dependency, uselessness, and lowered self-esteem. As a result, the dying often tried to find ways to contribute to their own care, concealed their own needs, focused on the needs of their caregiver, and engaged in planning for their deaths.

In an attempt to reduce the negative emotions associated with feeling that one is a burden, most eventually achieved a resigned acceptance while some focused on the positive aspects of the caregiver-care receiver relationship or expressed a sense of previously earned entitlement in an effort to reduce their feelings of being a burden. This study shows that a long dying trajectory changes previous roles and relationships in such a manner that the dying often experience distress and lowered self-esteem as they perceive that they are becoming a burden for their familial caregivers.

Family caregiver burden is a commonly reported outcome of providing care to dying and chronically ill family members. Only recently is it beginning to be reported that tremendous benefits for both the family caregiver and care recipient can also occur. These benefits include expressions of shared care and love, as well as opportunities to discharge duties and responsibilities that are openly and willingly accepted.

PREFERENCES FOR DYING AND DEATH

agree or disagree.

The shortest possible trajectory resulting in quick death is generally preferred over a long and lingering or dwindling dying trajectory (Aiken, 2001: 277). Indeed, the ideal death is often described as following a healthy and happy old age that ends suddenly and painlessly in one's sleep. This ideal reflects the so-called "natural" death from "old age." It can be illustrated by an anecdote told by a hairdresser whose father had been a barber. One day, a gentleman in his nineties came in for a haircut. After the man had been in the chair for a while, the barber noticed that his client seemed to have drifted off to sleep. In fact, he had quietly died. He had peacefully passed from life to death, and his hair cut turned out to be for his funeral. Stories like this illustrate the preferred way to die and can be contrasted with accounts of ways of dying that are less preferred.

mining stories

As discussed in Chapter 4, Lucas (1968) interviewed men who had been trapped underground for days in a coal mine disaster in Nova Scotia. The miners had no food, had run out of water and batteries to power their lights, and were surrounded by their dead and dying co-workers. The men began to speculate that death would come to them either from starvation, thirst, or suffocation from deadly gas or lack of oxygen. They had little fear of death itself but were more concerned about how they might die. They hoped to die painlessly, to just "go to sleep." They seemed to expect that poisonous gas would come eventually, and, indeed, gas was the preferred mode of death. The miners knew that when that gas came, they would just go to sleep, and death would follow quickly and painlessly.

As mentioned in Chapter 3, the dying and death of Sue Rodriguez received a great deal of public attention in the early 1990s (Wood, 1994; Bartlett, 1994; Ogden, 1994). In 1991, Rodriguez, an athletic woman who was just past 40 years of age, and who was the mother of a young son, began to experience symptoms that would eventually be diagnosed as amyotrophic lateral sclerosis (ALS). This disease leads to a progressive loss of muscle control, ending in paralysis, with death often coming from suffocation. Told by doctors that she had from two to five years to live, Rodriguez said that at first she felt panic, then numbness, and shock. She began to notice seniors, envying them because she would not get to experience old age (Bartlett, 1994). Although she was briefly defiant, thinking that she would beat the disease or at least live longer than predicted, its relentless progression soon put an end to such thoughts. Instead, she decided she would commit suicide at some future time when the quality of her life was sufficiently compromised. As she became increasingly dependent, however, she realized that she would need help to die and so began a much-publicized campaign for the legalization of doctor-assisted suicide in Canada.

The CBC-TV program *Witness* (Bartlett, 1994) followed Rodriguez through her final 18 months of life. The program intimately revealed to viewers both the person herself and the devastating effects of her disease. Rodriguez assessed her situation in a straightforward manner. She did not want to die, and, had she not gotten ALS, she would not be seeking to end her life. However, she observed that ALS is an awful disease to live with and from her point of view was a gruesome and unfair way to die. She wanted some control over her destiny and wanted a better death than the one that the disease promised. Early in 1994, completely dependent and barely able to speak, Rodriguez achieved her better, though still illegal, death through the assistance of an anonymous person. She was 43 years old at the time of her death, having lived not quite three years from the time she first experienced symptoms.

Like Sue Rodriguez in Canada, Professor Morris Schwartz, an American, died of ALS. As did Rodriguez, Schwartz faced his disease with great courage and dignity and with a desire to make his death meaningful. He spoke of the lessons learned in dying, lessons shared with and recorded by a former student. Indeed, the professor and the student collaborated on a book about the professor's experience with dying, his "last thesis" (Albom, 1997). As was the case with Sue Rodriguez, Schwartz's dying became public. In 1995 he came to the attention of Ted Koppel, host of the American television program *Nightline*, and interviews were aired on three different occasions as his disease progressed and death approached. The book about his dying and death, entitled *Tuesdays with Morrie*, became a best-seller

[handwritten: good contrast Rodriguez vs Schwartz]

and was made into a movie of the same name starring Academy Award winner Jack Lemmon.

Unlike Sue Rodriguez, Morris Schwartz did not campaign for assisted suicide. While both sought to gain control over their dying, they did so in different ways. Rodriguez wanted to control the final moment through assisted suicide, Schwartz by managing his emotions, acknowledging and then setting aside negative emotions such as self-pity and concentrating on positive emotions such as love. Schwartz accepted a natural death and made no effort to control its time or cause. In contrast to Rodriguez, who died at home presumably from assisted suicide, Schwartz died at home from the suffocating end of ALS, an end that Rodriguez had described as gruesome and unfair.

Although most people would say that ALS is not a good way to die, both Rodriguez and Schwartz could be cited as examples of good deaths. It is their manner of dealing with their terminal illness, rather than the illness itself, that tends to be applauded and portrayed as exemplary. As discussed earlier, however, dying peacefully in one's sleep in old age also tends to be considered a "good" death. In this scenario, there is only death — no dying, no pain, no suffering, no need for coping, and no test of character. It is an ideal death because it is an easy death. Note that the aim of hospice palliative care (discussed in previous chapters) is to promote a good death — one in which pain and other problems are prevented or successfully addressed.

Dying with ALS is not easy: it is a dying that tests, shapes, and reveals one's character. Cultural ideals value dignity, fortitude, courage, endurance, self-control, and making the best of the worst situation. Public accounts of people such as Rodriguez and Schwartz are designed to move others emotionally and to provide moral inspiration. Dying is not simply a biological process; it is also a process with psychological, social, moral, spiritual, and occasionally, as in the case of Sue Rodriguez, political dimensions. Public accounts of persons who die exemplary deaths are designed to remind us of these various dimensions and to describe and define the various pathways to a "good" death.

Professor Diana Austin at the University of New Brunswick, in an article originally published in the Toronto *Globe and Mail* (July 16, 1997), described the dying and death of her mother. Three years before her death, she "began her journey to death" when she experienced sudden liver failure at the age of 70. Her unexpected recovery from that initial event "led to a three-year celebration of life in the shadow of death." Austin wrote that her mother "continued to laugh and shop" and that "she chose to gauge the quality of her existence by the joy she found every day in her interaction with others." She resisted death, and even near the end said resolutely,

"I am not going." Noting that dying with dignity does not necessarily mean a quick and quiet death, Austin concluded, "Mom died slowly, but she died well" (quoted in McPherson, 2004: 439-40).

Austin's account shows that dying, despite its many drawbacks, can be a rewarding and meaningful time for the dying person, the family, and for others such as professional caregivers whose lives are touched by the dying person. It also illustrates a particular style of coping with dying. In this case, coping involved living life to its fullest extent, given the circumstances, and resisting death by fighting the good fight and never giving in. In this regard, Austin's mother illustrates a cultural ideal: the person who exercises her will to live, to extract as much meaning as possible from life, while holding death at bay for as long as possible. The notion that will power can extend life is part of our cultural mythology and reflects the social expectation that a person should make every effort to resist death. Austin's mother chose her own way of coping with her dying. Although we cannot know the extent to which she was influenced by cultural prescriptions, the telling of the story tends to reinforce these prescriptions.

The notion of dying well, as evident in the stories of Schwartz, Rodriguez, and Austin, is not solely a manifestation of Euro-Canadian values. The Cree living in Quebec near James Bay also value self-control and composure in the face of death (Preston and Preston, 1991). A story is told of a Cree man, Jimmy Moar, who was old and blind and who, one evening, announced his impending death by saying to his daughter, "I'm almost falling off from my chair. That's all I can sit here. I am very tired." He then told his daughter how much he loved her and his granddaughter, put on his best clothes, went to bed, and died (Preston and Preston, 1991: 142). This story is told as an example of a good death. Goodbyes were said, relationships were affirmed, and death was met with dignity and quiet competence.

FEAR OF DYING

The preference for a quick death suggests that dying is perceived to be distressing, even more than death itself (Lucas, 1968; Lévy et al., 1985: 31; Frank, 1991: 43). Although people generally prefer living to dying and prefer life to death, a person on a dying trajectory, such as Sue Rodriguez, may find dying so unpleasant that he or she asks for death. Indeed, following their demise, it is commonly said of such persons that death was a "blessing" for the deceased because it brought their suffering to an end.

Fear of dying is driven by concerns about loss and suffering (Lucas, 1968; Frank, 1991: 43) and tends to focus on the possibility of a long and lingering dying trajectory. A person entering such a dying trajectory faces loss of health, loss of control and independence, loss of competence and dignity, loss of status and social roles, loss of future plans and goals, and impending loss of life. Furthermore, fear of dying is motivated by concerns about prolonged suffering and, in particular, about pain (Lucas, 1968; Frank, 1991: 43).

With respect to fear of dying and loss of dignity, Chochinov *et al.* (2002) studied 213 terminally ill patients with cancer who were receiving palliative care in Winnipeg. They found that the majority of these patients reported that they were able to maintain their sense of dignity. Only a small number (8 per cent) reported frequent feelings of shame, degradation, or embarrassment. Those patients with a lessened sense of dignity tended to be younger rather than older and were cared for in hospital rather than being cared for at home. The authors note that a person's sense of dignity appears to be "a particularly resilient construct and, in most instances, is able to withstand the various physical and psychological challenges that face patients who are terminally ill" (Chochinov *et al.*, 2002: 2028). Nevertheless, it was noted that alterations in physical appearance coupled with feelings of being a burden, needing assistance with activities such as bathing, being in pain, and being hospitalized can undermine the dying person's sense of dignity, competence, autonomy, self-esteem, and sense of self worth (Chochinov, *et al.*, 2002: 2029).

AWARENESS OF DYING

Persons who are dying may be unaware that they are dying, either because they have not been informed of their terminal prognosis or because they are in denial. According to Glaser and Strauss (1965), two of the first researchers to focus on dying and death, persons who are aware that they are dying have two options. On the one hand, a drama of mutual pretence may be enacted in which the dying persons and the people around them do not speak of the dying process or of impending death. On the other hand, people may prefer to discuss the terminal prognosis openly. Today, dying persons are more likely to prefer to talk openly of dying and death (Novak, 1997: 304; Aiken, 2001: 295-96), although some ethnic groups have social norms that discourage open communication (Leming and Dickinson, 2007: 241; Kastenbaum, 1998: 297). Not speaking of dying and death maintains denial, hope, normalcy, and dignity, while avoiding unpleasant topics and issues. On the other hand, openly acknowledging dying facilitates the obtaining of information, allows for the expression and sharing of feelings, helps decision-making, and allows one to settle one's affairs and make final arrangements (Novak, 1997: 305).

The creation of the Internet has introduced a new method and opportunity for people to increase awareness and communication about dying and death. Radin (2006) studied online cyberspace communication about potentially fatal breast cancer. She detailed the history of an online community established in 1996 and sponsored by the nonprofit organization Breast Cancer Action Nova Scotia (BCANS; this virtual community can be found online at <http://bcans.net>). By 2003, this site was logging some 22,000 visits monthly. Radin argued that this new medium and form of communication breaks down established professional information monopolies and old ways of communicating. She observed that it provided a safe and supportive environment that fostered a "thick trust" and allowed persons with breast cancer and their supporters and survivors to communicate with each other about the various aspects of the disease and their experiences with it. This peer-to-peer communication provided mutual support and encouragement, facilitated the exchange of information and insight, empowered laypersons, provided a forum for advocates of change, and thereby facilitated social activism. Despite the potential for activism, an analysis of postings to this website indicated that the primary functions were the sharing of information and emotional support.

THE DYING PROCESS

Dying is a process that takes place over variable lengths of time. Elisabeth Kübler-Ross (1969), the physician who helped turn dying into an open affair, interviewed dying persons and, from these interviews, theorized that they typically go through stages in the course of their dying. This theoretical model is a generalization and does not necessarily apply in all aspects to any given individual. Furthermore, the model has been misused as a prescription about how one should feel in the course of dying and about how one should proceed through the process.

Kübler-Ross's model states that a typical initial reaction to a terminal diagnosis is denial. As reality overcomes denial, anger is a typical second reaction. A third stage involves "bargaining" for more time. In the fourth stage, depression sets in as the person reacts to their many losses and prepares for further losses. Finally, cognitive and emotional resistance give way to resigned acceptance. In other words, the stages might be characterized in the dying person's voice as: "Not me!" "Why me?" "Not yet," "Poor me," and finally "I give in."

More recently, David Kuhl, a palliative care physician living in Vancouver, suggested, "what dying people want is the same as what living people want" (2006: 2). Both, Kuhl argues, want to feel good about themselves, experience closeness to significant others, and feel that their lives are meaningful. Accomplishing this for the dying depends in part on controlling physical pain and facilitating open communication.

In 2003, legendary Canadian documentary filmmaker Allan King produced a two-and-a-half hour documentary titled *Dying at Grace*. It provides an intimate view of the dying and death of five patients in the palliative care unit at Grace Hospital in Toronto. Each of the patients is dying from a terminal cancer (ovarian, bladder, breast, lung, and brain cancer). Nichols (2005:143) reviewed this film and observed that it "is a poignant, in-depth exploration of the process of dying" and the reality of death. Nichols observed that: "dying is seen as a gradual loss of control" and "The events [dying and death] as they are documented speak for themselves. Death is seen as an anticlimax — the end of struggling for breath, the end of pain or suffering, a time of quiet after much activity, and the notable absence of struggle often after a prolonged period of suffering."

PERSONAL ACCOUNTS OF "BRUSHES WITH DEATH"

Occasionally people have an experience where, for a short moment or for some time, they come to think that they might be facing dying and death. A middle-aged man told the following story:

> In my early thirties, I began to experience frequent, extreme, and unexplainable fatigue often accompanied by anxiety, depression, and difficulty coping with everyday tasks. Visits to the doctor produced no explanation. Indeed, visits to the doctor were so unproductive and frustrating that at one point I swore I would never go back to a doctor again. I assumed that I was under stress from my employment and needed to develop better stress management strategies. However, nothing seemed to help.
>
> Things got worse over several years. I thought I might be losing my mind. In time, I became convinced that I was dying. The thought that I was dying came as a clear and certain realization. I remember being surprised that I felt no emotion attached to this realization. I was neither afraid nor angry. I was dying, most likely, and that was that. Indeed, I felt so miserable that death seemed to be the solution and dying seemed to be the explanation. I still wondered exactly what was wrong with me, but nevertheless, whatever was wrong, I felt that it was killing me.

think what would have been if I had more [strikethrough] time

I was pretty desperate when my wife made a doctor's appointment for me with a new doctor and told me that I was going to see him or else. I went. The doctor told me that I was probably losing my mind but agreed to do some blood tests. A week later he diagnosed Hashimoto's thyroiditis and shortly afterwards a specialist diagnosed pernicious anemia as well. I had a double whammy.

It seems melodramatic now to say that I was dying. These diseases are perfectly treatable today. But I was dying. A hundred years ago, I would have gone mad and then died. It would have been an unpleasant death for myself and for those around me, in particular for my wife and young children. While these two diseases will not kill me, I find myself wondering what will. Some day, sooner or later, I will get another diagnosis, and next time I may not be so lucky. (Personal communication, 1999)

For this storyteller, personal self-diagnosis was a cognitive exercise rather than an emotional one. While there was much emotional turmoil in his life, he exhibits an emotional detachment as he assesses his health status, concludes that he is dying, and attempts to deal with that realization. This story also reminds us that death has a certain capriciousness about it: many who are now reading this would already be dead if born at an earlier time in history or in some place where modern health care was not available. So many of the diseases that killed our ancestors are now either preventable or treatable. Similarly, those diseases that today are most likely to kill us at some time in our lives may yet be rendered impotent. When we die and how we die is in part a function of our time and place in history. Yet, the storyteller himself did not dwell on such academic observations. His concerns were more pragmatic: his perception was that he was dying, and his concern was what to do about it.

Persons who confront dying are often said to show anger, revealed, in part, in the form of questions such as "Why me?" or "Why now?" (Kübler-Ross, 1969). Such *we don't get to choose.* questions imply resistance and an unwillingness to accept fate. The storyteller above seems to be more fatalistic. It is as if his reaction is a bemused acknowledgment that these things happen haphazardly, and so "Why not me?" and "Why not now?"

A woman in her thirties told the following story:

It all started four and a half years ago driving home from a family ski trip with my husband and our two school-age daughters. I felt an itch behind my right ear, and as I was scratching I felt something unfamiliar to me. It felt like three bumps. My mind started to wander. Being an emergency nurse was not helping. I was thinking the worst. What if these were cancerous tumours?

because of awareness of terminal illness we tend to magnify simple health problems

It was a long trip home. I needed to get a proper look behind my ear. I was horrified to see the lumps. They were not anything I had seen before as a nurse (and believe me, I had seen it all). [The next day] I phoned my family doctor. I told the receptionist that I needed to see my doctor that day. They got me in to see him later that afternoon.

My doctor was not able to explain the lumps. His facial expression said it all, and then he started asking me a lot of questions. Questions I had heard over the years from my nursing experience. Questions that centred around signs and symptoms of cancer. I asked him bluntly. Is it cancer? He said he wasn't sure what they were, but he didn't like what he saw. In his attempt to be reassuring, he said, "If it is Hodgkin's disease, you are lucky. It is one of the best types of cancer to get. You could have up to a ten-year survival rate." Why was it that I wasn't feeling too lucky? Ten years did not seem like such a long time when I had one daughter in Grade Two and the other in Grade Three.

[The next day] I had an appointment with a surgeon. I was due to work the night shift but I called in sick. The charge nurse knew something was wrong immediately. She called me back at home and asked me what was wrong. In telling her my story, I broke down crying when I told her that the following day I was seeing a surgeon to see whether or not I had cancer. She was very understanding.

The next day was as fearsome and tense as the day prior. Waiting. Always waiting and wondering. I saw the surgeon. Again, the visit was not very encouraging. He thought the lumps looked suspicious. The only way to get a diagnosis would be to have a biopsy [of the lymph nodes in my neck. The surgeon] said he would schedule me for day surgery.

You may be wondering what was going through my mind these long days and nights. Well, I guess the first thing was fear. Not fear for myself, but fear for my daughters. If the news ends up being bad (malignant) what will happen to my girls? My husband works out of town, which means that they would have no mother and would see their father infrequently. Essentially they would be raised by a stranger (perhaps by a nanny). This is not something I wanted for my daughters. So I guess I was scared that my children would suffer tremendously if something were to happen to me.

Another concern was how to tell my children if the lumps turned out to be malignant. How do you tell your school-age daughters that their mom has cancer and may die within ten years? How do you prepare them for that? Well, my girls were very perceptive. They had never seen Mom quite so emotional before. I was crying all the time. Every time I saw them, my eyes would swell with tears. My voice was shaky and my mind fuzzy. I was definitely not my cheerful, upbeat, optimistic self. I was a stranger in my own body. My girls and I have a very open and honest relationship so I decided to tell them the truth. "Mommy is having minor surgery to see if these lumps on my neck are cancer." They took the news very well. No tears were shed, but many questions were asked. Not once did they let on that they were scared for me. It was only weeks later that one of the girls' schoolteachers told me that my youngest daughter was very concerned about me. Now I realize that they were trying to·be strong for me. Strangely enough, I did not give the process of dying a second thought.

to tell a child or not

The waiting game wasn't over. My surgery was two weeks away. Two more weeks of thinking and trying to prepare myself for the worst case scenario. I couldn't cope with working so I called the nurse manager. She agreed that it would be best if I took the time off until the biopsy was done. Once again, I had a lot of understanding from my immediate supervisors. But the support given to me by my husband was different.

I don't want to say that my husband wasn't supportive, I guess he thought I was getting myself all worked up for nothing. "Wait until we see what the results are. It may be nothing." My husband didn't go with me to either of my doctor appointments. I guess he thought that he wouldn't be much use to me. After all, I was the health care professional, not him. He wouldn't know what the doctor was saying anyway, so why miss a day's work. He also did not go with me to the hospital for my surgery. Again he felt that we wouldn't find out the results that day and he wouldn't be able to go in the treatment room so he chose once again to go to work. My mother knew that this would be a difficult day for me and drove me to the hospital, waited in the waiting room (picked my girls up from school while I was having my biopsy done), and drove me home. She cared for me like when I was a little girl. I know my mom was as worried about the outcome as myself. I don't think my mom knows how much that meant to me having her there, and I also don't think my husband knows how hurt I was not having him there. *now he dies)*

huge assumptions

[After the biopsy] I still had anywhere from four to seven days to wait for the results from the pathology report. On the fourth day following the biopsy, I phoned the surgeon. No results as yet. I phoned every day until the results were in. It took a full week.

What was frustrating during that week was the attitude of the surgeon. I knew he had no idea what I was going through emotionally and mentally. What was equally infuriating was that when my results did reach the surgeon's desk, he shuffled them aside when he saw that the diagnosis was benign. He did not call me with the results. He waited until I called him. When I asked him if he had the results he said yes, but couldn't remember what the report said. As he shuffled through the reports on his desk, he finally found mine. Oh yeah. The news is good. Nothing to report.

Does the story have a happy ending? The diagnosis was benign, and I wasn't going to die from Hodgkin's disease. But the story is not over. It will never be over. The surgeon told me to be continually checking my lymph nodes because even though they were benign that day, that may change in the future. The obsession continues. Every time I feel a lump, I feel the same anxiety I did four and a half years ago. The scar behind my ear is a constant reminder of those very stressful few weeks in my life and of my mortality. (Personal communication, 1999)

A casual reading of this story suggests that the storyteller was afraid that she might have cancer and might die. She highlights the anxiety and fear that she felt while waiting for a diagnosis. But what is she really afraid of? She indicates that she did not give any thought to the process of dying, nor did she seem to give any thought to death in purely personal terms. Instead, she focuses on relationships with her children, her family doctor, her supervisor at work, her surgeon, her mother, and her husband. Her greatest fear is that her young daughters will be left motherless, will be raised by a stranger, and might suffer because of the loss of their mother. She is also worried about how to tell her children about her health and how this will affect them.

The storyteller discusses her relationships during the time she waited for a diagnosis. She describes the women in her life as being very supportive: her daughters, her supervisor at work, and her mother are all sympathetic, understanding, and helpful. Her male family doctor sees her almost immediately and tries to be reassuring. The other men in the story are not perceived as being supportive. Her male surgeon does not acknowledge her concern or her need to know her diagnosis. Her husband minimizes the situation, refusing to get upset over something that "may be nothing." Not only does he distance himself emotionally from the situation, he distances himself physically by going to work.

The differences between the males and the females in this story can be explained in part by sex role socialization. Social norms for females legitimize emotional expression and nurturing responses (Aiken, 2001: 309). In contrast, social norms for males define emotional displays as deviant and unacceptable (Haas, 1977; Lucas, 1968). Consequently, males are less likely to show their emotions and are less likely to acknowledge the emotions of others.

The storyteller ends her account by pointing out that, while the initial lumps were benign, she nevertheless has to be continually on guard for new lumps. In the end, the experience serves as an ongoing reminder of her mortality. This event brought death into focus in a very close, personal, and threatening manner, when previously it had been only a distant eventuality. Death had become threatening because the storyteller wishes to raise her young daughters herself, an agenda that death would prevent. Death for this storyteller means suffering, not for herself, but for the daughters she would leave behind. For this reason, death is feared.

Another story about people who thought they were likely to die returns to the Nova Scotia coal miners referred to earlier in this chapter. Trapped underground, for the first three days the men tried to dig their way to safety. When their battery-powered lights gave out, they waited in total darkness. They would either be saved or they would die. Before becoming trapped, the miners in their daily routines had not discussed death with each other and said that they seldom thought of it individually, although they knew that coal mining was dangerous work. (Haas [1977] observed the same behaviour among the curiously named "high steel ironworkers," who erect the superstructures for high-rise buildings.) Even when trapped in the mine, the men maintained a psychological distance from dying and death by directing their lights away from the dying and dead and by speaking of the dying as if they were already dead, thereby using social death as a substitute for physical death. Furthermore, the miners knew that they were expected "to die 'like a man' with little expressive outcry, but with stoic determination" (Lucas, 1968: 16). Social norms against the expression of fear of dying are strong in male-dominated subcultures and may also exist in female-dominated work subcultures such as nursing (Reutter and Northcott, 1994).

The miners did express to each other in the mine certain regrets about dying. They spoke of things they had planned to do but would have to leave undone. They mentioned their roles as husbands, fathers, and providers, and expressed concern about not being able to fulfill these roles and the consequences for the survivors. In this regard, the miners were like the mother in the earlier story who worried more about the daughters she would leave behind in the event of her death than about herself. Finally, the miners engaged in a review of their lives in an attempt to affirm "that their achievements were creditable" (Lucas, 1968: 13). In summary, the miners who faced death did not express fear about their own impending deaths. They did express concern about how they might die, hoping for a quick and painless death, and about the consequences that their death would have for those they left behind.

Arthur Frank, a professor at the University of Calgary, published a personal account of his own experiences with two very different "brushes with death" (Frank, 1991). When he was 39 years old he had a heart attack, and at 40 he was diagnosed with cancer. He survived both life-threatening illnesses and wrote to tell his story.

Frank notes that serious illness takes a person to the edge of life. He refers to life-threatening illness as a "dangerous opportunity" to clarify what is important about life. The danger, of course, is that one might die; however, there is opportunity as well as danger. Standing at the edge of life, at the boundary between life and death, changes one's perception of both life and death. When death becomes personal, an immediate and real possibility, questions are raised about how one has lived one's life and how one should live one's life in the future should the illness not prove fatal.

Recovery from his heart attack meant that Frank returned to his previous life "as if nothing had happened." Of course, something had happened, but his inclination was to put the whole experience behind him. The diagnosis of cancer was different. The sense of being in remission rather than fully cured, coupled with the lengthy and demanding experience of cancer treatment, was transformative. Neither Frank, nor his wife, nor his life, nor their life together was the same again.

In analyzing his relations with his doctor, Frank observes that their communication involved a detached language of medical objectivity rather than the language of personal experience and subjective perceptions. In other words, communication was "cool" rather than emotional, impersonal rather than personal. Furthermore, the interaction focused on the management of the disease rather than on the experience of it. In short, both doctor and patient conformed to cultural rules that emphasize professionalism and technical and personal competence. In our society, emotionality is associated with incompetence. As a result, persons facing death tend to be denied legitimate expression of their fears, frustrations, and experiences.

Frank also wrote about the coherence and incoherence associated with serious illness. Incoherence is the loss of order in one's life and the loss of connection with others whose lives are ordered. Illness, pain, and dying separate a person from the normal biological and social order of lives. Because perceptions of order help a person to make sense of life, incoherence involves loss of a sense of understanding and meaning. Coherence involves (re-)gaining a sense of order, connection, and meaning. Frank observes that communication with others can facilitate the construction and maintenance of coherence. However, he distinguishes between communication in the form of detached medical talk, which promotes a sense of incoherence, and the communication of personal experience to sympathetic others, which promotes a sense of coherence.

Antonovsky (1987) has argued that a sense of coherence is very important to health and well-being. Coherence, he suggests, has three components: comprehensibility, manageability, and meaningfulness. Comprehensibility refers to the ability to make sense of things, to understand, to explain, and to predict. Although things may be either good or bad, it is helpful if they are at least understandable.

(1)

Manageability is the perception that one has adequate resources and supports to deal with problems. Meaningfulness is the ability to find meaning, purpose, and motivation. Life-threatening events, terminal illnesses, and the death of others can undermine a person's sense of coherence. From the perspectives of both Antonovsky and Frank, the challenge for the person facing death is to hang on to or to recreate their sense of coherence.

Frank describes the experience of a potentially terminal illness as alienating: one is separated from future plans and goals, from past health, from roles and relationships, and from "innocence" — that naïve sense of security that persists as long as death remains distant and abstract. Frank notes that all of these losses must be mourned. Yet, society tends to dictate the terms of mourning, and these *everything is taken away* are not always consistent with the needs of individuals who grieve for their losses in their own way and in their own time. Similarly, Frank complains that the medical system tends to take control of one's body, disease, identity, and even experience. One's identity becomes the disease; one's personal experience, expressed in subjective terms, is treated as largely irrelevant. The challenge for individuals facing death is to hang on to their personal identity and to acknowledge their personal experience in their own terms.

Robert Hughes, an art critic, writer, documentary maker, and a regular contributor to *Time* magazine, described his brush with death in a severe automobile accident that occurred in Australia (Hughes, 1999). Although he does not remember the collision itself, he remembers the hours he was trapped in the wreckage. Gasoline was leaking, and he begged a friend to shoot him if the car caught fire. Hughes preferred to be shot rather than face a fiery death; nevertheless, he wanted to live. He wrote: "At one point I saw Death ... I looked right down his throat, which distended to become a tunnel. He expected me to yield, to go in. This filled me with abhorrence, a hatred of non-being. In that moment I realized ... that the 'meaning of life' is nothing other than life itself, obstinately asserting itself against emptiness. Life was so powerful, so demanding, and in my concussion and delirium, even as my systems were shutting down, I wanted it so much."

Hughes's story gives voice to the common assumption that individuals have a strong will to live, find death repugnant, and accordingly resist death. Indeed, it has been argued that, in a non-religious age, the terror of death and the fear of non-being have led to the widespread denial of death (Becker, 1973). Nevertheless, Hughes's story also points out that some types of death are preferred to other types, especially in order to avoid unacceptable suffering.

The story of the car accident contrasts in many ways with the other stories reported above. Hughes's brush with death is sudden. In the other stories, the storytellers have more time to contemplate death's approach. In Hughes's story, death is hated and resisted because of the threat of "non-being." His concerns are immediate and personal, and he has little time to come to terms with death. The other storytellers, perhaps because they have more time to contemplate death, come to terms with their own death but resent it more for the disruption that it will cause the loved ones they will leave behind.

FEAR OF DEATH AND DENIAL OF DEATH

In Kübler-Ross's model of the dying process, denial is the initial reaction to learning that one is dying. This suggests that, initially, death is unwelcome and unthinkable. In the last stage of her model, however, the dying person accepts death (Kübler-Ross, 1969: 118). People who are closer to death often fear it less than persons more removed from it. Furthermore, dying may be feared more than death itself. Nevertheless, for most people death is an unwelcome eventuality.

According to Becker (1973), another early theorist, fear of death is fundamentally motivating and at the same time denied. Becker rewrote Freud's thesis by arguing that awareness of one's mortality, rather than one's sexuality, is the fundamental human motivation. Furthermore, because awareness of one's mortality gives rise to terror, it is also the fundamental repression. Becker thus argued that people repress their awareness of their mortality so that they can avoid the anxiety that this awareness provokes.

Becker further argued that an awareness of one's mortality provokes terror not only because it ends the individual life but also because it potentially invalidates the life lived. The individual prefers to believe that life is significant and has meaning and purpose. In Becker's terms, people have a need to see themselves as "heroes." The eventuality of death creates a problem for heroism, in that it calls into question the value of the individual life. In other words, awareness of one's ultimate demise creates an existential crisis centring on questions about the meaning of life. To deal with these unsettling questions and emotions, Becker argued that individuals either search for answers of their own creation or, more often, find answers in the form of socially constructed solutions, such as religion, notions of romantic love, or cultural prescriptions about how one can live a good and respected life. These ready-made answers provide direction and rationale that help the individual gain a sense of heroism, a sense that their life is meaningful. (For a contemporary extension of Becker's thesis, see terror management theory: Solomon *et al.*, 2004; Pyszczynski *et al.*, 1999; Greenberg *et al.*, 1997; Solomon *et al.*, 1991.)

Becker's thesis is hard to prove. If people admit that they fear death, then there is support for his thesis that death provokes terror. However, if people say that they do not fear death, then there is support for his thesis that death is denied. Heads Becker wins; tails he still wins. Nevertheless, his work has some merit. Death is widely "denied" both individually and collectively in contemporary Anglo-Canadian culture (Ramsden, 1991). Young people act and feel immortal (Aiken, 2001: 235). Death has been removed from polite conversation in the home and community (Aiken, 2001: 225; Ariès, 1981). Furthermore, death does seem to raise existential questions and anxieties. The dying person typically attempts to make sense of their impending death and to make sense of their life in the face of death (Marshall, 1986).

THE RELIGIOUS SOLUTION

Becker identified the "religious solution" to the problem of death as the most pervasive and enduring socio-cultural mechanism for defining death in terms that reduce anxiety. However, this solution may be irrelevant for those persons who do not have faith. Furthermore, the religious solution to the problem of death and the meaning of life has been undermined by secular trends. Interestingly enough, people who have strong religious beliefs and people with no religious beliefs tend to report less fear of death than persons with weak religious beliefs (Novak and Campbell, 2006: 323; Mirowsky and Ross, 1989: 108-11). It appears, then, that the religious solution can make death palatable for those who firmly believe; those people with no religious faith whatsoever also seem to be able to come to terms with death. Death seems to pose the greatest difficulty for those persons who are unsure about what lies beyond death.

THE SPIRITUAL SOLUTION

In a secular era, religion has little force in the lives of many individuals; yet some individuals continue to emphasize spirituality, even in the face of secularization. While spirituality may reflect religious discourses, at the beginning of the twenty-first century it is often linked with non-religious constructions that are designed to assign special meaning and significance to selected experiences such as dying and death (Chappell, McDonald, and Stones, 2008: 419). Durkheim (1965 [originally published in 1915]) observed that things and experiences can be defined as ordinary or special or, in Durkheim's terms, as profane or sacred. Thus, to construct a definition of something as having special significance and meaning is to define it as sacred. Once something is defined as sacred, then this thing tends to elicit reverence, respect, and deep consideration. Even in a secular society, there is a tendency to define life as sacred and to give the end of life special consideration. Perhaps the search for meaning and for significance in dying is inherently a spiritual quest.

RISKING DEATH

Gerald Kent (1996) describes himself as "yuppifying rapidly: 33 years old and somewhat paunchy; four young children; a ten-year marriage; a passion for golf and curling; and a busy law practice in Cranbrook, British Columbia." He writes: "I needed a weekend away! The stress and strain of home and practice was calcifying my soul" (81). His solution involved climbing Little Robson, a rock outcropping part of the way up Mount Robson, the highest peak in the Canadian Rockies. This was his first experience at rock climbing.

"After the descent," Kent writes, "the relief and happiness of being alive flooded my soul and I initially vowed never to return. I would stick to golf and curling and succumb to domestication at home with a thankful heart. Life was too precious to risk" (81). However, a year later he attempted a dangerous solo ascent of Mount Robson. He worried about leaving his children without a father and wondered how to deal with those who would ridicule him for risking his life. So why did he make the climb? He explains that he thought it "a great way to protest our society's obsession with physical health and security and its willingness to wink its eye at everything that is destructive to spirit and soul" (82).

Paradoxically, and metaphorically speaking, the moral of the story is that one can lose one's life while living it and find one's life by risking the loss of it. Kent was engaging in edgework — that is, in voluntary risk-taking (Lyng, 1990, 2005). Note that Kent characterizes his quest in spiritual terms, as an activity to free the spirit and to decalcify the soul. The experience is transcendent: the edgeworker transcends his or her own limitations and the petty circumstances of everyday life. Becker (1973) suggested that an awareness of our mortality undermines our sense of heroism, that is, our definition of ourselves as significant. Ironically, in edgework, coming face to face with mortality by purposely risking one's life is a means of achieving heroism and finding significance for one's life.

Edgework is evident in the current trend towards extreme sports, including skydiving, hang gliding, auto racing, dirt bike racing, triathlons, mountain climbing, mountain biking, whitewater kayaking and rafting, scuba diving, downhill skiing, heli-skiing, ice climbing, and bungee jumping. Edgeworkers acknowledge the risk of dying. Part of that acknowledgment typically involves making the sport as safe as possible — there is no death wish operating here. Edgeworkers want to live — they want to really live! They risk death because it makes them feel alive.

CHOOSING DEATH

While some persons risk death in order to affirm their life, some choose death voluntarily and purposely. The affirmation of life through edgework highlights the value of life both for the individual and for others in general. The choosing of death, on the other hand, may suggest that life has no value. Because others tend to think of life as inherently worthwhile, it can be particularly difficult for persons who have lost a loved one to suicide to understand and accept the decision of the person who chooses death.

Why would a person choose death over life? As noted above, dying generally tends to be feared more than death. In death, there is no life, no living, and therefore no pain, suffering, humiliation, and so on. Dying is feared when it involves a life with pain and suffering. In such a situation, the dying may prefer to "get it over with," and death may be viewed as a relief and a blessing.

While dying may involve suffering, living may also involve suffering to the point where life does not seem worth living. Suicide ideation — that is, thoughts about suicide — are common. People who are not otherwise facing death may prefer to actively seek death for a variety of reasons: depression, mental illness, grief, loneliness, unhappiness, chronic illness, pain, guilt, shame, low self-esteem, or feelings of failure (Kastenbaum, 2007: 195-231). Alternatively, death may be chosen to escape social sanctions such as imprisonment or public humiliation.

Farand *et al.* (2004) determined that adolescents involved with the child welfare and juvenile justice systems in Quebec were much more likely than adolescents in general to commit suicide. Factors thought to contribute to an increased risk of adolescent suicide included family disorganization, family violence, physical and sexual abuse, low support, substance abuse, behavioural problems, psychiatric disorders, and intervention by the juvenile justice system or child welfare services (e.g., removal of the adolescent from the family home and placement in a foster home).

Préville *et al.* (2005) examined the suicides of persons 60 years of age and older in Quebec and found that, in comparison to a matching control group of elderly persons who had died from natural causes, elderly persons who committed suicide were much more likely to have been suffering from psychiatric disorders, particularly depression. The suicides and controls did not differ in terms of the number of chronic physical health problems.

Achille and Ogloff (2003) surveyed 44 persons in the United States, Canada, and Britain who were dying from amyotrophic lateral sclerosis (ALS). This survey inquired about their attitudes toward assisted suicide. The majority (70 per cent) indicated that they felt assisted suicide was morally acceptable, and 60 per cent favoured legalization. Respondents who endorsed assisted suicide emphasized self-determination, dignity, and avoiding dependence and becoming a burden to others. Respondents who opposed assisted suicide tended to hold a religious perspective. Finally, this study also suggested that there is an association between depressive symptoms and the desire for assisted suicide.

Not all persons who attempt or commit suicide want to die. For some, suicidal behaviour is a desperate attempt to obtain help. For others, motivations may include getting attention or seeking revenge (Kastenbaum, 2007: 220-21). Suicide can even be "accidental" (Kastenbaum, 2007: 222): a person may intend to survive their suicide attempt but miscalculate the lethality of the means employed or may expect to be rescued but not be found in time. Suicide may also result from a momentary impulse when, for the most part, the victim would seem to prefer living. In summary, while some who commit suicide suffer chronically and reject a life without quality, others who commit suicide appear to be more ambivalent about the relative merits of life over death.

In 1984, the National Film Board (NFB) released a video entitled *The Last Right* (Fortier, Grana, and Howells), a docu-drama based on a true story. The video introduces us to three generations living together as an extended family. The grandfather develops a progressive dementia (formerly referred to as senility) resulting from hardening of the arteries in the brain. His behavioural and psychological symptoms include disorientation, memory loss, intermittent periods of lucidity and confusion, wandering, occasional outbursts of anger, and a sense of his own decreasing competence. The video depicts tender family moments and difficult times. There are tense family discussions about whether or not the situation is good for the two young children in the family and whether the grandfather should be placed in a nursing home.

One emotional discussion concerns whether the family should follow the grandfather's wishes. He had previously said that if he got really sick he wanted the family to just let him go, that he did not want to become a "zombie." He did not want to die like his brother, who had died a long, slow death. When the grandfather indicates that he has decided not to eat any more, the family members have an emotional discussion about how to respond. In the end, the grandfather does stop eating, and after three weeks he dies quietly at home.

This video raises questions about whether people should have some control over their dying. Does a person have a right to say how and when they will die? In this video, the grandfather decides to stop eating and thereby hastens his death and determines its cause. His final decision, implemented in his demented condition, is justified in terms of his earlier decision expressed before the onset of his dementia. It had been his expressed will that his life not be prolonged in such circumstances. In short, this video anticipates the so-called living will, more recently referred to as an advance directive (Novak and Campbell, 2006: 332).

In addition, the video focuses on the question of a "better" death. Is it better to die at home or in the hospital? Is it better to die under the care of loved ones or under the care of professionals who are strangers? Is it better to have some say in your dying or should control be given completely to others? The message here is that a person's last right is the right to have some say in dying, to exercise some control, and to have personal decisions respected.

PREFERRED LOCATION OF DYING AND DEATH

A "good death" has a number of characteristics. As discussed above, most individuals prefer a quick and peaceful death. Dying individuals may also want to be conscious, informed, and free to openly express themselves and to exercise some control by participating in the decision-making process. Finally, a good death may be seen as one that takes place at home, where one's surroundings are familiar, comfortable, and meaningful, and where family and friends can freely congregate (Des Aulniers, 1993: 45). Such deathbed ideals have been enshrined in pre-twentieth-century literature and art (Ariès, 1974: 12; Ariès, 1981). However, as discussed in Chapter 2, in the course of the twentieth century, the rise and successes of modern medicine resulted in dying and death being moved from the home to the hospital (Ariès, 1974: 87-89; Ariès, 1981: 570-71). Later in the twentieth century, the hospital was perceived as a good place to be saved from death but not as a good place to die. The health care community itself has also increasingly questioned the appropriateness of the acute care hospital for the dying. Furthermore, those contemplating dying have tended to characterize a hospital death in negative terms, using adjectives such as cold, technological, antiseptic, and impersonal.

By the late twentieth century and early in the twenty-first century, the preferences of the dying and their caregivers are resulting in dying being returned to the
home and to more home-like institutional environments such as palliative care
units and free-standing hospices (Kastenbaum, 2007: 147-72). As discussed in
Chapter 3, hospice palliative care, which administers to the family and to the dying
person's physical, emotional, psychological, spiritual, and social needs (Novak and
Campbell, 2006: 327), is increasingly preferred over futile attempts to maintain life.
The dying are typically more interested in comfort, dignity, and social support than
they are in prolonging their lives when prolongation means additional suffering,
indignity, and impersonal care.

In this vein, in 1980, the NFB released a video entitled *The Last Days of Living*
(Gilson and Daly, 1980), which outlines the work of the first palliative care unit
(PCU) in Canada, established in 1975 at the Royal Victoria Hospital in Montreal.
This unit was opened specifically to treat the terminally ill, a new concept at that
time (Novak and Campbell, 2006: 327). Another PCU was opened around the same
time at the St. Boniface Hospital in Winnipeg, Manitoba, and many more have been
established since that time across Canada. PCUs serve not only the dying person
but assist the grieving and bereaved family as well, with many offering services
both in the hospital and in the patient's home.

The Last Days of Living features a number of PCU clients who were dying from
cancer, including elderly and middle-aged men and women as well as a man in his
early twenties. The filmmakers try to show the needs of the dying and caregiver
responses to those needs. The patients' responses to their terminal illnesses are
shown as ranging from angry questioning and discouragement to philosophical
acceptance. A middle-aged woman who has had a mastectomy cannot fully accept
what has happened to her. "It is just not right," she says. One elderly man declines
an invitation to go out on the patio on a sunny day. He says that it holds no interest
for him and that it won't do him any good. Another elderly man says that he feels
lousy and complains that he can't even change his position in bed a half an inch.
"You ask for death," he says, meaning that he feels his life is so circumscribed he
wishes to die. A young man has decided to forego further treatment in the hospital
and to go home to die. He talks matter-of-factly about his impending death, observing that he finds it easier now that he knows that he will die, in comparison to the
"roller coaster" phase when he and his family lived with uncertainty and vacillated
between hope and despair. "We are all going to die," he says, and it is only the how
and the when that differ. As he expressed it, "There is no right age to die; any age is
the right age." His parents observe that his dying has scared his friends away — they

have stopped visiting. The video also shows the young man and his parents sharing meaningful time together until his death at home.

The Last Days of Living has two central messages. The first is that death comes to us all and comes in its own time: it can come early in life, in middle age, or in later life. The prominence in the video of the young man who dies at home emphasizes the capriciousness of the timing of death and highlights the vulnerability of persons of any age. Furthermore, his story suggests that dying at home can be a positive experience for all involved. This is the second central message of this video — it is an attempt to describe the good death or at least a better death. Dying with the assistance of hospice palliative care, whether in a PCU, hospice, or at home, is implicitly contrasted with dying in the hospital's intensive care unit while enduring heroic attempts to prolong life. Although this contrast is not made explicit, it is shown that hospice palliative care can make dying less painful and less lonely, thus helping the dying achieve a better death.

LIVING WITH DYING

Two other videos from the NFB show that living with dying can be a long process with both positive and negative aspects. In the video *Living with Dying* (Dolgoy and Phillips, 1991), the audience is introduced to Albert and Margaret Kerestes. Albert Kerestes was in his early sixties when he was told by a cancer specialist that he was terminally ill and had only weeks or perhaps months to live. Kerestes says that it is difficult to learn that you have only a couple of months. He notes that, initially, he was emotionally upset, but he got over it. Despite his acceptance, this was a difficult time for the couple. Their calendar was full of appointments at the cancer clinic, at the hospital, and with doctors. These medical appointments and regimens took control of their lives. They were glad when this phase came to an end and they were able to go home and regain some control over their own lives. Their home-care nurse emphasized the importance of people having a sense of personal control in such situations.

Kerestes's dying trajectory did not go as expected: his cancer went into remission. Although he still suffered many limitations and his prognosis was still terminal, he was now living with dying, and the time of his dying was no longer predictable. The home-care nurse began to describe him as a chronic palliative care client. Her initial focus had been on managing pain and symptoms and providing needed physical aids such as a wheelchair. During his long remission, she shifted her focus from active care to surveillance.

Albert Kerestes benefitted from the care received in doctors' offices and hospitals. At home he benefitted, in particular, from the care of his wife and from the visits of the home-care nurse. The local pharmacist helped make arrangements with Blue Cross to facilitate payments for medications. Other supports came from the Kerestes's extended family (grown children, grandchildren, siblings), friends and neighbours, and church officials and fellow parishioners; in addition to their faith and prayers, a move to a government-subsidized senior citizen apartment, which charged a fixed percentage of the Kerestes's income for rent and which was at ground level with no stairs to negotiate, also helped. Family and social gatherings and activities were frequent and enjoyable. The Kerestes indicated that they never felt alone.

In short, Albert Kerestes had expected to die and the remission of his cancer was unanticipated. He subsequently lived for years following his original diagnosis before finally dying. His home-care nurse said in the video that he wanted to live and that his wife and family wanted him to live. She noted that he defied the experts and stayed alive because he was a fighter.

This reference to the will to live is common in discussions about dying, reflecting a widespread belief that people have some control over the course of their dying and can will themselves to live or to die. There is some risk in making this assertion. For example, those who live tend to be congratulated for being a fighter and for their strong will to live, while those who die may be blamed for giving up or for lacking in will power. Both congratulation and blame may be misplaced. They both demonstrate our tendency to psychologize death, that is, to overemphasize the power of psychological processes and to underemphasize the power of biological processes. In terms of Albert Kerestes, other considerations besides will power — social supports, medical treatments and other health care, divine intervention, or the capriciousness of the disease — could be credited with prolonging life.

The reasons for the remission of Kerestes's cancer are not a particular concern of the filmmakers. Rather, the video shows that, while living with cancer and a terminal diagnosis bring pain and sorrow, living with dying can also have many meaningful and pleasurable moments. Another NFB video, *My Healing Journey: Seven Years with Cancer* (Viszmeg and Krepakevick, 1998), reinforces this point. In 1991, Joseph Viszmeg was in his mid-thirties when he was diagnosed with adrenal cancer and told that he would likely die within a year. Seven years later he directed, wrote, and edited a video describing his experience. The video shows him in 1991, a filmmaker and single parent raising a daughter. He is newly diagnosed with terminal cancer. Saying that his first reaction was disbelief, he then speaks of feeling cheated because of the anticipated shortness of his life. He tells his daughter that he has a tumour but does not mention cancer at that time. A risky surgery goes well, and a large tumour is removed. A year later Viszmeg marries, and the year after that he and his wife, Rachel, become parents to a baby boy.

Following his initial diagnosis and surgery, Viszmeg speaks of the many things he tried in an attempt to promote his health — Aboriginal healing practices, spirituality, macrobiotics, transcendental meditation, yoga, and shark cartilage. Nevertheless, many tumours grew back, and by 1993 he once again expected that he did not have long to live. He treated his time as a gift and concentrated on the moment. The new baby, in particular, brought much joy.

Then, unexpectedly, the cancer went into remission, which lasted for several years but was not permanent. In 1997, Viszmeg had surgery again and almost died. His recovery was slow, and he wondered how much time the surgery bought. Acknowledging all the difficulties, he said that sometimes he thought that it would have been better to have done nothing.

Finally, Viszmeg tried the chemotherapy that he had previously resisted because of its harsh side effects. At that point, he knew there was almost no chance of cure, but he hoped for relief from his constant pain. In 1991, his newly diagnosed cancer had seemed like a novelty; seven years later, it had become "a drag." He said he was bored with it, bored with the pain and nausea and weakness. He wanted the cancer to end. This did not mean that he wanted his life to end. He liked his life and wanted more: he just wanted the cancer to end. At the end of the video, he spoke of the importance of loving and of the wonderful events and people in his life. He died the following year, in 1999.

SUMMARY

Death inevitably raises questions about meaning — the meaning of life and the meaning to be found in both dying and death. Proximity to death because of terminal illness or old age tends to motivate an individual to reflect on the meaning of life and death.

A century ago, death was expected more often and earlier than it is today. Now, at the beginning of the twenty-first century, death is not expected, except in advanced old age. The premature death of a child, a young adult, or a middle-aged person has become almost entirely unexpected and thus often extremely difficult to accept.

While individuals generally do not wish to die, some deaths are preferred over others. The ideal death occurs suddenly or after a brief illness where final good-byes can be said, without pain, in a familiar setting, and in old age following a life lived to its fullest extent. People tend to fear the process of dying, with its potential losses, indignities, and suffering, more than they fear death itself. People facing death often express more concern for the loved ones that they will leave behind than they do for themselves.

This chapter has focused on perceptions of dying and death from the point of view of the person facing death. In the next chapter, the focus is on the perceptions of those persons who lose a loved one to death, that is, on survivors' perceptions of dying and death.

CHAPTER 6
SURVIVOR PERSPECTIVES ON DYING AND DEATH

This chapter examines perspectives on dying and death from the point of view of those persons who grieve the loss of a loved one. It begins with some brief comments on health care professionals. The primary focus of the chapter, however, is on the family and friends of the deceased.

Dying and death generally take place in a social context involving both professional caregivers and family members. While the health care system tends to take control of dying and death, health care professionals are not always willing participants in the process of dying. As we discussed in Chapter 3, doctors, who are generally trained to cure, have a tendency to view death as failure of treatment or medical care. Similarly, health care professionals of all kinds working in acute care hospitals typically work within a curative-care or medical model and so may not be equipped organizationally or even psychologically to deal with dying, palliative care, and death (Novak and Campbell, 2006: 324; Aiken, 2001: 284).

Health care workers, especially younger workers, may find caring for dying individuals and their distressed and grieving family members stressful. Some health care workers are threatened psychologically by death. Those who choose to work with the dying — in palliative care units, for example — are often better suited to, and have more positive attitudes for, dealing with the dying and the death of their patients (Novak and Campbell, 2006: 327).

There may be other issues with professional caregiving. For example, some health care workers may fear contamination and even death as a result of working with persons dying from infectious diseases. In the later 1980s, during the first decade of the AIDS epidemic, Reutter interviewed 13 nurses who cared for persons dying from AIDS in an active treatment hospital in western Canada (Reutter and Northcott, 1994). While the risk of contracting HIV/AIDS at work was small, the nurses expressed concern because of life-threatening consequences should they become infected with the disease. These nurses employed behavioural and cognitive strategies to gain a sense of control. They came to perceive risk as manageable by using precautions such as gloving and masking, reappraising risk as minimal or normal, and using distancing strategies including denial and avoidance of threatening thoughts and situations. They also accepted risk through finding meaning in their work (Reutter and Northcott, 1993) by accepting the AIDS patient as a person who needed and deserved care, by finding work enjoyable and worthwhile, and by emphasizing professional commitment to care. The notion of risk as meaningful and manageable gave the nurses a sense of security. However, when they were exposed to HIV-infected blood or body fluids, their feelings of security dissolved (Reutter and Northcott, 1995). They were instantly reminded of their own vulnerability and mortality. Many of the same issues arose in the more recent situation of the Severe Acute Respiratory Syndrome (SARS) epidemic, where nurses were once again exposed to infectious agents that placed them at considerable risk.

Professional caregivers who work with dying persons are reminded frequently, perhaps on a daily basis, of the mortality of others and presumably of their own mortality. Health care workers who care for the dying must therefore "come to terms" with dying and death if they are to provide quality care without undue personal distress.

GRIEF AND BEREAVEMENT

A vocabulary has developed to describe the loss of a close friend or family member. Persons who lose a loved one are often referred to as the bereaved and are said to go through a period of bereavement. The bereaved typically experience grief — that is, intense suffering — and go through a process of grieving. Bereaved persons who display their grief publicly are often referred to as mourners and are said to mourn or to be in mourning. If a distinction is to be made between grieving and mourning, it would be that grieving is personal and spontaneous while mourning tends to conform to social and cultural norms (Kastenbaum, 2007: 348-51; Aiken, 2001: 302; Counts and Counts, 1991).

Some people may suppress emotions that they feel; others may express emotions that they do not feel. In other words, there is not a one-to-one relationship between private and public grieving. Cultural rules describe what emotions can and should be expressed and when and where they are to be expressed. These rules shape the grieving process and can both facilitate and impede grieving. Although cultural rules can legitimate feelings and their expression, these rules also define what is appropriate, and the person who grieves too long or too intensely (or not enough) tends to be defined as abnormal, deviant, pathological, or a danger to self or others (Counts and Counts, 1991).

While individuals may be moved emotionally by the evening news, with its frequent accounts of tragedies around the world, the death of strangers is typically not associated with grief, mourning, or bereavement. It is the death of a significant other, a person with whom one has a personal relationship, which is distressing. In one sense, death ends the relationship; in another sense, it only transforms this relationship. While the deceased is no longer physically present, the relationship continues, although in an altered form, as evident in survivors' memories, thoughts, feelings, conversations, and behaviours.

A number of factors influence the extent of grief and the course of grieving. The timing of death can influence grieving — whether death is sudden and unexpected or if it occurs at the end of a long and certain dying trajectory. Grieving is also influenced by the nature of the death. Death from suicide, accident, or homicide may be seen as preventable, senseless, and tragic; death from cancer or Alzheimer's disease may be seen as unpreventable and perhaps even a "blessing" that brings an end to suffering (Aiken, 2001: 276; Marshall, 1986: 142).

Grieving is also influenced by the characteristics of the deceased, such as age. Inasmuch as death is expected in old age, it is generally more difficult to lose a loved one who is young than to lose a loved one who is old (Marshall, 1986).

Furthermore, grieving is influenced by the characteristics and personality of the survivor. A parent who has one child, for example, may have more difficulty losing that child than would a parent who has several children (Martin, 1998: 24). Someone who has never experienced the loss of a loved one may have more difficulty than a person who has experienced such a loss, although multiple losses can also be very difficult (Norris, 1994). Males may grieve differently than females (Kastenbaum, 2007: 364-67; Martin, 1998: 18-19; Martin and Elder, 1993: 81; Fry, 1997: 135; Aiken, 2001: 309), and the young may grieve differently than the old (Kastenbaum, 2007: 327-28).

Finally, grieving is influenced by the relationship the survivor had with the deceased. Grieving may differ for a parent who loses a young child, an adult who loses an aged parent, a wife who loses her husband, a husband who loses his wife, or an adult who loses a friend. Furthermore, while it may be difficult to lose someone with whom one had a good relationship, it may also be difficult to lose someone with whom relations were strained, given the feelings of regret and guilt that tend to exist in this situation.

In the context of the family, the loss of a loved one results in a change in social status and social roles. A wife who loses a husband becomes a widow, a husband who loses a wife becomes a widower, a parent who loses an only child becomes childless, and a child who loses a parent becomes fatherless or motherless while a child who loses both parents becomes an orphan. These changes in status and role imply changed relationships, changed circumstances, and alterations in personal and social identity. Adjustments following the death of a loved one involve coming to terms not only with the loss of the loved one but also with all of the associated disruptions to the survivor's life.

DEATH OF A CHILD

In the past, the death of a child was a frequent and expected event. Throughout much of the twentieth century, the death of a child became an increasingly rare event in Canada (Marshall, 1986: 132). Today, children are expected to grow up and grow old. Indeed, the death of a child at any age has come to be totally unexpected, and parents assume that they will most certainly predecease their children (Fry, 1997). Partly because of the unexpected nature of the event, it is particularly difficult for a parent to accept the death of a child (Martin, 1998: 4-5).

Braun (1992) interviewed ten Canadian mothers who had each lost a child. At the time of their death, the deceased children ranged from five months gestation to 25 years. Braun wanted to understand how bereaved parents develop an understanding of their child's death by focusing on the parents' existing "meaning structure" at the time of their child's death (1992: 62-63). Meaning structure refers to a person's understanding of the nature of life, including their beliefs and assumptions — a construction of reality that gives life meaning and purpose. For some parents, their existing construction of reality was able to provide a meaningful explanation of the death of their child. Other parents experienced disorientation when their meaning structures could not provide an adequate explanation. Disorientation took the form of a deconstruction of existing beliefs. Adjustment involved a process of reconstructing meaning. Braun (1992: 89) points out that parents who ask "why?" are indicating that they do not have a readily accessible meaning structure in place that they can use to make sense of their child's death.

A person who believes that whatever happens is a manifestation of God's plan has an explanation for a child's death, while a person who believes that God should be looking out for the innocent has a problem. Similarly, a person who believes that there are no guarantees in life has an explanation of a sort, while a person who believes that being a good parent will protect a child has a problem. A child's death can raise questions about whether there is a caring God and whether life is just, fair, safe, meaningful, manageable, predictable, purposeful, and ordered. Furthermore, because a child can give a parent's life meaning and purpose, the loss of that child can then be particularly difficult. According to Braun, loss of meaning resulting from a child's death is associated with guilt, placing blame, anger, incomprehension, feeling disconnected from the world, a wish for the parent's own death, thoughts of suicide, loss of a sense of security, lack of hope for the future, loss of motivation, and lack of interest, as well as loss of a sense of personal control and purpose. The process of adjustment then involves searching for an explanation for the child's death and searching for a new sense of meaning and purpose in life.

Martin (1998) also studied the reactions of Canadian parents to the death of their child. In Martin's study, the children all died as a result of sudden infant death syndrome (SIDS). In this situation, parental grief tends to be particularly intense because SIDS takes the life of a baby, occurs suddenly, without warning, has no known cause, and is investigated by legal authorities that include the police and the medical examiner.

Reviewing the existing research on SIDS, Martin noted that bereaved parents manifest a wide range of individual grief reactions including emotional manifestations such as shock, numbness, sorrow, depression, anxiety, anger, and fear. Cognitive reactions include "flashbacks" to the moment of discovering the deceased baby, obsessive reviewing of the circumstances prior to the baby's death, preoccupation, difficulty concentrating, dreams about the baby, self-reproach, guilt, and difficulty controlling thoughts. Physical reactions include problems sleeping, headaches, stomach problems, fatigue, dizziness, chest pain, and loss of appetite. Regarding spiritual reactions, some parents rely on their faith, while others question or lose faith. For some, life loses meaning and purpose. Behavioural reactions include crying, restlessness, moving to a new residence, losing interest in social activities, difficulties at work, ineffective functioning, taking medications, and increased smoking or drinking. Some consider or attempt suicide.

The studies that Martin reviewed also showed that spousal relationships are affected by the loss of an infant to SIDS. The husband and wife may grieve in different ways, and their grieving may follow different timelines. These differences can be a source of marital strain. Yet, while some couples experience increased marital difficulties, others are strengthened.

When there are other children in the family, SIDS takes a baby away from both its parents and its siblings. The other children may feel guilt that they are somehow responsible for the baby's death. They may show anger or anxiety, have nightmares, ask repeated questions, and exhibit behavioural problems. The loss of the baby also affects the relationships among the surviving children and their parents. Both the parents and the surviving children are changed because of their grief and loss. The siblings have to cope with a changed relationship with their grieving parents, and the parents have to cope with their children who are also grieving, each child grieving in her or his own way. Sometimes children become angry with their parents. Parents can become distant from their children or, alternatively, can become overprotective.

Martin's research featured in-depth interviews with nine couples and another three mothers, each of whom had lost a baby to SIDS. The deaths ranged from as recently as less than one year prior to the study to over 25 years previously. In reviewing the wide range of reactions of individual parents to the loss of their baby, Martin concluded that underlying these various individual reactions was the undermining of the foundation upon which the parents had built their lives. The baby's death abruptly and substantially altered each parent's life. Not only was the baby suddenly gone, but also the seeming randomness of SIDS undermined each parent's sense that the world is ordered, comprehensible, predictable, manageable, just, and meaningful. Accordingly, the baby's death led to a "search for reason" in an attempt to find the cause and meaning of the baby's death. Parents sought to make sense not only of their baby's death but also of their own lives once again.

Grieving for a deceased baby involves emotional pain, but searching for the reason for the baby's death is also a reaction to cognitive, intellectual, and spiritual pain (Martin, 1998). Death occasions various kinds of pain and various responses to suffering. At a cognitive level, Martin observed that some parents were able to reconcile the loss of their baby with their previous world-view. Other parents constructed a new world-view, some "for the better and some for the worse." Still others were unable to make any sense of their baby's death. The perspective that parents took "made the difference between eventual healing or continual hell" (Martin, 1998: 219).

Martin (1998: 229-32) described five phases of the grief process. Parents who had lost a baby spoke of the loving attachment that had developed prior to the baby's death. They then spoke of being devastated, trying to carry on while struggling for control, learning to let go, and being changed. She argued that "being changed" does not necessarily imply recovery, resolution, or healing. Indeed, she challenged "the myth" that people can ever fully recover. According to Martin, "Since some people improve and some people never function well again, I propose that we stop using the word 'recovery' to describe the goal of the grief process. We need to start talking about how traumatic experiences can change survivors. My study clearly shows that the death of a child changed the parents, some negatively and some positively" (232). She concluded by commenting on the power and potential of the human mind to construct interpretations of devastating events such as the death of a child, constructions that often help the bereaved deal with their grief.

The following is an account written by a father who experienced the unthinkable — the unexpected loss of two of his four children in separate fatal accidents:

"When a loved one dies, a part of you also dies." This cliché, is in fact, true. The moment someone close to you dies, you are a changed person. Instantaneously. Your whole being transforms the moment a close one departs from his or her earthly existence. They exit, and in reality, your being as you knew it also exits. You immediately become a different person. Whether you like it or not, or wish to acknowledge it, it's true. If you don't believe it, a perception check of those immediately around you should make you aware of this fact. The world's perception of you changes. This truism is all the more pronounced when one loses a close one tragically. Instantaneously. One second a loved one is here. A second later gone. Your total world goes numb. You hope that it is just a bad dream, a nightmare, which you will awake from and get on with normal living. Deep down you know this is only wishful thinking. Your world, as you knew it, has changed forever. You walk around in a daze, put up a brave front, and proceed to do all the normal things like nothing has happened. Pick up the mail, wash the dishes, all the while fighting a deep depression that totally engulfs your whole being, from the tips of your toes to the bristling hairs on your head. You reflect on how life was a few moments ago, a few days ago, and yearn for the clock to be turned back just enough to by-pass the tragedy you are now faced with, But in your heart you know you have to somehow muster the strength to deal with the situation at hand, impossible and unreal as it might seem.

No one has prepared you for this moment. You read about it happening to other people; the sudden loss of a child — It sent shivers down your spine, made you feel totally uncomfortable and vulnerable. Something to quickly forget. A parent's worst nightmare; sudden death of a child. Now it has happened to you. Not once, but twice, in the matter of a couple of years. Moments earlier, your daughter was healthy and alive. Now the policeman, in your living room, at three o'clock in the morning, tells you she is dead. How can this be possible? Two years later, one o'clock in the morning. Two policemen on your back step. Your son has been in an accident, they're working on him, we'll drive you to the hospital. Body language and the words of the police tell me that our son is indeed dead. We drive to the hospital and meet reality face to face. Another child suddenly departed. Without warning. How does one cope; where is one's statute of limitations on grief and pain? Numbness, depression, a longing for moving the clock back, just a couple of hours.

Years earlier, the phone rang at approximately five o'clock on a Saturday afternoon in early February. A relative is on the other end. "There's been an accident, your mother is dead." I was introduced into the real world of grief, pain, and coping with loss. Anxiety, depression, and sense of loss. Ongoing. How to muster enough energy to get through a day; this was an ongoing battle. Now two children dead in the short span of just over two years. When does one's reservoir run dry? I remember, at this time, using the quote attributed to William Irwin Thompson: "The future is beyond knowing, but the present is beyond belief."

When our daughter died, I felt that I was regressing in grief and despondency. After six months I felt worse than after the first week. I was fortunate that a counsellor gave me some materials on "coping with loss." I then recognized the grief cycle I was going through; first six months, a year, and so on. It didn't make it easier, but at least I became aware that there are some usually predictable happenings in the grief cycle, and one usually has to go through the full grief cycle before one can return to cope with a "normal" life again. Not dealing effectively with grief can leave one stranded in "grief limbo" endlessly fighting a futile battle until the end of one's mortal existence.

What coping mechanism worked for me? I have no magic answer. Daily, I have to deal with memories, an enormous sense of loss. However, I feel that part of our difficulty in dealing with the death of close ones, and those others in our immediate environment, is that it puts us in direct touch with our own mortality. Realizing this, one has to acknowledge the minute shortness of time one has on earth. To live to 80, or 8, the time spent on earth in comparison to eternity is minuscule. I look around, and death is continuous. A close friend, a neighbour, a relative. Everyone dies a mortal death. Thus, it makes it all the more important that we make the most of the few minutes we do have on earth. We should not become a victim of a close death; by martyring oneself to the memory of a departed close one, we in fact also become a victim of the initial death. However, it is much easier said than done. Our emotions, our sense of loss can be overwhelming.

A close friend of mine passed away, shortly after my daughter's death. A couple of years ago I saw his widow on the street. I asked her how she was doing. She said, "It's okay to remember, but not to dwell."

I found that co-workers, friends, neighbours, and acquaintances have difficulty in acknowledging your dilemma. We are all good at sending cards, flowers, and attending the immediate functions such as the funeral and luncheons. Then it is over. You are on your own, to grieve your loss in a vacuum. Very few want to enter this domain. It becomes your own personal battleground. Everyone gets back to their life, their worries, their concerns. You feel isolated, despondent, abandoned. The pain of loss is usually too much for "outsiders" to comprehend. It is better to stay a safe distance away. Most everyone wants to be "associated" with someone whom "lady luck" shines down on – the sweepstakes winner, the person who visibly is on a positive track in life. The opposite holds true for those perceived to be "down on their luck." Whether we like it or not, there is a general perception that we are in control of our destiny; we reap what we sow. Death is not where it's at. Avoidance of the situation is most prudent for most concerned. I have no problem with that — when I was younger I tried to avoid thinking of death — a casket was cause for concern. However, the reality is that death is a major part of life. No one can escape it. We must all some day face death head on.

Personally, I sincerely believe that on earth we are but travellers, passing through a transition period. A very short trip in an eternal spectrum. But a very important trip. We are not human beings having a spiritual experience. We are spiritual beings having a human experience. In my mind, this belief brings reason to an otherwise meaningless existence.

How does one really cope with extreme grief? With great difficulty. I found that some very close friendships can add some comfort, family pets, physical activity such as weights and tennis, walking, a strong belief in the "hereafter," a loving wife, a sense of humour, and most of all the avoidance of the word "why?" As other factors/ individuals played significant roles in the demise of our two children, I was initially adamant that these said parties formally acknowledge responsibility for their actions. In both cases, neither party was willing to do so. I have accepted this as something I have no control over, and life must go on. However, I think it indicates a common significant human factor in coping with the sudden death of a loved one; someone or something is perceived to be totally or partially responsible for the tragic sudden ending. Surely it is more than just "chance."

Also, I found that in the cases of all three deaths [mother, daughter, son], I felt a strong urgency to have their memories live on. It seems that the moment a person dies, he or she becomes a nonentity to the rest of the earthly living population, with the exception of the immediate loved ones. Therefore, any dedication to their memory was and is most important to me. I find that most people have trouble talking about the "dead" … It is like a pretence that they never existed. I find this disheartening. These departed individuals are still family. The fact that they have departed earth a few minutes before me does not change their status. They are still loved ones, my family members.

Death, tragic or otherwise, of loved ones, weighs heavily on the minds and souls of those left behind. Coping is an ongoing process. And like a member of Alcoholics Anonymous, the survivor must take one day at a time. Grief can overtake one instantaneously, if one leaves the door open. Honour those that have gone before you, and fill your remaining days on earth with good works. (Personal communication, 1999)

This father's story of the deaths of his daughter and son contains four themes: change, personal feelings of grief, personal coping, and social reactions. The father notes that the loss of each child brings change. He feels that part of him has died, his world as he knew it has changed forever, he feels different, and he believes that others see him differently. Yearning for life as it was before tragedy struck, for his normal life, he nevertheless recognizes that his previous life is irretrievable. For friends and neighbours, disruption is temporary. The father's life, however, is permanently altered. There is no going back, and going forward involves coping with grief.

The second theme is personal feelings of grief. The grieving father experiences a range of emotions including numbness and feeling dazed, yearning and longing, depression and despondency, isolation and abandonment, pain and a sense of loss. He writes of feeling worse months after the initial tragedy and of going through the motions of daily living while fighting deep depression. Keeping the memories of his deceased children alive becomes a goal. He suggests that one never fully recovers from grief, for it can intrude again in an instant.

With regard to the third theme, the father describes coping as an ongoing process. He writes about putting on a brave front, mustering strength and energy to deal with immediate situations, and acting normal as if nothing has happened. His coping is facilitated by his wife, some close friends, his pets, physical activity, and a sense of humour. Although he notes that going through the "full grief cycle" helps one to cope, at the same time he observes that grief is ongoing and can surface and overwhelm at any moment, "if one leaves the door open."

In the process of coping, he is initially adamant that the people who were directly involved in the tragedies acknowledge the part they played and accept responsibility for their actions. Otherwise, he explicitly avoids asking "why?" Indeed, he adds "that I have always felt that it is pointless to pose the question 'why' when a death occurs — I feel strongly that part of my survival gear for coping is to never let 'Why did this happen?' be part of my repertoire" (Personal communication). Instead, he finds assurance in his beliefs in spiritual existence and eternal life. From his beliefs, he gains a sense that human life and, therefore, human events ultimately happen for a reason and have meaning.

In addition, he uses an intellectual strategy to normalize death. He comments on the pervasiveness of death: sooner or later everyone dies. He himself has experienced the death of loved ones; he knows others who have lost loved ones; he acknowledges his own mortality. This normalization of death, tied to his beliefs in eternal life, renders death more acceptable.

Finally, this father comments on the social reactions to his family's losses. He makes three points, all of which relate to the concept of stigma. First, he notes that the world's perception of him has changed. He is now seen as one of the unlucky, one of the unfortunate. In this new social status, he receives sympathy but also blame, reflecting the tendency for people to assume that the unfortunate are in some way responsible for their misfortune. This social reaction is both victim-blaming and stigmatizing, and supports the argument of Posner (1976), discussed in Chapter 4, that people associated with death are stigmatized because death itself is stigmatized. The father acknowledges this lack of social acceptance when he notes that people avoid the unlucky and unfortunate.

Second, the father recollects a widow saying to him, "it's okay to remember, but not to dwell." He interpreted this comment positively. He understood her to say that "it is important and okay to remember a dearly departed one, but one should not dwell on the memory to a point that one gets depressed and regresses into deep depression" (Personal communication). The widow's comment conveys encouragement and advice and reflects society's rules for the bereaved. The widow encourages him to remember but also to be careful not to wallow in self-pity.

Third, the father observes that, after the initial events of tragedy and funeral, others go back to their normal lives and distance themselves from the grieving family. These people have difficulty acknowledging or participating in the family's grieving. Indeed, avoidance is the typical response. On this point, the father says: "I find that most people have trouble talking about the 'dead.' ... It is like a pretence that they never existed." This avoidance indicates social stigma. When people are faced with social stigma, they experience discomfort, distance themselves, use avoidance, and act as if nothing is wrong. The father finds this social response disappointing and unsupportive.

Woodgate (2006) interviewed in-depth 28 parents in a western Canadian city who had experienced the death of a child. The children had died at ages ranging from three days to 28 years, and their deaths had occurred recently for some parents and years ago for others. Regardless of how recently or long ago their child had died, the parents indicated that they had not experienced a "sense of closure," nor did they want to. They equated closure with forgetting their deceased child, something they did not want to do. In this sense, parents do not "get over" the death of a child; instead, parents live with their loss for the rest of their life.

While it seems to be the case that parents never completely recover from the death of a child, Grant Kalischuk and Hayes (2003) suggested that a degree of "healing" is possible, even in the case of a youthful family member's suicide. Healing was defined in this study as "letting go of the negative impact of the suicide and achieving a sense of health and well being" (59). These authors interviewed parents and other family members of nine males who had committed suicide between the ages of 14-19 and of another two males who had committed suicide at the ages of 24 and 29. The families lived in rural and small urban communities in three western Canadian provinces. Most of the suicides had occurred from six months to four years previously, although one suicide had occurred six years ago and another 12 years ago. Parents and family members spoke of being wounded by the suicide of their relatively young family member and of wishing to regain a sense of normalcy and wholeness. This healing process or "journeying toward wholeness," as the authors labelled it, was facilitated by letting go of the question "why" regarding the deceased's motivations for committing suicide, releasing themselves from responsibility for their family member's suicide, and believing that healing was possible and making a conscious decision to move toward healing.

Like natural parents who grieve the death of a child, there is also evidence that foster parents tend to grieve deeply when a child placed in their care dies. Schormans (2004) interviewed in-depth eight foster parents in Ontario who had experienced one or more deaths from two to 14 years ago of disabled foster children placed in their permanent care. The author noted that the foster parents thought of themselves as parents having a parent-child relationship with their disabled foster children. They viewed their foster children as family members and reported that they experienced the death of their disabled foster children as difficult as the death of a birth child. Despite the grief they experienced, these foster parents reported that their grief was not always recognized or legitimated but was often disenfranchised and unsupported.

When parents lose a child, grandparents also lose a grandchild. Fry (1997) studied 152 grandparents in Alberta who had lost a grandchild in the previous three years. Although most of the grandchildren were under 19 years of age at the time of their deaths, some were young adults. Fry found that grandparents often reported survivor guilt; that is, they felt that it was their turn to die and that the grandchild should not have died. Fry's analysis of responses to an open-ended questionnaire and to in-depth interviews shows the multidimensionality, complexity, and diversity of the grief reactions of grandparents to the loss of a grandchild. Finally, Kastenbaum (2007: 372) observed that, when grandparents lose a grandchild, they grieve not only for the deceased grandchild but also for their own child who is the grieving parent of the deceased.

DEATH OF A SPOUSE

Many marriages end with the death of one of the spouses. Because women have a longer life expectancy than men and tend to be younger than their male partners, the husband is more likely to die before his wife, leaving her a widow. Indeed, in Canada there are currently about five widows for every widower. Widowhood typically occurs in the older years, and the likelihood of being a widow or widower increases with age (Chappell, McDonald, and Stones, 2008: 125, 277-79; Martin Matthews, 1991: 2-7; Northcott, 1984).

The death of a spouse tends to be experienced as a particularly stressful event. In some cases, however, a widowed person may view the death of a spouse as a positive thing, as in the case of the death of an alcoholic or abusive spouse (Martin Matthews, 1991: 17-19). Vezina et al. (1988; see also Ducharme and Corin, 1997) studied older persons who had lost a spouse and found that, while bereavement tends to be generally stressful, some of the bereaved were at greater risk for depression and anxiety than others. Waskowic and Chartier (2003) showed that the nature of the spousal relationship before the death of a spouse affects the experience of grief for the surviving spouse. In particular, persons who had been securely attached to their spouses before their spouses' deaths experienced more moderate symptoms of grief, were better able to resolve their grief, and maintained a better ongoing relationship with the deceased. Belicki *et al.* (2003) suggested that dreams of the deceased spouse may express and help to maintain the ongoing relationship of the surviving spouse with the deceased spouse.

Widowhood later in life tends to be more "expected" than early in life (Martin Matthews, 1991: 20; Martin Matthews, 1987). There is a complicated relationship between the timing of widowhood (i.e., early or late in life), anticipation of the spouse's death (i.e., whether widowhood is expected or not), the intensity of grief, and the resolution of the grieving process. Some evidence indicates that widowhood is most stressful when it is unexpected and occurs early in life (Martin Matthews, 1991: 19-23, 25). In contrast, women who are widowed when they are older may find that widowhood is less disruptive to their sense of identity and self-image in contrast to women who are widowed when they are younger (van den Hoonaard, 1999). Nevertheless, the death of a spouse in old age can jeopardize a lifestyle that depends on two persons cohabitating and assisting each other in managing life in old age.

In marriage, spouses tend to develop a shared identity and a shared life. The loss of a spouse may undermine this shared identity and transforms the life of the surviving spouse. Furthermore, the social status of the surviving spouse is devalued, even stigmatized to a degree. Widowhood may be psychologically and socially disorienting. Adjustment for many widowed persons — both male and female — tends to occur within several years. Some even come to see widowhood as an opportunity for growth and a time of autonomy, independence, and freedom (Van den Hoonaard, 2001; Martin Matthews, 1991: 23-29, 33-34, 119; see also Gee and Kimball, 1987: 89-90).

Widowhood may affect men and women differently. Women are more likely than men to be economically disadvantaged by the loss of their spouse. Further, men and women may have different coping strategies and tend to have different social support networks, which they access differently. Although it may be experienced somewhat differently, the loss of a spouse may be equally difficult for both men and women (see Norris, 1994; Martin Matthews, 1991: 89).

Van den Hoonaard (1997) analyzed ten published autobiographical accounts of widowhood written by widows in Canada and the United States, most of whom had experienced widowhood while still relatively young. Most of the authors lost their husbands after long illnesses. The stories of their marriages and the dying of their husbands were integral parts of these stories of widowhood, indicating what was lost and how it was lost. Despite long dying trajectories and the anticipation of death, the women experienced shock at the time of their husbands' deaths.

Because they were written for an audience, mostly other widows, these accounts are both descriptive and instructive; that is, the stories are descriptive personal accounts with which a reader can empathize; at the same time, the accounts provide guidance for a reader who is seeking to know what to do in a similar situation.

Van den Hoonaard's analysis of these accounts of widowhood yields common themes relating to loss of identity and its reconstruction. In a process that van den Hoonaard terms "identity foreclosure," the loss of the husband and of social interactions (including friendships) that depended on being a couple undermined the widows' sense of self. At the death of the husband, the old identity as a wife and as a couple became obsolete. The widows described themselves as no longer knowing who they were nor how they fit into society. A new identity as a widow was thrust upon them, an identity that was not chosen, not welcomed, and that was perceived as a devalued social status. Being called a widow or filling out a form and having to select "widow" for one's marital status for the first time became "identifying moments" in which the wife's new status as a widow was often shockingly and painfully driven home. In these moments, the widows came to know that their identity had been transformed and that they were viewed differently by society. They were made to feel that they were different, and they were treated differently in a couples-oriented society.

According to van den Hoonaard, the transformation of identity is a process in which the previous identity as a wife is lost and replaced with the socially imposed identity as a widow. The loss of the old identity is disorienting, and the imposition of the new one is distressing. In time, however, a new and positive identity is created. The authors of these stories tend to describe themselves as becoming "new women" with new characteristics such as greater self-reliance and increased independence.

Women who are widowed when they are older may be less likely to experience identity foreclosure and may find widowhood less threatening to their self-image, according to van den Hoonaard (1999; 2001) who interviewed 28 widows over 50 years of age in New Brunswick whose husbands had died within the past five years. Van den Hoonaard noted that these older widows readily volunteered to tell their husbands' death stories and that these stories, and the telling of them, seemed to provide comfort for the storytellers and to create meaning regarding "their sense of themselves and their lives as widows" (1999: 69). These older widows, in part through the telling of their husbands' death stories, were able to hold on to their identity as wives, maintain a positive self-image, and facilitate their difficult transition into widowhood.

Widowhood can be real or anticipated. Sometimes a spouse has a "brush with death" that leads her or his partner to contemplate the possibility of loss and the life that would result from that loss. For example, a woman in her thirties tells about her reaction to her husband's brush with death:

I have been married to my husband for 15 years. My husband spends about 50 per cent of the year out of the country on business, leaving me and our three children alone to cope without a husband or a father. Needless to say, I have become a part-time single parent. I have gotten used to this over the years, but never did I think that part-time single parenting could potentially become full-time single parenting. Last week my husband had a brush with death that would have left me a widow and our three children without a father.

My husband travels frequently to Taiwan on business, experiencing small earth-quakes on almost all of his trips. So, I didn't get too hysterical when I was told of another earthquake in Taiwan, this time registering 7.6 on the Richter scale. My friend, who informed me of the most recent Taiwan earthquake, was surprised that I was so calm. She wondered if I was in a state of shock. But I knew that what you heard on the radio or saw on TV was the worst damage caused by the earthquake and that my husband was probably just fine. Meanwhile, my husband left voice mail on our answering machine that he was alive and well.

When I received his message, I returned his call immediately. I was relieved to hear that he was well but didn't really expect that I would hear any differently. My husband told me to call all our family to let them know that he was fine should they watch the evening news and panic. Being in the middle of the day, most of our family members were working, so I just left messages on their answering machines. My voice was cheerful and reassuring. But when I got a live person on the end of the phone, that's when my whole outlook changed.

When I talked to my husband's sister, I fell apart. She started the conversation by asking (as she always does), "How are you?" That's when it happened. I fell apart. I could hardly get a word out. I was crying uncontrollably. I could hardly speak between sobs. I guess it was at that point in time that I realized I could have been a widow at a very young age. I wasn't prepared to be a widow and a single mother of three children. The possibility of becoming a widow was terrifying. I was used to being alone and a part-time single mother, but I always knew that this was a temporary situation. In a few days or weeks, my husband would be arriving home and we would share the parenting role once more. It took about ten minutes before I gained some sort of composure.

Within minutes another one of my friends phoned. Once again, my tears took me by surprise. So why was this happening now? I concluded that it must be because at the time I was talking to my husband, I was just grateful that he was all right. I didn't really think about the "what ifs?" I didn't really think about potentially becoming a widow until I started talking to more and more people.

This emotional period was short-lived. In the end, I realize that I have no time or energy to dwell on the "what ifs," and therefore my fleeting thoughts of widowhood were just that, fleeting. (Personal communication, 1999)

At first, the storyteller cognitively assesses the odds of her husband being killed in the earthquake and concludes confidently and unemotionally that everything is most likely all right. Concern expressed by others, however, cues her and leads her to re-evaluate her own level of concern — to consider the "what ifs," as she puts it. This draws out an intense, although brief, emotional reaction.

Why did the "what ifs" upset her? A family is a set of relationships, roles, circumstances, and patterns, and all of these are disrupted by the death of one of its members. In this story, the person who might have been killed occupies the roles of husband and father, roles that would have been vacated and left unfilled by his death. The family's circumstances and patterns would have been disrupted, and the survivors' roles and social statuses would have been transformed — from wife to widow, from part of a parenting couple to a single parent, and from children with a father to fatherless children. These transformations were things that the storyteller had not really considered previously, was not prepared for, and found terrifying. Death is disruptive. While death is the final disruption of the life of the deceased, death also disrupts the lives of the surviving family members. The family, as it had been, no longer exists. The family is transformed, and the survivors have to adjust to a new life.

DEATH OF A PARENT

The preceding storyteller describes her husband's brush with death and her thoughts about being left a widow. The storyteller's two eldest daughters, aged 12 and 13, also described their reactions to the question "What if Dad had died?" Nina, (not her real name), aged 12, writes:

As my mom was explaining that my dad was in a near death experience (Taiwan earth-quake), the question "What if my dad were to die" flashed through my mind. Shortly after she was done talking and said that my dad was all right, I stopped thinking about it. I thought about the question for about one minute, and after that I thought about it a bit occasionally, but after I found out he was okay all the questions just slowly disappeared. Although I only thought about it a little while, I still cared just as much as someone who couldn't get their mind off it. (Personal communication, 1999)

While the question "What if my dad were to die?" flashed into her mind, Nina was quickly reassured. Her dad was safe, so there was no reason to get upset. She did not dwell on what might have happened but instead focused only on what did happen. Her last comment suggests slight defensiveness, as if she felt that she might be criticized for her reaction. However, she saw no reason for concern, reminding the reader that this does not mean that she does not care.

This story contains a 12-year-old's honest report of her reaction and, at the same time, an acknowledgment of her awareness that others may have expectations about how she should react. As people age, it perhaps becomes increasingly difficult to distinguish one's unique personal reactions from one's socialized reactions that reflect one's understanding of society's expectations.

Nina's 13-year-old sister, Mackenzie (a pseudonym), also gives her thoughts on the question "What if my dad had died?" She writes:

"Do you want the good news or the bad news first?" was my mom's question introducing the terrible disaster that happened. My mom told my sister and me that my dad was okay, however, he was in an earthquake. A million questions went through my mind at that time. Such as, how big was this earthquake? How many lives did it take? I was relieved that my dad was all right but couldn't help but wonder how many kids had lost their dads. After my mom said that dad was all right, I didn't think much of it. I thought about it, but it wasn't on my mind every waking moment. People kept calling and asking how I was feeling and if I was okay. My dad was fine, so what more did I have to worry about? I feel bad for people that lost someone close to them.

"What if my dad had died?" That is a question that I thought about a little more than once. It was weird to think my dad wouldn't come home after work and say hello to all of us. Or that I would never get to spend time with him again or even talk with him because he would be gone. The last words that I said to my dad was to go away and turn off the lights. I said that because it was like 6:00 a.m. and I was half asleep. If my dad was to die, then I wouldn't want those to be my last words to him. That was probably what I thought about the most. I thank God for sparing my dad's life. I pray for all of those who lost someone close to them. (Personal communication, 1999)

Mackenzie, like her sister, is quickly reassured that her dad is fine, and sees no reason to get upset. Nevertheless, she identifies and sympathizes with children who did lose their fathers. She acknowledges that, if her dad had died, it would have been "weird" — her life would have been transformed by the loss of both her father and the familiar pattern of her relationship with him. She would also have regrets. For example, she would regret the last words that she said to him when he woke her early in the morning to say goodbye as he left for his business trip. Mackenzie recognizes that the loss of a loved one implies not only the loss of a relationship but also the loss of the familiar and the necessity of adjusting to a new and unanticipated life.

Silverman, Nickman, and Worden (1995) studied children aged 6 to 17 who had recently lost a parent to death. They found that the children constructed connections to the deceased that helped them maintain a relationship with their dead parent. Five things helped in this process. First, the children tended to locate their dead parent, often in heaven. Second, they experienced the deceased in dreams or in feelings, for example, by feeling that the parent was watching them. Third, they reached out to the dead parent by visiting the cemetery or by speaking to the deceased. Fourth, they thought about and remembered the parent. Finally, they held on to certain objects that served as reminders of the deceased. While the connection that the child constructs with the deceased parent tends to evolve over time, it does not end. Silverman *et al.* (1995: 269) wrote: "Bereavement should not be viewed as a psychological state that ends or from which one recovers. The emphasis should be on negotiating and renegotiating the meaning of loss over time, rather than on letting go."

Schultz (2007) interviewed six women in western Canada who were 18-25 years of age and whose mothers had died three to nine years earlier, when they were 15-20 years of age. The loss of a mother in adolescence tended to redefine the daughter's life and influence her sense of self. For example, the daughters in this study tended to demarcate their lives before and after their mothers' deaths: there was life before when one was cared for by one's mother and life after when one had to care for oneself. Further, the daughters tended to report feeling different from their peers and had a sense of inferiority as a result. While these young women often formed attachments with mother substitutes (such as an aunt or friend's mother), their memories of their deceased mothers also continued to shape their developing sense of self. They were defined, in part, by their mothers' lives and their mothers' deaths. That is, the lives and deaths of their mothers became both a part of their life history and an integral part of their developing identity.

Most often though, the death of a parent occurs when the child has grown into an adult or even into a senior. The loss of a parent, and particularly the last parent, can have profound meaning for children who are middle-aged or seniors already. The buffer between them and death is no longer there (Colarusso, 1999; Moss *et al.*, 1997). As such, the death of a parent has additional meanings and implications beyond the grief that is experienced for the deceased parent. To this point, one of the authors of this book (Herbert C. Northcott) recalls the funeral of his father-in-law's mother. His father-in-law said that his mother's funeral was particularly difficult for him, given that his father had died previously and now his mother was dead, and as he put it, "Now I am next."

DEATH OF A GRANDPARENT

Ens and Bond (2005) surveyed 226 adolescents who were 11-18 years of age and lived in Manitoba. They found that 138 (61 per cent) had experienced the death of one or more family members (one mother, six fathers, seven siblings, and 183 grandparents) including 124 (55 per cent) who had experienced only the death of one or more grandparents and no other family members. This study determined that grief and anxiety about death were correlated such that those adolescents who reported grief due to the death of a grandparent also reported higher levels of anxiety about death.

DEATH OF A FRIEND

A young adult woman was asked if she had had any experience with dying and death. She answered with the following account about the death of a school acquaintance:

When you first asked if I had experienced death in my life, I initially thought of family situations, of which I have no close experiences. It surprised me when I remembered that a friend, Joyce, died when I was in high school. For all the time that I had known her she had leukemia. We met in junior high school when her family moved [to the city] to be closer to the hospitals for her sake. She never really seemed sick. Except for the initial rumours that circulated when she first came to our school, none of us really thought about it much.

I got to know her well in high school as we had English class together. We talked about a lot of things including her illness. I remember her being a lot of fun and very strong willed. During that same year her cancer started to progress. I don't really know all of the medical things that were happening to her. Some friends and I went to visit her in the hospital; she seemed in great spirits. We never really thought that anything bad was really happening. We all got sick; we all got better.

Things progressed pretty quickly. She slipped into a coma and was put into intensive care. Then we arrived at school one day and her closest friend came up to us in tears and we knew that she had died. The first class I had that day was English. During the announcements they informed us that she had died, and we had a moment of silence. One girl in the class started sobbing, and I remember a guy in the back saying something like, "I don't know why she's crying, she didn't even know her." I didn't cry. I remember wondering why since I had known her pretty well. I continued going to classes through the day until someone told me that people who had known Joyce were in the guidance counsellor's office. I went because I wanted to make sure that some of my other friends were okay. A number of them met me in the hall because they had been looking for me. Many were crying, but I still wasn't.

It was very surreal. None of us really knew what to do. We decided that we should go to the funeral home. So the night before the funeral, we decided to go together. One thing that sticks out clearly in my mind was that we did not know what we were supposed to do. It was strange because Joyce's mom was the one that took us under her wing and led us into the room where the casket was laying.

The casket was closed because she had wasted [away] a great deal and the family thought it would be better. As we stood around the casket, I was wishing that the casket were open so that I could really believe that she was gone. It was difficult to really believe it. I stared at the picture of Joyce on the casket and thought over and over again how it was her lying inside, that we would not see her again. That was when the tears started to come. It was overwhelming. I don't think I had ever really sobbed in my life, but I was right there in front of a bunch of strangers, but I wasn't thinking about that at all. My crying touched off the rest, so the five or six of us stood there sobbing our hearts out for a good long time. Joyce's mom and aunt were comforting us. They seemed to want to take care of us.

One of our friends had experienced death in her family a great deal more than the rest of us. We looked to her for guidance. There was a kneeling bench in front of the casket, so I whispered to ask her if it was for praying. I knelt and prayed for Joyce's family and for us. After our tears had dried up, we went to the lounge and talked together. I think everyone felt very badly for us. We decided to go back to my house together because my parents were away. We just wanted to be together for a while.

We just talked, watched some TV, and played Twister. I think we wanted to laugh. We talked about Joyce a bit but mostly we chatted about nothing.

The next day was the funeral. I had a lot of anxiety because the only nice clothes I had were light colours and I thought that was sacrilegious but I wore them anyway. I remember a lot of detail from that day even though it was seven years ago. I remember Joyce's mother, brother, and sisters coming in along with Joyce's boyfriend. I remember the minister's eulogy, how we laughed at Joyce's aggressive basketball skills but also reminisced about her tender concern for others. Everything about the funeral was new to me. I think it was the very first funeral I had ever been to. Again, I didn't cry. I think that [may have been seen] as a sign that I didn't really care but it was more that I don't cry very often. The outpouring at the funeral home was a great shock to me.

The reception seemed strange to me. To be sitting around eating, laughing, joking, chitchatting while Joyce was dead. It was awkward for me. After the funeral we talked about Joyce less and less. I would think of her in English class, wishing she was there so we could gossip in the back row, but life went back to normal quickly for us. When there was a write-up about Joyce in our graduating yearbook, two years after she died, I wondered why it was there. Nobody seemed to remember her. She would have accomplished a lot in her life; she had accomplished a lot by the time she died at 15. I suppose some of that came from knowing that she had a terminal illness.

I'm not sure how much of my grief was for Joyce and how much was over the fact that someone my age was dead. Her opportunities were over. As I think about all this now I am wondering what if. What if she had lived to be 23 years old, as I have? What would she be doing now? Would she be proud of me? Have I used the years wisely that she didn't have? It's hard to think about those things; perhaps that was why she was so far from my consciousness when we discussed my experience with death. (Personal communication, 1999)

The storyteller, who faced dying and death for the first time in her relatively young life, speaks of the strangeness of dying and death. At first the schoolmate who died is not perceived to be sick, despite her terminal illness, and the storyteller indicates that nobody really thought of the possibility of her dying. Even when the girl is obviously sick and in the hospital, her schoolmates still assume that she will recover. Death is not known: it is a stranger to these young people.

When death does come, the storyteller describes the situation as surreal, as dreamlike and without context. Accordingly, Joyce's schoolmates did not know what to do. Once again, death is described in terms of its strangeness. The one schoolmate who had experience with death was looked to for guidance by those who were not experienced.

The storyteller speaks of her and her friends' intense, though brief, outpouring of grief at the funeral home, the night before the funeral. She notes that this was out-of-character for her and that she was shocked at her emotional display. Leming and Dickinson (2007: 346-47) observe that funeral rituals "become rites of intensification whereby feelings and emotional states are intensified by ritual participation.... Oftentimes the function of death rituals is to intensify feelings and emotions and then provide a means by which individuals can express their sentiments." This seems to have been the case for Joyce's friends as they gathered at the funeral home. Furthermore, while the grief expressed was because of Joyce's death, it seems to have also been occasioned by a loss of naïvety — by the realization that a young person can die and that so much unlived life can be lost. The moral taken from the story focuses on the value of life and the importance of living life wisely.

Finally, the salience of another's death tends to recede from active consciousness as survivors get on with the business of everyday life. While the story of Joyce is not a memory that the storyteller visits every day, it was nevertheless a significant event, a socializing event in the sense of providing instruction about dying and death, and a memory that the storyteller calls upon when she thinks of dying and death and their meaning for her.

A SECOND-ORDER ACCOUNT OF DYING

The young woman's story of her experience of the death of another, told above, is a personal account, that is, an account of the first order. First-order accounts of dying and death take the form of Y's account of Z's dying and death. For example, a wife's account of her husband's dying is a first-order account, which gives the wife's version of how she experienced the dying and death of her husband.

Second-order accounts, on the other hand, take the form of X's account of Y's experience of Z's dying and death (also known as third-person accounts). X's account may be a more or less accurate representation of Y's experience. Accurate or not, X's account reveals X's subjective understanding and often evaluation of Y's experience. Consider the following second-order account provided by a young woman:

I am really concerned about my aunt. My uncle is dying with stomach cancer. It was a great shock when he was diagnosed last year and the doctor determined that he would not survive. Over the year he has been in and out of hospital a great deal undergoing a number of surgeries to relieve some of his pain and to help his digestive system. I have been pretty removed from the whole situation; even though I was living very close to my aunt and uncle, I only saw my uncle once since he was diagnosed and saw my aunt only a few more times than that.

My aunt has spent a lot of time trying to deny the fact that her husband is dying. She didn't tell their children for a time after she found out that his cancer was terminal. Each time my uncle has had to return to the hospital, it serves as a reminder that he is dying but then when he is again released it seems that she tries to forget the end prospect. She has done very little planning for a future without him; I recently found out that a will has not even been signed. When I think of the difficulties that she has been dealing with and will have to deal with, I wonder how she will get out of bed every day.

She is my father's sister and is relying on him for a great deal. Any time she has a crisis he is the first one she calls. When I speak with him on the phone, I notice the toll that it is taking. My aunt is expecting when my uncle dies that my father will make all of the funeral arrangements and bail her out of the difficulties of not having a will, etc. All this time I think that my father is facing his own fears of death. I think that for him cancer is very frightening and stomach cancer the most frightening of all. His grandfather died of stomach cancer; he fears that he is in line as cancer can be hereditary. Watching the suffering of my uncle is no doubt bringing back memories as well as touching on a great fear for his own health. (Personal communication, 1999)

While this woman's account of her aunt's reaction to her husband's dying is empathetic, it is also critical. The storyteller indicates her concern for her aunt. However, while acknowledging her aunt's distress, shock, and denial, and her difficulty facing the dying and impending death of her husband, the storyteller is also critical. She feels that her aunt should face reality, plan more adequately, cope better, and be more self-reliant. The aunt is portrayed as overly reliant on her brother (the storyteller's father). Finally, the storyteller is concerned for her father, whom she perceives to be overly burdened by his sister's difficulties and distressed by concerns for his own health, which are exacerbated by his brother-in-law's dying of a feared disease.

Accounts such as the one above are both descriptive and prescriptive. On the one hand, they describe the storyteller's perception of the facts of the situation. At the same time, in describing the difficulties a distressed spouse is having in the face of her husband's dying and the problems that inadequate coping brings, the storyteller prescribes how the distressed person should respond. The telling of such stories serves more than the simple communication of a person's perceptions of a distressing situation; it also creates and reinforces collective norms about how one should cope with the dying of a loved one.

PATHWAYS FOR THE GRIEVING

Clark (1993) studied six persons from Alberta who were having difficulty with their grieving. The subjects of this study were a young woman who had lost her 16-year-old sister in a motor vehicle accident; a man who had lost his 79-year-old father in a motor vehicle accident; a man who had lost his wife at the age of 52 to breast cancer; a woman who had lost her daughter at the age of 34 to a diabetic coma; a woman who had lost her mother at the age of 77 to complications following surgery; and a man whose 16-year-old son had been murdered. The death of most of the loved ones had occurred from one to three years prior to the study; in one case the death had occurred seven years earlier.

Difficulties with grieving arose for various reasons. One subject had difficulty coming to terms with her loss of connection with her sister. She also experienced the loss of her sense of security because of the nature of her sister's sudden, unexpected, and horrifying death. A son had difficulty because his love for his father was intertwined with resentment towards the man who had never made him feel loved and respected. A husband suffered intensely following the loss of his beloved wife and the life that they had shared. A mother felt that there must have been something she could have done to save her daughter. A daughter felt that there were things health care professionals could have done to save her mother or at least to give her mother more dignity in dying. A father remained confused about how to deal with the various emotions he felt regarding his son's death.

The subjects expressed various emotions, including intense sorrow, anguish, depression, bitterness, anger, rage, regret, self-blame, guilt, loneliness, pessimism, hopelessness, despair, confusion, emptiness, and numbness. They experienced fatigue, lack of motivation, low self-esteem, feelings of failure, a sense of personal vulnerability, loss of faith, loss of meaning, and loss of purpose. Alienation from other surviving family members was not uncommon. Some turned to thoughts of suicide, looked forward to their own death, or displayed inappropriate behaviour. Clark (1993: 149-51) points out that each person's grieving is, to a degree, personal and unique and reflects the particular circumstances of that person's life, the relationship with the deceased, the circumstances of the death, and the survivor's coping style and resources. In a sense, each person follows his or her own path in the course of grieving.

Martin and Elder (1993) wrote about "pathways through grief." The use of the plural, "pathways," emphasizes the uniqueness and the individuality of grief. Martin and Elder suggest that each person tends to grieve in a unique way and to find his or her own pathway through grief. They acknowledge that, while there are commonalities among individuals, there are always differences as well.

Despite Martin and Elder's phrase "pathways through grief," they argue that grief is not a process with a beginning, an ending, and well-defined steps between the two. A person does not necessarily ever get "through" grief, in the sense of being done with it or getting beyond it. Instead they proposed a figure-eight model of grief. In this model there is no end point and an individual can return to a "place" where they have been before. The "places" in the model include protest, despair, and detachment in one-half of the figure eight, and exploration (of ways to rebuild a disrupted life), hope, and investment in new relationships in the other half.

At the intersection of the two circles, the authors located meaning, their central concept. Meaning refers to interpretations individuals use to define and make sense of their loss and of their lives. Different individuals take different meanings, and the meanings taken influence the pathway that an individual then follows.

Following bereavement, intense grief may dissipate and return, rise and fall. Martin and Elder's model allows for the cyclical nature of grief. It also acknowledges that some people follow better or perhaps more positive and adaptive pathways than others. Regardless of the pathway, however, grief is never truly over.

SUMMARY

It is hard to lose a loved one to death. While, in one sense, death ends the relationship with the loved one, in another sense it transforms the relationship, which continues in the survivor's memories, thoughts, feelings, conversations, and behaviours. Because the relationship continues, albeit in a transformed way, grieving for the presence of the deceased is ongoing. While the intensity of grief tends to wane over time, grief does not completely disappear. It comes and goes and returns again.

To the extent that our lives are made up of our relationships with others, the death of a loved one transforms our own life. Part of us dies with the deceased. Life is never completely the same again. We grieve for the deceased and we grieve for ourselves, for what we have lost of ourselves. Nevertheless, out of loss and despair, many find meaning, purpose, and hope. To paraphrase the father who lost two children to unexpected and premature deaths: we can remember the dead and honour them, we can accept our own mortality as the natural order of things, and we can do good works while we are among the living.

CONCLUSION

Dying and death reflect the material and social conditions of society. In the pre-contact era, living conditions for Aboriginal peoples in Canada were such that life expectancy was perhaps 30 to 40 years, about the same as in Europe at that time. While death often came early in life for Aboriginal people, some individuals survived to old age. Nevertheless, dying and death were common, visible, and expected occurrences. Aboriginal social practices and cultural definitions reflected these realities and, in turn, shaped the experience of dying and death.

Contact with Europeans brought devastation to the Aboriginal peoples of Canada. Infectious diseases previously unknown in North America increased death rates and decimated whole populations. The gradual destruction of Aboriginal economies and ways of life further contributed to high rates of death. In addition, European culture, brought by missionaries and traders, had an impact on

Aboriginal social practices and cultural definitions, and tended to transform the social and personal experience of dying and death. Christian religious views of life and death sharply contracted the values common among First Nations. For Aboriginal peoples, death was more likely to be a natural or unavoidable part of life, explained by their cosmology and given meaning by their spirituality. Death began to take on a new significance when viewed in the Christian context of heaven and hell.

While the infectious diseases brought to Canada by the Europeans were especially devastating for the Aboriginal peoples, they did not spare European explorers, traders, and settlers. The harsh climate, rough pioneer existence, low standards of living, and unsanitary practices contributed to many early deaths in the colonies. Infant mortality was high, as was maternal mortality, and life expectancy, in general, was low. Health care was relatively ineffective, and the few hospitals that existed were considered to be places of death. It was not until the late nineteenth century that the newly emerging public health movement began to have a positive impact on health and life expectancy by improving sanitation and the safety of food and water. Subsequent advances in health care in the twentieth century brought dramatic improvements in life expectancy. The causes of death shifted from infectious to chronic diseases. The timing of death shifted increasingly to later life. The care of the dying was transferred from family members to health care professionals, and dying and death were moved from the home and community to the hospital. Death, which had been common and familiar, became unfamiliar and expected only in old age.

At the beginning of the twenty-first century, the most common causes of death are circulatory disease and cancer, although causes of death vary depending on personal characteristics such as age, sex, and social class. Young adults are most likely to die of accidents, injuries, and suicide. In the older age groups, cancer and circulatory disease dominate as causes of death. The timing of death has become noticeably discrepant for males and females, with females outliving males by a number of years on the average. This gender differential in life expectancy emerged during the twentieth century but in recent years has begun to decrease. Disadvantaged social classes and relatively disadvantaged groups such as Aboriginal people continue to have life expectancies below the Canadian norm. Nevertheless, deaths occurring early in life have come to be unexpected and have been labelled premature.

Social institutions such as the family, religion, the health care system, the legal system, and the funeral industry influence views of dying and death, along with practices related to these phenomena. Families have become much less likely to be involved as primary caregivers for the dying. Increasingly, professional caregivers attend to the dying, often in an institutional setting rather than in the dying person's home. Furthermore, families have become much less involved with the processing of the dead body. Instead, processing of the dead body and management of the funeral rituals are now typically provided by the funeral industry, which has become "big business" consistent with a general trend towards the corporatization, bureaucratization, professionalization, and secularization of dying and death. Increasingly, the funeral ritual has moved from the home, community, and church, to the profit-driven funeral industry.

Religion has played a significant part in giving meaning to dying and death and continues to do so for those who maintain a religious commitment. Furthermore, religion continues to play an active role in social debates about end-of-life issues such as euthanasia and assisted suicide. Nevertheless, the influence of religion for many has been undermined by secular trends.

The successes of twentieth century medicine in curing disease and forestalling death led to the dominance of the curative model in modern medicine, which emphasized cure and tended to resist death, viewing it as a failure of the health care system. Towards the end of the twentieth century, the hospice palliative care movement gained momentum; it emphasized the quality of life for the dying by focusing on managing symptoms rather than engaging in futile attempts to cure. This movement has raised legal questions, and while the Criminal Code of Canada continues to define active euthanasia as murder and assisted suicide as illegal, there is a trend towards legalizing advance directives that authorize the withholding or withdrawing of treatment and care for those persons who are terminally ill.

Despite the twentieth-century trends towards the hospitalization, bureaucratization, and professionalization of dying and death, there appears to be a move towards bringing dying and death back to the home and to the family, who once again may become the primary caregivers, functioning with the assistance of health care professionals, in providing palliative home care.

There is a diversity of views as to what death is and what it means. For some, death is a transition to a better life. Others view it as the final end. For many, death is a mystery or, as Shakespeare put it in *Hamlet*, "the undiscovered country from whose bourn no traveller returns" (Act III, Scene I). People facing death tend to interpret it, to give it meaning, but the specific meaning assigned to death tends to vary from one individual to another. Similarly, those facing death often engage in a review of their life, examining their biography to give it meaning in the face of death. Just as the specific meaning assigned to death tends to vary from one individual to another, so does the meaning assigned to one's life. Because each individual's biography is personal and unique, the construction of life's meaning and the construction of the meaning of dying and death are both personal and unique.

The dying tend to view the process of dying as more distressing than the prospect of death itself. Pain and suffering are not welcome. Furthermore, the dying do not welcome the various losses — of health, future, competence, independence, social roles, social status, and personal relationships — that they face. Although, they may express concern for those who will survive them and for the relationships that will be disrupted by their death, they may welcome death itself as an end to suffering.

There are many different kinds of deaths and many different ways of dying. Similarly, there are many different ways to grieve. While shock and numbness often attend the sudden loss of a loved one, and while sadness is commonly experienced by the bereaved, different people grieve in their own way and in their own time. While intense grieving does end, grieving may nevertheless last a lifetime.

Losing a loved one means losing a relationship with that person, a relationship that is part of oneself. It follows that the loss of a significant other involves a loss of oneself to some degree. Loved ones are not forgotten; they are remembered from time to time with varying degrees of emotion. In that sense, grieving does not end. Furthermore, the process of making sense of loss and of finding meaning in death and in life is often ongoing. Nevertheless, over time personal grieving is likely to become less "disruptive" to one's personal and social functioning.

While dying and death, bereavement and grieving are intensely personal experiences, and while reactions vary from one individual to another, nevertheless, society and culture do provide definitions and guidelines for grieving. When personal grief violates these guidelines — for example, when a person continues to grieve intensely beyond the time allotted for grieving — then such grief becomes defined as complicated, prolonged, chronic, unresolved, deviant, abnormal, pathological, or as a sign of individual failure and weakness. Definitions such as this fail to legitimize individual differences in grieving and put pressure on people to hide their personal grief while in public.

People may manage their emotions and behaviours in public to conform to social expectations, showing grief or hiding it when appropriate. Public displays of either grief or non-grief should not be mistaken for the private and the personal. Similarly, the homogeneity of public displays should not blind one to the heterogeneity of personal experiences. Dying and death, bereavement and grieving are, in the end, highly personal experiences.

APPENDIX
SELECTED SOURCES OF INFORMATION ON DYING AND DEATH

http://ancestorsatrest.com/deaths_by_location.shtml

This website has information about finding your ancestors through death record searches in Canada, the United States, and Britain. It includes free databases for coffin plates, death cards, funeral cards, wills, church records, family bibles, and cenotaph and tombstone inscriptions. Links to other great death records like cemeteries, vital statistics, and obituaries are also provided, as well as information on finding death records off the Internet.

http://dir.blogflux.com/cat/death.html

This website is a death blog directory, with links to over 80,000 sites where individuals or groups from 239 countries have discussed their views or experiences with dying and death.

http://www.forestofmemories.org/

http://www.naturalburial.ca/about-the-co-operative/founding-members/

These two websites were created by volunteers who wish to have "green" or environmentally friendly burial and death-observance practices in Canada and the United States.

Bibliography of Native North Americans (BNNA)

This is a library database comprising over 100,000 citations for books, essays, journal articles, and government documents of the United States and Canada, from the sixteenth century to the present. A wide range of topics are found on Native North American culture, history, and life.

http://www.gov.ns.ca/heal/downloads/preparing_at_home.pdf

"Preparing for a Death at Home," Nova Scotia Department of Health and Home Care Nova Scotia (no date).

http://www.health.gov.bc.ca/hcc/pdf/elcpaper.pdf

"Discussion Paper on a Provincial Strategy for End-of-Life Care in British Columbia," British Columbia Ministry of Health Services (October 2002).

http://www.health.gov.bc.ca/hcc/pdf/framework.pdf

"A Provincial Framework for End-of-life Care," British Columbia Ministry of Health (May 2006).

http://www.chpca.net/public_policy_advocacy/pan-canadian_gold_standards.htm

"The Pan-Canadian Gold Standards in Palliative Home Care: Toward Equitable Access to High Quality Hospice Palliative and End-of-Life Care at Home," Canadian Hospice Palliative Care Association (December 2006).

http://www12.statcan.ca/english/census01/products/analytic/cda01pymd.swf

"Age Pyramid of Canada of Population July 1, 1901 to 2001," Statistics Canada. This is a website showing the change in population size and age over 100 years.

http://www.vifamily.ca/about/about.html

The Vanier Institute of the Family, an Ottawa organization, has a vision to make families as important to Canadian society as they are to the lives of individual Canadians.

http://www.dyingwithdignity.ca/

This is a Canadian organization that supports and provides information about the right-to-die movement.

http://www.compassionandchoices.org/

A website for the right-to-die or choices group, which evolved from the Hemlock Society, is called Compassion & Choices. Their website states that "Compassion & Choices is a nonprofit organization working to improve care and expand choice at the end of life. As a national organization with over 60 chapters and 30,000 members, we help patients and their loved ones face the end of life with calm facts and choices of action during a difficult time. We also aggressively pursue legal reform to promote pain care, put teeth in advance directives, and legalize physician aid in dying."

http://www.compassionandchoices.org/hemlock/

The website for the original right-to-die group, called the Hemlock Society, states: "Hemlock is committed to providing information regarding options for dignified death and legalized physician aid in dying. To strengthen our ability to serve the terminally ill, and forward aid-in-dying laws across the country, Hemlock is now partnered with the national leader in aid in dying, Compassion & Choices. To learn more about the choice-in-dying movement and Compassion & Choices' Client Support Program, legal and legislative advocacy work, and educational outreach programs, visit www.compassionandchoices.org or call 800-247-7421."

Other right-to-die groups are: Death With Dignity National Center, Euthanasia Research & Guidance Organization (ERGO), and Final Exit Network.

http://www.nrlc.org/

In contrast, a predominant US right-to-life organization — National Right to Live — also has this website.

http://www.campaignlifecoalition.com/

This is the website for a Canadian right-to-life organization. It states: "Campaign Life Coalition is the political wing of the pro-life movement in Canada. We are working to restore the right to life, from conception to natural death, at all levels of government — federal, provincial, and municipal. We support any legislative measure to end anti-life practices, either directly or indirectly, on the condition such a measure does not compromise our basic pro-life beliefs. We defend the sanctity of human life against threats posed by abortion, euthanasia, doctor-assisted suicide, reproductive and genetic technologies, cloning, infanticide, eugenics, population control, and threats to the family."

REFERENCES

Achille, M.A., and Ogloff, J.R.P. (2003). Attitudes toward and desire for assisted suicide among persons with amyotrophic lateral sclerosis. *Omega*, 48(1), 1-21.

Adelson, N. (2005). The embodiment of inequity: health disparities in Aboriginal Canada. *Canadian Journal of Public Health*, 96(Suppl 2), S45-S61.

Agnew, G.H. (1974). *Canadian Hospitals, 1920-1970*. Toronto: University of Toronto Press.

Aiken, L.R. (2001). *Dying, Death, and Bereavement* (4th ed.). Mahwah, NJ: Lawrence Erlbaum.

Ajemian, I.C. (1990). Palliative care in Canada: 2000. *Journal of Palliative Care*, 6(4), 47-58.

Ajemian, I.C. (1992). Hospitals and health care facilities. *Journal of Palliative Care*, 8(1), 33-37.

Alberta Health. (1992-97). *Annual Report*. Edmonton: Author.

Albom, M. (1997). *Tuesdays with Morrie*. New York: Doubleday.

Allard, P., Dionne, A., and Potvin, D. (1995). Factors associated with length of survival among 1081 terminally ill cancer patients. *Journal of Palliative Care*, 11(3), 20-24.

Amyot, G.F. (1967). Some historical highlights of public health in Canada. *Canadian Journal of Public Health*, 58(8), 337-41.

Anderson, H. (1980). The death of a parent: Its impact on middle-aged sons and daughters. *Pastoral Psychology*, 28(3), 151-67.

Anonymous. (2004). Employment Insurance Compassionate Care Benefit. Important information for doctors and health administrators. *Canadian Family Physician*, 50, 420-21.

Antonovsky, A. (1987). *Unraveling the Mystery of Health: How People Manage Stress and Stay Well*. San Francisco, CA: Jossey-Bass.

Ariès, P. (1974). *Western Attitudes toward Death: From the Middle Ages to the Present*. Baltimore, MD: The Johns Hopkins University Press.

Ariès, P. (1981). *The Hour of Our Death*. New York: Knopf.

Aronson, K.J., Howe, G.R., Carpenter, M., and Fair, M.E. (1999). Surveillance of potential associations between occupations and causes of death in Canada. *Occupational and Environmental Medicine*, 56(4), 265-69.

Asada, Y., and Kephart, G. (2007). Equity in health services use and intensity of use in Canada. *BMC Health Services Research*, 7, 41.

Audette, A. (1964). Nursing care in cardiovascular surgery. *Canadian Nurse Journal*, 60(3), 259-68.

Baillargeon, L. (2003). Editorial. Palliative care at home. Dying at home: An increasingly important trend. *Canadian Family Physician*, December, 2-3.

Bartlett, S. (Director and Producer). (1994). *Who owns my life? The Sue Rodriguez story*. From the television series *Witness* [Video]. Canadian Broadcasting Corporation.

Baumgart, A.J. (1992). Evolution of the Canadian health care system. In A.J. Baumgart and J. Larsen (eds.), *Canadian Nursing Faces the Future* (2nd ed., pp. 23-41). Toronto: Mosby.

Beaton, J.I., and Degner, L.F. (1990). Life and death decisions: The impact on nurses. *Canadian Nurse Journal*, 86(3), 18-22.

Becker, E. (1973). *The Denial of Death*. New York: Free Press.

Belicki, K., Gulko, N., Ruzycki, K., and Aristotle, J. (2003). Sixteen years of dreams following spousal bereavement. *Omega*, 47(2), 93-106.

Bettman, O.L. (1956). *A Pictorial History of Medicine*. Springfield, IL: C.C. Thomas.

Bibby, R.W., and Brinkerhoff, M.B. (1994). Circulation of the saints, 1966-1990: New data, new reflections. *Journal for the Scientific Study of Religion*, 33(3), 273-80.

Blishen, B.R. (1991). *Doctors in Canada: The Changing World of Medical Practice*. Toronto: University of Toronto Press.

Blouin, M. (1995). Care-in-dying: A call to action. *Catholic Health Association of Canada Review*, 23(1), 23.

Bourette, S., and Milner, B. (1999, June 2). No-frills funerals changing an already evolving industry. *Globe and Mail*, B11.

Bowman, K.W., and Singer, P.A. (2001). Chinese seniors' perspectives on end-of-life decisions. *Social Science and Medicine*, 53, 455-64.

Boyd, K.J. (1993). Palliative care in the community: Views of general practitioners and district nurses in East London. *Journal of Palliative Care*, 9(2), 33-37.

Bradley, L.O. (1958). The changing role of hospitals. *Canadian Nurse*, 54(6), 550-58.

Braun, M.J. (1992). Meaning Reconstruction in the Experience of Parental Bereavement. Unpublished masters thesis, University of Manitoba, Winnipeg.

Brazil, K., Krueger, P., Bedard, M., Kelley, L., McAiney, C., Justice, C., and Taniguchi, A. (2006). Quality of care for residents dying in Ontario long-term care facilities: Findings from a survey of directors of care. *Journal of Palliative Care*, 22(1), 18-25.

Bresnahan, J.F. (1993). Getting beyond suspicion of homicide: Reflections on the struggle for morally appropriate care of the dying under high technology medical care. *Trends in Health Care, Law and Ethics*, 8(1), 31-38.

Brockopp, D.Y., King, D.B., and Hamilton, J.E. (1991). The dying patient: A comparative study of nurse caregiver characteristics. *Death Studies*, 15(3), 245-58.

Brown, J.S.H. (1980). *Strangers in Blood: Fur Trade Company Families in Indian Country*. Vancouver: University of British Columbia.

Bryce, G. (1902). *The Remarkable History of the Hudson's Bay Company* (2nd ed.). London: Sampson Low Marston.

Buckley, S. (1988). The search for the decline in maternal mortality: The place of hospital records. In W. Mitchinson and J.D. McGinnis (eds.), *Essays in the History of Canadian Medicine* (pp. 148-63). Toronto: McClelland and Stewart.

Bulkin, W., and Lukashok, H. (1991). Training physicians to care for the dying. *American Journal of Hospice and Palliative Care*, 8(2), 10-15.

Burch, E.S. (1988). *The Eskimos*. Norman, OK: University of Oklahoma Press.

Burke, M.A., Lindsay, J., McDowell, I., and Hill, G. (1997). Dementia among seniors. *Canadian Social Trends*, Summer, 24-27.

Burkhardt, S., La Harpe, R., Harding, T. W., and Sobel, J. (2006). Euthanasia and assisted suicide: Comparison of legal aspects in Switzerland and other countries. *Medicine, Science and the Law*, 46(4), 287-94.

Campbell, N.R.C., Onysko, J., Johansen, H., and Gao, R. (2006). Changes in cardiovascular deaths and hospitalization in Canada. *Canadian Journal of Cardiology*, 22(5), 425-27.

Campion, B. (1994). Is there a place for a good death? *Catholic Health Association of Canada Review*, 22(1), 4-5.

Canadian Cancer Society/National Cancer Institute of Canada. (2007). *Canadian Cancer Statistics 2007*. Toronto, ON: Author.

Canadian Healthcare Association. (2007). Online: http://www.cha.ca/

Canadian Hospice Palliative Care Association. (2007). Online: http://www.chpca.net/home.htm.

Canadian Institute for Health Information. (2004). *Improving the Health of Canadians*. Ottawa: Author.

Canadian Institute for Health Information. (2005). *Exploring the 70/30 Split: How Canada's Health Care System Is Financed*. Ottawa: Author.

Canadian Institute for Health Information. (2006). *Health Care in Canada 2006*. Ottawa: Author.

Canadian Nurses Association. (1964). Submission on Aging. *Canadian Nurse Journal*, 60(8), 741-44.

Canadian Nurses Association, Public Policy Division. (2006). *2005 Workplace Profile of Registered Nurses in Canada*. Ottawa, ON: Author.

Canadian Palliative Care Association. (1997). *The Canadian Directory of Services: Palliative Care and HIV/AIDS, 1997*. Ottawa: Author.

Carstairs, S. (2000, June). Quality end-of-life care: The right of every Canadian. Final report of the Subcommittee to Update "Of Life and Death" of the Standing Senate Committee on Social Affairs, Science and Technology. Ottawa: Author.

Carter, W.H. (1973). *Medical Practices and Burial Customs of North American Indians*. London, ON: Namind.

Catholic Health Association of Canada. (1991). *Health Care Ethics Guide*. Ottawa: Author.

Chappell, N. (1992). *Social Support and Aging*. Toronto: Butterworths.

Chappell, N., McDonald, L., and Stones, M. (2008). *Aging in Contemporary Canada* (2nd ed.). Toronto: Pearson Prentice Hall.

Charlton, R., and Dovey, S. (1995). Attitudes to death and dying in the UK, New Zealand, and Japan. *Journal of Palliative Care*, 11(1), 42-47.

Chasteen, A.L., and Madey, S.F. (2003). Belief in a just world and the perceived injustice of dying young or old. *Omega*, 47(4), 313-26.

Chee, J.H., Filion, K.B., Haider, S., Pilote, L., and Eisenberg, M.J. (2004). Impact of age on hospital course and cost of coronary artery bypass grafting. *American Journal of Cardiology*, 93(6), 768-71.

Chen, J., Wilkins, R., and Ng, E. (1996). Health expectancy by immigrant status, 1986 and 1991. *Health Reports*, 8(3), 29-38.

Chin, A.E., Hedberg, K., Higginson, G.K., and Fleming, D.W. (1999). Legalized physician-assisted suicide in Oregon: The first year's experience. *New England Journal of Medicine*, 340(7), 577-83.

Chochinov, H.M., Tataryn, D., Clinch, J.J., and Dudgeon, D. (1999). Will to live in the terminally ill. *The Lancet*, 354, 816-19.

Chochinov, H.M., Hack, T., Hassard, T., Kristjanson, L.J., McClement, S., and Harlos, M. (2002). Dignity in the terminally ill: A cross-sectional, cohort study. *The Lancet*, 360, 2026-30.

Choudhry, N.K., Ma, J., Rasooly, I., and Singer, P.A. (1994). Long-term care facility policies on life-sustaining treatments and advance directives in Canada. *Journal of the American Geriatrics Society*, 42(11), 1150-53.

Clark, G.T. (1993). *Personal Meanings of Grief and Bereavement*. Doctoral dissertation. Edmonton, University of Alberta.

Claxton-Oldfield, S., Tomes, J., Brennan, M., Fawcett, C., and Claxton-Oldfield, J. (2005). Palliative care volunteerism among college students in Canada. *American Journal of Hospice and Palliative Medicine*, 22(2), 111-18.

Clifton, J.A. (1991). Folklore. In R. Lachmann (ed.), *The Encyclopedic Dictionary of Sociology* (4th ed., p. 115). Guilford, CT: Dushkin.

CMA Policy Summary. (1995). Joint statement on resuscitative interventions (Update 1995). *Canadian Medical Association Journal*, 153(11), 1652A-52C.

Colarusso, C.A. (1999). The development of time sense in middle adulthood. *Psychoanalytic Quarterly*, 68(1), 52-83.

Coleman, V. (1985). *The Story of Medicine*. London: Robert Hale.

Colman, P. (1997). *Corpses, Coffins, and Crypts: A History of Burial*. New York: Henry Holt and Company.

Cook, D.J., Uyatt, G.H., Jaeschke, R., Reeve, J., Spanier, A., King, D., Molloy, D.W., Willau, A., and Streiner, D.L. (1995). Determinants in Canadian health care workers of the decision to withdraw life support from the critically ill. *Journal of the American Medical Association*, 273(9), 708-99.

Corlett, W.T. (1935). *The Medicine-Man of the American Indians and His Cultural Background*. Springfield, IL: Charles C. Thomas.

Counts, D.R., and Counts, D.A. (1991). Conclusions: Coping with the final tragedy. In D.R. Counts and D.A. Counts (eds.), *Coping with the Final Tragedy: Cultural Variation in Dying and Grieving* (pp. 277-91). Amityville, NY: Baywood.

Cremation Association of North America. (2007). Canadian statistics. Online: http://www.cremationassociation.org/docs/WebCanFigures.pdf.

Curran, W.J., and Hyg, S.M. (1984). Quality of life and treatment decisions: The Canadian Law Reform report. *New England Journal of Medicine*, 310(5), 297-98.

D'Amico, M., Agozzino, E., Biagino, A., Simonetti, A., and Marinelli, P. (1999). Ill-defined and multiple causes of death certificates: A study of misclassification in mortality statistics. *European Journal of Epidemiology*, 15(2), 141-48.

Davies, B., and Steele, R. (1996). Challenges in identifying children for palliative care. *Journal of Palliative Care*, 12(3), 5-8.

Death with Dignity Act Annual Report. (2007). Year 9 — 2006 summary. Online: http://www.
oregon.gov/DHS/ph/pas/ar-index.shtml.

Decker, J.F. (1991). Depopulation of the northern plains natives. *Social Science and Medicine*,
33(4), 381-93.

Decker, J.F. (1997). The York Factory medical journals, 1846-52. *Canadian Bulletin of Medical
History*, 14(1), 107-31.

Des Aulniers, L. (1993). The organization of life before death in two Quebec cultural configura-
tions. *Omega*, 27, 35-50.

DeSpelder, L.A., and Strickland, A.L. (2005). *The Last Dance: Encountering Death and Dying*
(7th ed.). Boston: McGraw-Hill.

de Beauvoir, S. (1973). *Old Age*. (Patrick O'Brien, Trans.). London: Deutsch

Dickason, O.P. (1984). *The Myth of the Savage and the Beginnings of French Colonialism in the
Americas*. Edmonton: University of Alberta Press.

Doka, K.J. (1995). Disenfranchised grief. In L.A. DeSpelder and A.L. Strickland (eds.), *The Path
Ahead: Readings in Death and Dying* (pp. 271-75). Mountain View, CA: Mayfield.

Dolgoy, R. (Director), and Phillips, D. (Producer). (1991). *Living With Dying* [Video]. National
Film Board of Canada.

Donnelly, S.M., Michael, N., and Donnelly, C. (2006). Experience of the moment of death at
home. *Mortality*, 11(4), 352-67.

Downe-Wamboldt, B. (1985). Hospice program eases fear, pain and loneliness. *Dimensions*,
28-29, 37.

Ducharme, F., and Corin, E. (1997). Le veuvage chez les hommes et les femmes âgés: une étude
exploratoire des significations et des stratégies adaptatives. *Canadian Journal on Aging*, 16,
112-41.

Duffy, C.M., Pollock, P., Levy, M., Budd, E., Caulfield, L., and Koren, G. (1990). Home-based palliative care for children, Part 2: The benefits of an established program. *Journal of Palliative
Care*, 6(2), 8-12.

Durkheim, E. ([1915] 1965). *The Elementary Forms of Religious Life*. New York: Free Press.

Eastaugh, A.N. (1996). Approaches to palliative care by primary health care teams: A survey.
Journal of Palliative Care, 12(4), 47-50.

Edmonds, P., Karlsen, S., Khan, S., and Addington-Hall, J. (2001). A comparison of the palliative care needs of patients dying with chronic respiratory disease and lung cancer. *Palliative
Medicine*, 15, 287-95.

Ellison, L.F., Morrison, H.I., de Groh, M.J., and Villneuve, P.J. (1999). Health consequences of
smoking among Canadian smokers: An update. *Chronic Diseases in Canada*, 21(1), 36-39.

Emke, I. (2002). Why the sad face? Secularization and the changing function of funerals in
Newfoundland. *Mortality*, 7(3), 269-84.

Eng, B., and Davies, B. (1992). Canuck Place: A hospice for children. *Canadian Oncology Nursing
Journal*, 2(1), 18-20.

Ens, C., and Bond, J.B. Jr. (2005). Death anxiety and personal growth in adolescents experiencing the death of a grandparent. *Death Studies*, 29, 171-78.

Epp, J. (1986). *Achieving Health for All: A Framework for Health Promotion*. Ottawa: Minister of
Supply and Services Canada.

Erichsen-Brown, C. (1979). *Use of Plants for the Past 500 Years*. Aurora, ON: Breezy Creeks
Press.

Ericksen, J., Rodney, M.P., and Starzomski, R. (1995). When is it right to die? *Canadian Nurse*,
91(8), 29-34.

Ewart, W.B. (1983). Causes of mortality in a subarctic settlement (York Factory, MB.), 1714-1946.
Canadian Medical Association Journal, 129(6), 571-74.

Faber-Langendoen, K., and Bartels, D.M. (1992). Process of forgoing life-sustaining treatment
in a university hospital: An empirical study. *Critical Care Medicine*, 20(5), 570-77.

Fair, M. (1994). The development of national vital statistics in Canada, Part 1: From 1605 to 1945.
Health Reports, 6(3), 355-72.

Farand, L., Chagnon, F., Renaud, J., and Rivard, M. (2004). Completed suicides among Quebec
adolescents involved with juvenile justice and child welfare services. *Suicide and Life-
Threatening Behavior*, 34(1), 24-35.

Farncombe, M.L. (1991). Symptom control in a regional cancer centre: An innovative outpatient
approach. *Journal of Palliative Care*, 7(4), 21-25.

Feldman, D.E., Platt, R., Dery, V., Kapetanakis, C., Lamontagne, E., Ducharme, A., Giannetti, N., Frenette, M., and Beck, E.J. (2004). Seasonal congestive heart failure mortality and hospitalization trends, Quebec 1990-1998. *Journal of Epidemiology and Community Health*, 58(2), 129-30.

Fishbane, S. (1989). Jewish mourning rites: A process of resocialization. *Anthropologica*, 31, 65-84.

Flynn, D. (1993). *The Truth about Funerals. How to Beat the High Cost of Dying (An Insider's Perspective)*. Burlington, ON: Funeral Consultants International.

Foot, R. (1997, December 23). Doctor convicted in aiding suicide: Toronto AIDS physician pleads guilty to two charges of giving potent pills to HIV patients. *Edmonton Journal*, A7.

Fortier, R. (Director), and Grana, S., Fortier, R., and Howells, B. (Producers). (1984). *The Last Right* [Video]. National Film Board of Canada.

Frank, A.W. (1991). *At the Will of the Body: Reflections on Illness*. Boston, MA: Houghton Mifflin.

Fries, J.F. (1980). Aging, natural death, and the compression of mortality. *New England Journal of Medicine*, 303(3), 130-35.

Fry, P.S. (1997). Grandparents' reactions to the death of a grandchild: An exploratory factor analytic study. *Omega*, 35, 119-40.

Fry, R. Sr., and Schuman, J.E. (1986). Providence expands palliative care to meet patients' needs better. *Dimensions*, 63(8), 31-33.

Gardner-Nix, J.S., Brodie, R., Tjan, E., Wilton, M., Zoberman, L., Barnes, F., Friedrich, J., and Wood, J. (1995). Scarborough's palliative "at-home" care team (PACT): A model for a suburban physician palliative care team. *Journal of Palliative Care*, 11(3), 43-49.

Gee, E.M. (1987). Historical change in the family life course of Canadian men and women. In V.W. Marshall (ed.), *Aging in Canada: Social Perspectives* (2nd ed., pp. 265-87). Markham, ON: Fitzhenry and Whiteside.

Gee, E.M., and Kimball, M.M. (1987). *Women and Aging*. Toronto: Butterworths.

Gilson, M. (Director), and Daly, T. (Producer). (1980). *The Last Days of Living* [Video]. National Film Board of Canada.

Glaser, B.G., and Strauss, A.L. (1965). *Awareness of Dying*. Chicago, IL: Aldine.

Glaser, B.G., and Strauss, A.L. (1968). *Time for Dying*. Chicago, IL: Aldine.

Goffman, E. (1963). *Stigma*. Englewood Cliffs, NJ: Prentice-Hall.

Goodridge, D., Bond, J.B. Jr., Cameron, C., and McKean, E. (2005). End-of-life care in a nursing home: a study of family, nurse, and healthcare aide perspectives. *International Journal of Palliative Nursing*, 11(5), 226-32.

Grant, J.H.B. (1946). Immunization in children. *Canadian Medical Association Journal*, 55, 493-97.

Grant Kalischuk, R., and Hayes, V.E. (2003). Grieving, mourning, and healing following youth suicide: A focus on health and well being in families. *Omega*, 48(1), 45-67.

Gray, R.E. (1993). Suicide prevention consultation in Canada's Northwest Territories: A personal account. In J.D. Morgan (ed.), *Personal Care in an Impersonal World: A Multidimensional Look at Bereavement*. Amityville, NY: Baywood.

Greaves, L., Hankivsky, O., Livadiotakis, G., and Cormier, R. (2002). *Final Payments: Socioeconomic Costs of Palliative Home Caregiving in the Last Month of Life*. Vancouver, BC: British Columbia Centre of Excellence for Women's Health.

Greenberg, J., Solomon, S., and Pyszczynski, T. (1997). Terror management theory of self-esteem and cultural worldviews: Empirical assessments and conceptual refinements. *Advances in Experimental Social Psychology*, 29, 61-139.

Haas, J. (1977). Learning real feelings: A study of high steel ironworkers' reactions to fear and danger. *Sociology of Work and Occupations*, 4, 147-70.

Hafferty, F.W. (1988). Cadaver stories and the emotional socialization of medical students. *Journal of Health and Social Behavior*, 29, 344-56.

Hailstone, P. (1979). The growing role of the hospice. *Health Care in Canada*, 21(4), 44-45.

Hall, E. (1947). Health problems of an aging population. *Canadian Nurse Journal*, 43(8), 591.

Hall, G.S. (1922). *Senescence, The Last Half of Life*. New York: Appleton and Company.

Hall, P., Schroder, C., and Weaver, L. (2002). The last 48 hours of life in long-term care: a focused chart audit. *Journal of the American Geriatrics Society*, 50(3), 501-06.

Hall, P., Weaver, L., Fothergill-Bourbonnais, F., Amos, S., Whiting, N., Barnes, P., and Legault, F. (2006). Interprofessional education in palliative care: a pilot project using popular literature. *Journal of Interprofessional Care*, 20(1), 51-59.

Hamilton, G. (1997, July 22). Murder charge revives euthanasia debate: Killing them with kindness? *Edmonton Journal*, A1.

Harding le Riche, W. (1979). Seventy years of public health in Canada. *Canadian Journal of Public Health*, 70(3), 155-63.

Harrold, J., Rickerson, E., Carroll, J.T., McGrath, J., Morales, K., Kapo, J., and Casarett, D. (2005). Is the palliative performance scale a useful predictor of mortality in a heterogeneous hospice population? *Journal of Palliative Medicine*, 8(3), 503-09.

Hartling, R.N. (1993). *Nahanni: River of Gold, River of Dreams*. Hyde Park, ON: The Canadian Recreational Canoeing Association.

Harvey, J. (1997). The technological regulation of death: With reference to the technological regulation of birth. *Sociology*, 31(4), 719-35.

Hasselback, D., Schreiner, J., and Kuitenbrouwer, P. (1999, June 2). Loewen files for bankruptcy protection. *Financial Post*, C1.

Hauser, D.J. (1974). Seat belts: Is freedom of choice worth 600 deaths a year? *Canadian Medical Association Journal*, 110(12), 1418-22.

Hawranik, P.G., and Strain, L.A. (2000). *Health of Informal Caregivers: Effects of Gender, Employment, and Use of Home Care Services*. Winnipeg, MB: Prairie Women's Health Centre of Excellence.

Hayter, J. (1968). Organ transplants: A new type of nursing? *Canadian Nurse Journal*, 64(11), 49-53.

Heagerty, J.J. (1928). *Four Centuries of Medical History in Canada*. Toronto: Macmillan.

Heagerty, J.J. (1940). *The Romance of Medicine in Canada*. Toronto: Ryerson Press.

Health Canada. (2001). Organ donation in Canada. Online: http://www.hc-sc.gc.ca/ahc-asc/media/nr-cp/2001/2001_36bk1_e.html.

Health Canada, Division of Aging and Seniors. (2002). *Canada's Aging Population*. Ottawa, ON: Minister of Public Works and Government Services Canada.

Hebert, M.P. (1998). Perinatal bereavement in its cultural context. *Death Studies*, 22, 61-79.

Heffner, J.E., Fahy, B., Hillings, L., and Barbieri, C. (1996). Attitudes regarding advance directives among patients in pulmonary rehabilitation. *American Journal of Respiratory and Critical Care Medicine*, 154(6/1), 1735-40.

Heyland, D.K., Frank, C., Groll, D., Pichora, D., Dodek, P., Rocher, G., and Gafni, A. (2006). Understanding cardiopulmonary resuscitation decision-making: Perspectives of seriously ill hospitalized patients and family members. *Chest*, 130(2), 419-28.

Higginson I.J., and Sen-Gupta, G.J.A. (2000). Place of care in advanced cancer: a qualitative systematic literature review of patient preferences. *Journal of Palliative Medicine*, 3, 287-300.

Hill, G., Forbes, W., Berthelot, J., Lindsay, J., and McDowell, I. (1996). Dementia among seniors. *Health Reports*, 8(2), 7-10.

Hornby, K., Shemie, S.D., Teitelbaum, J., and Doig, C. (2006). Variability in hospital-based brain death guidelines in Canada. *Canadian Journal of Anaesthesia*, 53(6), 613-19.

Howarth, G., and Willison, K.B. (1995, March). Preventing crises in palliative care in the home. *Canadian Family Physician*, 41, 439-44.

Hughes, R. (1999, October 11). In death's throat. *Time*, 78-79.

Industry Canada. (2007). Consumer tips — funerals. Online: http://consumer.ic.gc.ca/epic/site/oca-bc.nsf/en/ca01492e.html.

Iribarren, C., Crow, R.S., Hannan, P.J., Jacobs, D.R., Jr., and Luepker, R.V. (1998). Validation of death certificate diagnosis of out-of-hospital sudden cardiac death. *American Journal of Cardiology*, 82(1), 50-53.

Jack, D. (1981). *Rogues, Rebels, and Geniuses: The Story of Canadian Medicine*. Toronto: Doubleday.

Johansen, H., Nair, C., and Bond, J. (1994). Who goes to hospital? An investigation of high uses of hospital days. *Health Reports*, 6(2), 253-77.

John-Baptiste, A., Naglie, G., Tomlinson, G., Alibhai, S.M., Etchells, E., Cheung, A., Kapral, M., Gold, W.L., Abrams, H., Bacchus, M., and Krahn, M. (2004). The effect of English language proficiency on length of stay and in-hospital mortality. *Journal of General Internal Medicine*, 19(3), 221-28.

Johnson, N., Cook, D., Giacomini, M., and Willms, D. (2000). Towards a "good" death: End-of-life narratives constructed in an intensive care unit. *Culture, Medicine and Psychiatry*, 24, 275-95.

Joint Statement on Resuscitation Interventions. (1995). Online: http://www.cma.ca/index.cfm/ci_id/33236/la_id/1.htm

Joint Statement on Terminal Illness. (1984). A protocol for health professionals regarding resuscitation intervention for the terminally ill. *Canadian Nurse*, 80(6), 24. Online: http://www. pubmedcentral.nih.gov/articlerender.fcgi?artid=1483518

Joseph, S.E. (1994). Coast Salish Perceptions of Death and Dying: An Ethnographic Study. Unpublished masters thesis. University of Victoria, Victoria.

Joseph, K.S., Kramer, M.S., Allen, A.C., and Sauve, R. (2005). Infant mortality in Alberta and all of Canada. *Canadian Medical Association Journal*, 172(7), 856-57.

Kastenbaum, R.J. (1998). *Death, Society, and Human Experience* (6th ed.). Boston, MA: Allyn and Bacon.

Kastenbaum, R.J. (2007). *Death, Society, and Human Experience* (9th ed.). Boston, MA: Pearson/ Allyn and Bacon.

Kaufert, J.M., and O'Neil, J.D. (1991). Cultural mediation of dying and grieving among Native Canadian patients in urban hospitals. In D.R. Counts and D.A. Counts (eds.), *Coping with the Final Tragedy: Cultural Variation in Dying and Grieving*, (pp. 231-51). Amityville, NY: Baywood.

Kelm, M., and Townsend, L. (eds.). (2006). *In The Days of Our Grandmothers: A Reader in Aboriginal Women's History in Canada*. Toronto: University of Toronto Press.

Kendall, D., Murray, J.L., and Linden, R. (2000). *Sociology in Our Times* (2nd Cdn. ed.). Scarborough, ON: Nelson.

Kennedy, P., and Milner, B. (1999, June 2). Family at root of Loewen's fall shows sympathy. *Globe and Mail*, B11.

Kent, G. (1996, June/July). Robson: A climber's baptism. *Explore*, 15th Anniversary Issue, 80-83.

Kerr, M., and Kurtz, J. (1999). *Facing a Death in the Family*. Toronto: John Wiley and Sons.

Kissane, D.W., Street, A., and Nitschke, P. (1998). Seven deaths in Darwin: Case studies under the *Rights of the Terminally Ill Act*, Northern Territory, Australia. *Lancet*, 352(9134), 1097-102.

Koop, P.M., and Strang, V.R. (2003). The bereavement experience following home-based family caregiving for persons with advanced cancer. *Clinical Nursing Research*, 12(2), 127-44.

Kouwenhoven, W.B., Jude, J.R., and Knickerbocker, G.G. (1960). Closed-chest cardiac massage. *Journal of the American Medical Association*, 173, 1064-67.

Kristjanson, L.J., and Balneaves, L. (1995). Directions for palliative care nursing in Canada: Report of a national survey. *Journal of Palliative Care*, 11(3), 5-8.

Kübler-Ross, E. (1969). *On Death and Dying*. New York: Macmillan.

Kuhl, D. (2006). *Facing Death, Embracing Life: Understanding What Dying People Want*. Toronto: Doubleday.

Kurti, L.G., and O'Dowd, T.C. (1995). Dying of non-malignant diseases in general practice. *Journal of Palliative Care*, 11(3), 25-31.

Lalonde, M. (1978). *A New Perspective on the Health of Canadians: A Working Document*. Ottawa: Minister of Supply and Services.

Landry, F.J., Kroenke, K., Lucas, C., and Reeder, J. (1997). Increasing the use of advance directives in medical outpatients. *Journal of General Internal Medicine*, 12(7), 412-15.

Langham, P., and Flagel, D. (1991). Medical intervention and the effectiveness of the health care delivery system: A Canadian perspective. *Holistic Nursing Practice*, 5(3), 77-84.

Laurence, M. (1964). *The Stone Angel*. Toronto: McClelland and Stewart.

Lavigne-Pley, C., and Levesque, L. (1992). Reactions of the institutionalized elderly upon learning of the death of a peer. *Death Studies*, 16(5), 451-61.

Lee, D.S., Johansen, H., Gong, Y., Hall, R.E., Tu, J.V., and Cox, J.L. (2004). Regional outcomes of heart failure in Canada. *Canadian Journal of Cardiology*, 20(6), 599-607.

Leftwich, R.E. (1993). Care and cure as healing processes in nursing. *Nursing Forum*, 28(3), 13-17.

Leming, M.R., and Dickinson, G.E. (2007). *Understanding Dying, Death, and Bereavement* (6th ed.). Belmont, CA: Thomson Wadsworth.

Lessard, R. (1991). *Health Care in Canada during the Seventeenth and Eighteenth Centuries*. Ottawa: Canadian Museum of Civilization.

Lévy, J.J., Dupras, A., and Samson, J. (1985). La religion, la mort et la sexualité, au Québec. *Cahiers de Recherches en Sciences de la Religion*, 6, 25-34.

Levy, M., Duffy, C.M., Pollock, P., Budd, E., Caulfield, L., and Koren, G. (1990). Home-based palliative care for children, Part 1: The institution of a program. *Journal of Palliative Care*, 6(1), 11-15.

Lindsay, C. (1999). Seniors: A diverse group aging well. *Canadian Social Trends*, 52 (Summer), 24-26.

Lindsay, E. (1991). Life at all costs. *Canadian Nurse Journal*, 87(3), 16-18.

Lloyd-Jones, D.M., Martin, D.O., Larson, M.G., and Levy, D. (1998). Accuracy of death certificates for coding coronary heart disease as the cause of death. *Annals of Internal Medicine*, 129(12), 1020-26.

Lucas, R.A. (1968). Social implications of the immediacy of death. *Canadian Review of Sociology and Anthropology*, 5, 1-16.

Lyng, S. (1990). Edgework: A social psychological analysis of voluntary risk taking. *American Journal of Sociology*, 95, 851-86.

Lyng, S. (ed.). (2005). *Edgework: The Sociology of Risk-Taking*. New York: Routledge.

Lynn, J. (2001). Perspectives on care at the close of life. Serving patients who may die soon and their families: The role of hospice and other services. *Journal of the American Medical Association*, 285(7), 925-32.

MacDougall, H. (1994). Sexually transmitted diseases in Canada, 1800-1992. *Genitourinary Medicine*, 70(1), 56-63.

MacKillop, H.I. (1978). Effects of seat belt legislation and reduction of highway speed limits in Ontario. *Canadian Medical Association Journal*, 119(10), 1154-58.

MacLean, M.J., and Kelley, M.L. (2001). Palliative care in rural Canada. *Rural Social Work*, 6(3), 63-67.

Malette v. Schulman. (1992). 72 OR (2d) 417 (Ont CA).

Malkin, S. (1976). Care of the terminally ill at home. *Canadian Medical Association Journal*, 115(2), 129-30.

Manuel, D. G., Leung, M., Nguyen, K., Tanuseputro, P., and Johansen, H. (2003). Burden of cardiovascular disease in Canada. *Canadian Journal of Cardiology*, 19(9), 997-1004.

Marquis, S. (1993). Death of the nursed: Burnout of the provider. *Omega*, 27(1), 17-33.

Marsh, J.H. (1985). Disease. In J.H. Marsh (ed.), *The Canadian Encyclopedia* (pp. 833-34). Edmonton: Hurtig.

Marshall, V.W. (1980). *Last Chapters: A Sociology of Aging and Dying*. Monterey, CA: Brooks/ Cole.

Marshall, V.W. (1986). A sociological perspective on aging and dying. In V.W. Marshall (ed.), *Later Life: The Social Psychology of Aging* (pp. 125-46). Beverly Hills, CA: Sage.

Martin, K. (1998). *When a Baby Dies of SIDS: The Parents' Grief and Search for Reason*. Edmonton, AB: Qual Institute Press (International Institute for Qualitative Methodology).

Martin, K., and Elder, S. (1993). Pathways through grief: A model of the process. In J.D. Morgan (ed.), *Personal Care in an Impersonal World: A Multidimensional Look at Bereavement* (pp. 73-86). Amityville, NY: Baywood.

Martin Matthews, A. (1987). Widowhood as an expectable life event. In V.W. Marshall (ed.), *Aging in Canada: Social Perspectives* (2nd ed., pp. 343-66). Markham, ON: Fitzhenry and Whiteside.

Martin Matthews, A. (1991). *Widowhood in Later Life*. Toronto: Butterworths.

McGinnis, J.D. (1985). Public health. In J.H. Marsh (ed.), *The Canadian Encyclopedia* (pp. 1507-08). Edmonton, AB: Hurtig.

McGowan, S.A. (Director), and Bowen, C. (Producer). (1990). *When the Day Comes* [Video]. National Film Board of Canada.

McPhail, A., Moore, S., O'Connor, J., and Woodward, C. (1981). One hospital's experience with a "do not resuscitate" policy. *Canadian Journal of Cardiovascular Nursing*, 125(8), 830-36.

McPherson, B.D. (2004). *Aging as a Social Process: Canadian Perspectives* (4th ed.). Don Mills, ON: Oxford University Press.

McPherson, C.J., Wilson, K.G., and Murray, M.A. (2007). Feeling like a burden: Exploring the perspectives of patients at the end of life. *Social Science and Medicine*, 64, 417-27.

McPherson, K. (1996). *Bedside Matters: The Transformation of Canadian Nursing, 1900-1990*. Toronto: Oxford University Press.

McWhinney, I.R., Bass, M.J., and Orr, V. (1995). Factors associated with location of death (home or hospital) of patients referred to a palliative care team. *Canadian Medical Association Journal*, 152(3), 361-67.

McWhinney, I.R., and Stewart, M.A. (1994). Home care of dying patients. *Canadian Family Physician*, 40, 240-46.

Menec, V.H., Lix, L., Nowicki, S., and Ekuma, O. (2007). Health care use at the end of life among older adults: Does it vary by age? *Journals of Gerontology Series A — Biological Sciences and Medical Sciences*, 62(4), 400-07.

Mikos, C.A., and Wilson, S.M. (2003). Advance directives for artificial nutrition and hydration. One lesson from the Terry Schiavo case. *Florida Nurse*, 51(4), 15-24.

Millar, W.J. (1995). Life expectancy of Canadians. *Health Reports*, 7(3), 23-26.

Millar, W.J., and Hill, G.B. (1995). The elimination of disease: A mixed blessing. *Health Reports*, 7(3), 7-13.

Miller, L.G. (1960). Geriatric nursing in the home. *Canadian Nurse Journal*, 56(7), 606-09.

Mirowsky, J., and Ross, C.E. (1989). *The Social Causes of Psychological Distress*. New York: Aldine de Gruyter.

Mitchell, W.O. (1947). *Who Has Seen the Wind*. Agincourt, ON: Macmillan.

Molzahn, A.E., Starzomski, R., McDonald, M., and O'Loughlin, C. (2004). Aboriginal beliefs about organ donation: Some Coast Salish viewpoints. *Canadian Journal of Nursing Research*, 36(4), 110-28.

Molzahn, A.E., Starzomski, R., McDonald, M., and O'Loughlin, C. (2005). Chinese Canadian beliefs toward organ donation. *Qualitative Health Research*, 15(1), 82-98.

Morrison, S. (2004). Canada achieves lowest perinatal mortality ever. [erratum appears in CMAJ, 4 Jan. 2005, 172(1), 19]. *Canadian Medical Association Journal*, 171(9), 1030.

Morton, D. (2006). *A Short History of Canada* (6th ed.). Toronto: McClelland and Stewart.

Moss, M.S., Resch, N., and Moss, S.Z. (1997). The role of gender in middle-age children's responses to parent death. *Omega*, 35(1), 43-65.

Mount, B., and Flander, E.M. (1996). Morphine drips, terminal sedation, and slow euthanasia: Definitions and facts, not anecdotes. *Journal of Palliative Care*, 12(4), 31-37.

Murrant, G., and Strathdee, S. (1992, Summer). AIDS, hospice and volunteers. The Casey House volunteer program. *Journal of Volunteer Administration*, 11-17.

Murray, M. (1981). Palliative care. *Canadian Nurse*, 77(5), 16-17.

Myers, K.A., and Farquhar, D.R. (1998). Improving accuracy of death certification. *Canadian Medical Association Journal*, 158(10), 1317-23.

Nancarrow Clarke, J. (2004). A comparison of breast, testicular, and prostate cancer in mass print media (1996-2001), *Social Science and Medicine*, 59, 541-51.

Nancarrow Clarke, J. (2006). Death under control: The portrayal of death in mass print English language magazines in Canada. *Omega*, 52(2), 153-67.

Nault, F. (1997). Narrowing mortality gaps, 1978 to 1995. *Health Reports*, 9(1), 35-41.

Nault, F., and Ford, D. (1994). An overview of deaths in Canada in 1992. *Health Reports*, 6(2), 287-94.

Nichols, D. (2005). Review of *Dying at Grace*, directed by Allen King, 2003. *The Gerontologist*, 45(1), 141-43.

No charges in death of girl, 10. (1999, December 3). *Edmonton Journal*, A19.

No jail time for mother who tried to kill child. (1999, December 1). *Edmonton Journal*, A13.

Norris, J. (1994). Widowhood in later life. *Late-life Marital Disruptions. Writings in Gerontology*, Number 14. Ottawa: National Advisory Council on Aging.

Northcott, H.C. (1984). Widowhood and remarriage trends in Canada, 1956 to 1981. *Canadian Journal on Aging*, 3, 63-78.

Noseworthy, T.W. (1997). Canada deserves a national health system. *Healthcare Management Forum*, 10(1), 39-46.

Novak, M. (1997). *Aging and Society: A Canadian Perspective* (3rd ed.). Toronto: ITP Nelson.

Novak, M., and Campbell, L. (2006). *Aging and Society: A Canadian Perspective* (5th ed.). Toronto: Nelson Thomson.

Ogden, R. (1994). The right to die: A policy proposal for euthanasia and aid in dying. *Canadian Public Policy*, 20, 1-25.

Oneschuk, D., MacDonald, N., Bagshaw, S., Mayo, N., Jung, H., and Hanson, J. (2002). A pilot survey of medical students' perspectives on their educational exposure to palliative care in two Canadian universities. *Journal of Palliative Medicine*, 5(3), 353-61.

Ontario Coalition of Senior Citizens Organizations. (1995). *Life before Medicare: Canadian Experiences*. Toronto: Author.

Osgood, R. (1994). Palliative care and euthanasia: A continuum of care? *Journal of Palliative Care*, 10(2), 82-85.

Ostbye, T., and Crosse, E. (1994). Net economic costs of dementia in Canada. *Canadian Medical Association Journal*, 151(10), 1457-64.

Ott, B.B., and Nieswiadomy, R.M. (1991). Support of patient autonomy in the do not resuscitate decision. *Health and Lung*, 29(1), 66-72.

Palda, V.A., Bowman, K.W., McLean, R.F., and Chapman, M.G. (2005). "Futile" care: do we provide it? Why? A semistructured, Canada-wide survey of intensive care unit doctors and nurses. *Journal of Critical Care*, 20(3), 207-13.

Pannuti, F., and Tanneberger, S. (1992). The Bologna eubiosia project: Hospital-at-home care for advanced cancer patients. *Journal of Palliative Care*, 8(2), 11-17.

Patterson, R.M. ([1954] 1989). *Dangerous River*. Toronto: Stoddart.

Payne, S., Hawker, S., Kerr, C., Seamark, D., Roberts, H., Jarrett, N., and Smith, H. (2007). Experiences of end-of-life care in community hospitals. *Health and Social Care in the Community*, 15(5), 494-501.

Phillips, J.R. (1992). Choosing and participating in the living-dying process: A research emergent. *Nursing Science Quarterly*, 5(1), 4-5.

Posner, J. (1976). Death as a courtesy stigma. *Essence*, 1, 39-49.

Preston, R.J., and Preston, S.C. (1991). Death and grieving among northern forest hunters: An East Cree example. In D.R. Counts and D.A. Counts (eds.), *Coping with the Final Tragedy: Cultural Variation in Dying and Grieving* (pp. 135-55). Amityville, NY: Baywood.

Préville, M., Hébert, R., Boyer, R., Bravo, G., and Seguin, M. (2005). Physical health and mental disorder in elderly suicide: A case-control study. *Aging and Mental Health*, 9(6), 576-84.

Priest, A. (1987). Care for the dying. *Registered Nurses' Association of British Columbia News*, 19(5), 11-13.

Public Health Agency of Canada. (2007). Leading causes of death and hospitalization in Canada. Online: http://www.phac-aspc.gc.ca/publicat/lcd-pcd97/mrt_mf_e.html.

Pyszczynski, T., Greenberg, J., and Solomon, S. (1999). A dual-process model of defense against conscious and unconscious death-related thoughts: An extension of terror management theory. *Psychological Review*, 106, 835-45.

Quan, H., Fong, A., De Coster, C., Wang, J., Musto, R., Noseworthy, T.W., and Ghali, W.A. (2006). Variation in health services utilization among ethnic populations. *Canadian Medical Association Journal*, 174(6), 787-91.

Quill, T., and Kimsma, G.K. (2006). How much suffering is enough? *Medical Ethics*, 13(2), 10-11.

Radin, P. (2006). "To me, it's my life": Medical communication, trust, and activism in cyber-space. *Social Science and Medicine*, 62, 591-601.

Ramos, H., and Gosine, K. (2002). "The Rocket": Newspaper coverage of the death of a Québec cultural icon, a Canadian hockey player. *Journal of Canadian Studies*, 36(4), 9-31.

Ramsden, P.G. (1991). Alice in the afterlife: A glimpse in the mirror. In D.R. Counts and D.A. Counts (eds.), *Coping with the Final Tragedy: Cultural Variation in Dying and Grieving* (pp. 27-41). Amityville, NY: Baywood.

Randhawa, J., and Riley, R. (1995). Trends in hospital utilization, 1982-83 to 1992-93. *Health Reports*, 7(1), 41-49.

Rasooly, I., Lavery, J.V., Urowitz, S., Choudhry, S., Seeman, N., Meslin, E.M., Lowy, F.H., and Singer, P.A. (1994). Hospital policies on life-sustaining treatments and advance directives in Canada. *Canadian Medical Association Journal*, 150(8), 1265-70.

Reutter, L.I., and Northcott, H.C. (1993). Making risk meaningful: Developing caring relation-ships with AIDS patients. *Journal of Advanced Nursing*, 18, 1377-85.

Reutter, L.I., and Northcott, H.C. (1994). Achieving a sense of control in a context of uncertain-ty: Nurses and AIDS. *Qualitative Health Research*, 4, 51-71.

Reutter, L.I., and Northcott, H.C. (1995). Managing occupational HIV exposures: A Canadian study. *International Journal of Nursing Studies*, 32, 493-505.

Robb, N. (1998). The Morrison ruling: The case may be closed but the issues raised are not. *Canadian Medical Association Journal*, 158(8), 1071-72.

Roberts, D. (1997). *Profits of Death*. Chandler, AZ: Five Star Publications.

Rocker, G.M., Cook, D.J., O'Callaghan, C.J., Pichora, D., Dodek, P.M., Conrad, W., Kutsogiannis, D.J., and Heyland, D.K. (2005). Canadian nurses' and respiratory therapists' perspectives on withdrawal of life support in the intensive care unit. *Journal of Critical Care*, 20(1), 59-65.

Rodney, P. (1994). A nursing perspective on life-prolonging treatment. *Journal of Palliative Care*, 10(2), 40-44.

Rodney, P., and Starzomski, R. (1993). Constraints on the moral agency of nurses. *Canadian Nurse*, 89(9), 23-26.

Roland, C. (1985). History of medicine. In J.H. Marsh (ed.), *The Canadian Encyclopedia* (pp. 1112-14). Edmonton: Hurtig.

Romanow, R. (2002). *Building on Values: Final report of the Commission on Health Care in Canada*. Ottawa: Communication Canada.

Rosenberg, M.W., and Moore, E.G. (1997). The health of Canada's elderly population: Current status and future implications. *Canadian Medical Association Journal*, 157(8), 1025-32.

Rutman, D. (1992). Palliative care needs of residents, families, and staff in long-term care facilities. *Journal of Palliative Care*, 8(2), 23-29.

Scalena, A. (2006). Defining quackery: An examination of the Manitoba medical profession and the early development of professional unity. *Journal of the Canadian Chiropractic Association*, 50(3), 209-18.

Schormans, A.F. (2004). Experiences following the deaths of disabled foster children: "We don't feel like 'foster' parents." *Omega*, 49(4), 347-69.

Schriever, S.H. (1990). Comparison of beliefs and practices of ethnic Viet and Lao Hmong concerning illness, healing, death, and mourning: Implications for hospice care with refugees in Canada. *Journal of Palliative Care*, 6, 42-49.

Schultz, L.E. (2007). The influence of maternal loss on young women's experience of identity development in emerging adulthood. *Death Studies*, 31, 17-43.

Scott, J.F. (1992). Palliative care education in Canada: Attacking fear and promoting health. *Journal of Palliative Care*, 8(1), 47-53.

Senate of Canada. (1995). *Of Life and Death: Report of the Special Senate Committee on Euthanasia and Assisted Suicide*. Final report. Ottawa: Author.

Senior sentenced for wife's death. (2006). CBC News. Online: http://www.cbc.ca/canada/story/2006/04/20/jaworski060420.html.

Service Canada. (2007). Employment Insurance (EI) Compassionate Care Benefits. Online: http://www.hrsdc.gc.ca/en/ei/types/compassionate_care.shtml.

Service Corporation International. (2007). Annual report, 2006. Online: http://library.corporate-ir.net/library/10/108/108068/items/238742/2006annualreport.pdf.

Sheth, T., Nair, C., Nargundkar, M., Anand, S., and Yusuf, S. (1999). Cardiovascular and cancer mortality among Canadians of European, South Asian, and Chinese origin from 1979 to 1993: An analysis of 1.2 million deaths. *Canadian Medical Association Journal*, 161(2), 152-53.

Shields, M., and Martel, L. (2006). Healthy living among seniors. *Health Reports*, 16 Suppl, 7-20.

Silverman, P.R., Nickman, S., and Worden, J.W. (1995). Detachment revisited: The child's reconstruction of a dead parent. In L.A. DeSpelder and A.L. Strickland (eds.), *The Path Ahead: Readings in Death and Dying* (pp. 260-70). Mountain View, CA: Mayfield.

Simmons-Tropea, D., and Osborn, R. (1987). Disease, survival, and death: The health status of Canada's elderly. In V.W. Marshall (ed.), *Aging in Canada: Social Perspectives* (2nd ed., pp. 399-423). Richmond Hill, ON: Fitzhenry and Whiteside.

Smith, G.P. (1995). Restructuring the principle of medical futility. *Journal of Palliative Care*, 11(3), 9-16.

Smith, R. (2000). Editorial. A good death: An important aim for health services and for us all. *British Medical Journal*, 320, 129-30.

Sneiderman, B. (1993). The case of Nancy B: A criminal law and social policy perspective. *Health Law Journal*, 1, 25-38.

Solomon, S., Greenberg, J., and Pyszczynski, T. (1991). A terror management theory of social behavior: The psychological functions of self-esteem and cultural worldviews. In M. Zanna (ed.), *Advances in Experimental Social Psychology* (Vol. 24, pp. 91-159). Orlando, FL: Academic Press.

Solomon, S., Greenberg, J., Schimel, J., Arndt, J., and Pyszczynski, T. (2004). Human awareness of mortality and the evolution of culture. In M. Schaller and C. Crandall (eds.), *The Psychological Foundations of Culture*. Hillsdale, NJ: Lawrence Erlbaum.

Statistics Canada. (1991). *Canada Yearbook, 1992*. Ottawa: Author.

Statistics Canada. (1997). *National Population Health Survey Overview, 1996-97*. Ottawa: Minister of Industry.

Statistics Canada. (1998). *Canada Yearbook, 1999*. Ottawa: Minister of Supply and Services.

Statistics Canada. (2002a). *Profile of the Canadian Population by Age and Sex: Canada Ages*. Ottawa: Author. Catalogue no. 96F0030XIE2001002.

Statistics Canada. (2002b). Deaths subject to autopsy, Canada, provinces and territories, 2002. CANSIM table number 01020510. Online: http://www.statcan.ca/english/freepub/84F0211XIE/2002/tables/html/t013_en.htm.

Statistics Canada. (2006). *Canada Yearbook, 2006*. Ottawa: Author.

Statistics Canada. (2007). Life expectancy at birth, by sex, by province. Online: http://www40. statcan.ca/l01/cst01/health26.htm.

Status of Women. (2003). Economic impact of health, income security and labour policies on informal caregivers of frail seniors. Online: http://www.swc-cfc.gc.ca/pubs/pubspr/ 0662654765/200103_0662654765_8_e.html.

Stephenson, P.H. (1992). "He died too quick!" The process of dying in a Hutterian colony. In L.A. Platt and V.R. Persico, Jr. (eds.), *Grief in Cross-Cultural Perspective: A Casebook* (pp. 293-303). New York, NY: Garland Publishing.

Stokes, J., and Lindsay, J. (1996). Major causes of death and hospitalization in Canadian seniors. *Chronic Diseases in Canada*, 17(2), 63-73.

Stone, E. (1962). *Medicine Among the American Indians.* New York: Hafner.

Storch, J.L., and Dossetor, J. (1994). Public attitudes towards end-of-life treatment decisions: Implications for nurse clinicians and nursing administrators. *Canadian Journal of Nursing Administration*, 7(3), 65-89.

Stroebe, M., Gergen, M.M., Gergen, K.G. and Stroebe, W. (1995). Broken hearts or broken bonds: Love and death in historical perspective. In L.A. DeSpelder and A.L. Strickland (eds.), *The Path Ahead: Readings in Death and Dying* (pp. 231-41). Mountain View, CA: Mayfield.

Sudnow, D. (1967). *Passing On: The Social Organization of Dying.* Englewood Cliffs, NJ: Prentice-Hall.

Symons, D. (1992). Palliative response team. *Canadian Nurse*, 88(9), 36-37.

Tanuseputro, P., Manuel, D.G., Leung, M., Nguyen, K., and Johansen, H. (2003). Risk factors for cardiovascular disease in Canada. *Canadian Journal of Cardiology*, 19(11), 1249-59.

Teno, J.M., Branco, K.J., Mor, V., Phillips, C.D., Hawes, C., Morris, J., and Fries, B.E. (1997). Changes in advance care planning in nursing homes before and after the *Patient Self-Determination Act*: Report of a 10-state survey. *Journal of the American Geriatrics Society*, 45(8), 939-44.

The Canadian Encyclopedia. (2007a). Native people, demography. Online: http:// thecanadianencyclopedia.com/index.cfm?PgNm=TCEandParams=A1ARTA0005644.

The Canadian Encyclopedia. (2007b). The wake. Online: http://www.thecanadianencyclopedia. com/index.cfm?PgNm=TCEandParams=A1SEC821012.

The Organ Donation and Transplant Association of Canada. (2007). Fact. Online: http://www. organdonations.ca/.

Trovato, F. (2001). Aboriginal mortality in Canada, the United States, and New Zealand. *Journal of Biosocial Science*, 33(1), 67-86.

Trudeau, R. (1997). Monthly and daily patterns of death. *Health Reports*, 9(1), 43-50.

Tully, P., and Mohl, C. (1995). Older residents of health care institutions. *Health Reports*, 7(3), 27-30.

Turner, K., Chye, R., Aggarwal, G., Philip, J., Skeels, A., and Lickiss, J.N. (1996). Dignity in dying: A preliminary study of patients in the last three days of life. *Journal of Palliative Care*, 12(2), 7-13.

Valentine, P.E.B. (1994). A female profession: A feminist management perspective. In J.M. Hibberd and M.E. Kyle (eds.), *Nursing Management in Canada* (pp. 372-90). Toronto: W. B. Saunders.

van den Hoonaard, D.K. (2001). *The Widowed Self: The Older Women's Journey through Widowhood*. Waterloo, ON: Wilfrid Laurier University Press.

van den Hoonaard, D.K. (1999). No regrets: Widows' stories about the last days of their husbands' lives. *Journal of Aging Studies*, 13(1), 59-72.

van den Hoonaard, D.K. (1997). Identity foreclosure: Women's experiences of widowhood as expressed in autobiographical accounts. *Ageing and Society*, 17, 533-51.

Van der Maas, P., van der Wal, G., Haverkate, I., Graff, C., Kester, J., Onwuteaka-Philipsen, B., van der Heide, A., Bosma, J., and Willems, D.L. (1996). Euthanasia, physician-assisted suicide, and other medical practices involving the end of life in the Netherlands, 1990-1995. *New England Journal of Medicine*, 335(22), 1699-705.

Van Weel, H. (1995). Euthanasia: Mercy, morals, and medicine. *Canadian Nurse*, 91(8), 35-36.

Vanier Institute of the Family. (2007). The Vanier Institute of the Family defines family. Online: http://www.vifamily.ca/about/about.html.

Veatch, R.M. (1989). *Death, Dying, and the Biological Revolution: Our Last Quest for Responsibility* (rev. ed.). New Haven, CT: Yale University Press.

Vezina, J., Bourque, P., and Belanger, Y. (1988). Spousal loss: Depression, anxiety, and well-being after grief periods of varying lengths. *Canadian Journal on Aging*, 7, 388-96.

Viszmeg, J. (Director, Writer, and Editor), and Krepakevich, J. (Producer). (1998). *My Healing Journey: Seven Years with Cancer* [Video]. National Film Board of Canada.

Vital Statistics Council of Canada. (2007). Welcome to the Vital Statistics Council of Canada. Online: http://www.vscouncil.ca/e_index.html

Waldie, P., and Kennedy, P. (1999, June 2). Loewen files for court protection. *Globe and Mail*, B1.

Waskowic, T.D., and Chartier, B.M. (2003). Attachment and the experience of grief following the loss of a spouse. *Omega*, 47(1), 77-91.

Webb, M. (1997). *The Good Death: The New American Search to Reshape the End of Life*. New York: Bantam Books.

Wells, L.M. (1990). Responsiveness and accountability in long-term care: Strategies for policy development and empowerment. *Canadian Journal of Public Health*, 81(5), 382-85.

Wilinsky, C.F. (1943, January). Hospitals have place in public health programme. *Canadian Hospital*, 36, 12.

Wilkins, K., and Park, E. (1997). Characteristics of hospital users. *Health Reports*, 9(3), 28-36.

Wilkins, K., and Park, E. (1998). Home care in Canada. *Health Reports*, 10(1), 29-37.

Williams, A., Crooks, V.A., Stajduhar, K.I., Allan, D., and Cohen S.R. (2006). Canada's Compassionate Care Benefit: Views of family caregivers in chronic illness. *International Journal of Palliative Nursing*, 12(9), 438-45.

Williamson, J.B., Evans, L., and Munley, A. (1980). *Aging and Society*. New York: Holt, Rinehart and Winston.

Willison, K.D. (2006). Integrating self-care and chronic disease management through a community based research approach. Ontario Health Promotion E-Bulletin. Online: http://www.ohpe.ca/:/index.php?option=com_contentandtask=viewandid=7747andItemid=77.

Wilson, D.M. (1993). Supporting life through tube feeding: Factors influencing surrogate decision-making. *Canadian Journal on Aging*, 12(3), 298-310.

Wilson, D.M. (1996). Highlighting the role of policy in nursing practice through a comparison of "DNR" policy influences and "no CPR" decision influences. *Nursing Outlook*, 44(6), 272-79.

Wilson, D.M. (1997). A report of an investigation of end-of-life patient care practices in health care facilities and the influences for those practices. *Journal of Palliative Care*, 13 (4), 34-40.

Wilson, D.M. (2002). The duration and degree of end-of-life dependency of home care clients and hospital inpatients. *Applied Nursing Research*, 15(2), 81-86.

Wilson, D.M. (2006, December 30). Research Report: Caritas Health Services Utilization and Client Trends. Final Caritas health services and client trends research report. Edmonton: Author.

Wilson, D.M., Anderson, M.C., Fainsinger, R.L., Northcott, H.C., Smith, S.L., and Stingl, M.J. (1998). *Social and Health Care Trends Influencing Palliative Care and the Location of Death in Twentieth-Century Canada*. NHRDP Final Report. Edmonton: Author.

Wilson, D.M., Kinch, J., Justice, C., Thomas, R., Shepherd, D., and Froggatt, K. (2005). A review of the literature on hospice or palliative day care. *European Journal of Palliative Care*, 12(5), 198-202.

Wilson, D.M., Northcott, H.C., Truman, C.D., Smith, S.L., Anderson, M.C., Fainsinger, R.L., and Stingl, M.J. (2001). Location of death in Canada: A comparison of 20th-century hospital and nonhospital locations of death and corresponding population trends. *Evaluation and the Health Professions*, 24(4), 385-403.

Wilson, D.M., Smith, S., Anderson, M., Northcott, H., Fainsinger, R., Stingl, M., and Truman, C.D. (2002). Twentieth-century social and health-care influences on location of death in Canada. *Canadian Journal of Nursing Research*, 34(3), 141-61.

Wilson, D.M., Truman, C., and Northcott, H.C. (1999, May). *Hospital Utilization by Terminally Ill Albertans, 1992/93 to 1996/97*. Preliminary Report. Edmonton, AB: Author.

Wilson, D.M., Truman, C., Huang, J., Sheps, S., Thomas, R., and Noseworthy, T. (2005b). The possibilities and realities of home care. *Canadian Journal of Public Health*, 96(5), 385-89.

Wilson, D.M., Truman, C., Huang, J., Sheps, S., Birch, S., Thomas, R., and Noseworthy, T. (2007). Home care evolution in Alberta: How have palliative clients fared? *Healthcare Policy Journal*, 2(4), 44-56.

Wilson, K. (1983). *The Fur Trade in Canada*. Toronto: Grolier.

Winterfeldt, E. (1991). Historical perspective, Part 1: Dietary management of diabetes mellitus, 1675-1950. *Topics in Clinical Nutrition*, 7(1), 1-8.

Wood, C. (1994, February 28). The legacy of Sue Rodriguez. *Maclean's*, 21-25.

Wood, G.C., and Martin, E. (1995). Withholding and withdrawing life-sustaining therapy in a Canadian intensive care unit. *Canadian Journal of Anaesthesia*, 42(3), 186-91.

Woodgate, R.L. (2006). Living in a world without closure: Reality for parents who have experienced the death of a child. *Journal of Palliative Care*, 22(2), 75-82.

World Health Organization. (1989). *Health of the Elderly: Report of a WHO Expert Committee*. Geneva: World Health Organization.

Zilm, G., and Warbinek, E. (1995). Early tuberculosis nursing in British Columbia. *Canadian Journal of Nursing Research*, 27(3), 65-81.

Zimmermann, C. (2004). Denial of impending death: A discourse analysis of the palliative care literature. *Social Science and Medicine*, 59(8), 1769-80.

INDEX

Aboriginal burial customs, 23-24; Aboriginal
    medicine/Native healers, 21, 26-27
Advance care directives, 83, 115, 145
Alienation, 139, 175
Amyotrophic lateral sclerosis (ALS), 127-28, 144
Antonovsky, Aaron, 138-139
Ariès, Philippe, 117, 145
Assisted suicide, 81-82, 84 86, 127-28

Becker, Ernest, 140-42
Beothuk, 26
Bereavement, 153, 169
Berton, Pierre, 99

Cadaver stories, 97-98
Cancer, 39-40, 42-45, 56, 130-38, 146-49
Cardiopulmonary resuscitation (CPR), 33,
    75-76, 81
Centenarians, 53-55
Cholera, 27, 30
Chronic diseases, 33-36, 49-50
Circulatory disease, 39-44
Coherence, sense of, 138-39
Comprehensibility, 138, 156-57, 161

Cremation, 87
Criminal Code of Canada, 80
Cystic fibrosis, 57

Darwin Awards, 99-100
Death, biological 106; certificate, 41; denial of,
    91-92, 139, 140-41; disenfranchised, 107; eu-
    phemisms, 95-96; fear of, 124, 129-30, 136-37,
    139, 140-41; home, 60, 145-47; ideal, 126,
    129, 137, 145-47; industry, 87-89; infant and
    child, 23, 30, 55, 105, 124, 154-63; legal, 107;
    media coverage, 100-01; media portrayals,
    101; natural, 126; perinatal, 112-14; personal,
    106; premature, 56-57, 105, 124; psychologi-
    cal, 106; psychosocial, 106; rate, 31-32; social,
    106-07; strangeness of, 172
Dementia, 144-45
Dignity, 130
Diphtheria, 30, 32
Do not resuscitate order (DNR), 76
Durkheim, 141-42
Dying, end-stage, 47-48; stages of, 131, 133, 140;
    trajectory, 125-26

Edgework, 142-43
Embalming, 88
Emotional socialization, 136-38, 153, 161
End-of-life care, ethical guidelines, 73, 81, 83
Euthanasia, 81-82, 84-86

Folklore, 96-99
Frank, Arthur, 137-39
Funeral home, funeral director, 71-72, 102-03;
    costs, 87; rituals, 109-10; services, 87-89,
    171-73

Grief, 153-54, 160-63, 169-73, 175-76

Heart disease, 41-44, 137-38
Hemlock Society, 83
Hospices, 78
Hospice Palliative care, 35-36, 76-79, 85, 146-47
Hospitals, 34-35, 48, 50-51, 60-63, 69, 72, 74-78,
    145
Hughes, Robert, 139
Human Papilloma Virus, 32
Humphry, Derek, 83

Identifying moments, 165
Identity foreclosure, 165
Infanticide, 23
Infectious diseases, 25-28, 30, 32-33
Influenza, 30, 32-33

Kent, Gerald, 142
Kerestes, Albert and Margaret, 147-48
Kevorkian, Dr. Jack, 86
Kübler-Ross, Dr. Elisabeth, 131, 140

Latimer, Robert and Tracy, 85
Laurence, Margaret, 92
Life expectancy, 21-22, 26, 29-32, 57-59
Life review, 137
Living wills, 83-84, 145
Longevity, 21, 53-55

Malette v. Schulman, 82
Manageability, 139, 156
Martin, Karen, 155-57, 175-76
Maternal mortality, 29-30
Meaningfulness, 138-39, 155-56, 161, 176
Meaning structure, 155-57
Measles, 26, 30
Mitchell, W.O., 93
Modernism, 117
Morrison, Dr. Nancy, 85-86
Mourning, 153
Mutual pretence, 93, 130

Nahanni, 98-99
Nancy B., 82
Nurses, 34-35, 70, 74, 152

Organ and tissue donation, 70-71, 115

Palliative Care Unit, Royal Victoria Hospital,
    146-47
Patterson, R.M., 98
Pneumonia, 34
Polio, 32
Popular culture, 96-99, 101
Postmodernism, 117
Potential years of life lost (PYLL), 56
Public health, 20, 30-34, 36

Quarantine, 27
Quinlan, Karen Ann, 81-83

Right-to die groups, 83
Right-to life groups, 83
Rodriguez, Sue, 85, 127-28
Romanticism, 117

Schwartz, Professor Morris, 127-28
Schiavo, Terri, 82, 84
Scurvy, 27
Senescence, 53-54
Seniors, abandonment of, 21
Smallpox, 25, 31-32
Social supports, 148
Spirituality, 141-42
Stigma, courtesy, 108, 161
Sudden infant death syndrome (SIDS), 125,
    155-57
Suicide, 143-45, 162
Survivor guilt, 163
Syncretism, 116

Taboo, death as, 13, 20, 97
Television, 101-02
Terminal illness, 47
Terror management theory, 140
Tuberculosis, 30, 33, 59

Urban legends, 96-99

Viszmeg, Joseph, 148-49
Vital statistics, 19

Whooping cough, 32
Widowhood, 154, 163-67
Withdrawing and withholding care, 74-76,
    81-86
Will to live, 129, 139, 148